arts of the
POLITICAL

arts of the
POLITICAL

NEW OPENINGS FOR THE LEFT

ash amin + nigel thrift

Duke University Press   Durham + London   2013

© 2013 Duke University
Press. All rights reserved.
Printed in the United States of
America on acid-free paper ∞

Designed by Courtney Leigh
Baker and typeset in Arno Pro
by Tseng Information Systems, Inc.

Library of Congress
Cataloging-in-Publication Data
Amin, Ash.
Arts of the political : new openings for
the left / Ash Amin and Nigel Thrift.
p. cm.
Includes bibliographical
references and index.
ISBN 978-0-8223-5387-4
 (cloth : alk. paper)
ISBN 978-0-8223-5401-7
 (pbk. : alk. paper)
1. Political sociology. 2. Right and left
(Political science). 3. Social justice.
4. Social change. I. Thrift, N. J. II. Title.
JA76.A474 2013 320.53—dc23
2012033719

contents

acknowledgments vii   prologue ix

1   THE GROUNDS OF POLITICS 1

2   LEFTIST BEGINNINGS 17

3   REINVENTING THE POLITICAL 39

4   CONTEMPORARY LEFTIST THOUGHT 77

5   ORGANIZING POLITICS 111

6   EUROCRACY AND ITS PUBLICS 135

7   AFFECTIVE POLITICS 157

epilogue 187   notes 201   references 211   index 229

acknowledgments

We embarked on this project in 2005. It has taken some years to come to fruition, and more could be written even on the eve of publication, for the political terrain on which counter-currents can be forged never remains still. Along the way a number of people have helped us to clarify our arguments. We thank Jonathan Darling, Shari Daya, Michele Lancione, and Helen Wilson for helping to source material for some of the chapters; Laurent Frideres for so expertly finalizing the references; Peter Wissoker for improving the legibility of the manuscript; and Courtney Berger for guiding us through the various stages with tact and commitment. Above all, we thank the two anonymous readers for critical but always helpful suggestions to sharpen and clarify the argument.

Parts of chapter 7 are drawn from Nigel Thrift, *Non-Representational Theory: Space, Politics, Affect* (London: Routledge, 2007), with permission of the publisher.

prologue

This is a book about how the Left, particularly in the West, can move forward in the struggle to voice a politics of social equality and justice. But it does not provide a manifesto, a template, or even a plan. The reason for this seeming absence of guidance is straightforward. We believe that the Left needs to invest much more effort in understanding both the political and the process of politics when it seeks to steer toward a particular outcome. Compared with times past, when the Left did indeed manage to capture hearts and minds and found itself able to alter the course of history for the many rather than just the few, too many of the forces that profess to be of the Left take the political as given and, for that reason, fail to disclose or enable new futures. That, at least, is the thesis of this book. Thus, the book is about what it means to be "Left" once the political is given the attention it deserves. Too often lately, the Left has been unsuccessful because it has allowed itself to be constrained by a politics that is grounded in habitual ways of thinking and acting — to the advantage of conservative forces. The Left needs to repopulate the political with new visions, new desires, and new modes of organization — that is, with the three arts of imagination, persuasion, and fulfilment without which a different future cannot be seen or desired and the present is viscerally understood as closed to any kind of renewal. Only then will the Left be able to make its case successfully for a fair and equal society.

How this case is made, however, is part of the problem. The organized Left — not just in the West, but the world over — has spent too much time telling people what the future ought to be and too little time thinking about ways in which that future can be brought about by like-minded people who have been able to find one another. We believe that new futures can be built only by trusting to the organizational capacities and enthusiasm of these people to a much greater extent than has been typical so far. Accordingly, a considerable part of this book is concerned with how we can boost people's hopes and ambitions for the future—how we can give them a sense that something uplifting and worthwhile exists around the corner—rather than fixating on drawing up the map that gets them there.

None of this is to say that we do not have views on what the future of the Left should be, but we are also aware that we are in the middle of a set of circumstances that are very likely to change those views and redirect political energies as we go along. Who, for example, would have predicted only twenty years ago that climate change would have become such a pressing issue for the Left as it has now become? Or take shorter time scales. Who would have predicted just a couple of years ago that a good part of the Arab world would try to throw off the shackles of dictatorship? Who would have predicted just a year ago the outbreak of rioting in British cities? So if the future is not predictable, what kind of leftist politics can we still do?

Before progressing any further, we need to offer three clarifications. First, there is what we mean by the "political." This is a much debated term, but our interest lies in the art of imagination as an integral part of political practice. We focus on the process by which an organized force aims to set out in a particular direction, producing the tools not just to persuade others to move with it, though that is important, but to craft the contours of the political field itself so that proponents of that political direction can have the confidence that they are being held through the turbulence of social experience and are able to produce a continuity of being. We want to consider the implications of seeing politics as an art form, but one with rather more consequences than the average landscape painting. A more general art is at issue here—an art of moving forward without getting stuck in the old and, as a corollary, making progress without having too strong a notion of what is coming next. That knowledge has to be created—carefully, never indiscriminately—as part of what this art form is. The book therefore is less concerned with understanding the political as a set of arguments between Left and Right, as a space of representation, or as a sphere in its own right that is separated from other sites of social interaction than with how the desire for a different future can be threaded into people's lives as both a set of existential territories and an *expressive* allegiance so they believe that they, too, can have a stake in the world. Our thesis is that the Left has largely lost sight of the political as an art of expressing new desires and ambitions for the world as it is now, a world that has real urgencies and needs. It is this loss of the ability to stir the imagination that explains the Left's greatly reduced standing in, at least, the Western capitalist world—a world in which, ironically, so much of the imagination has been tethered in so many spheres of human action.

Second, there is what we mean by the Left. We mean a set of different political forces grouped around common matters of concern and affinity; although they are often very different in their character and contours, they cleave to the notion that all is not right with the world and, specifically, that the recurring evils of inequality, oppression, and exploitation need to be fought. We also mean a movement with a positive vision of futures in which people are able to develop their full potential and contribute freely, but for the common good rather than as "individuals" just out for themselves. In addition, we believe that the Left is the only set of established political forces that—fitfully and imperfectly, it is true—has glimpsed a vision of futures in which human beings are open to what they might want to become. That is an extravagant outlook on history, if you like, but one that has never been more necessary in a world that is creaking at the seams. Given the scale of the problems that the world currently faces, we can see no other actor that wants to make sufficient change to ensure that its problems might be solved—or, at the very least ameliorated—in the interests of those (humans and nonhumans) most affected by them. Finally, we associate the Left with being a force for change, radical or reformist, that is democratic in intent, if not practice, but that does not shy away from a realistic understanding that not everyone can be or wants to be roped into the political process.

Then there is the issue of why we want to focus on the Left in the way we are suggesting. We want to reinvent the Left but without losing hold of its enduring concerns and values. Many of the challenges the world faces today mean taking an explicit stance against grotesque levels of inequality and frightening forms of injustice. But they must be addressed in ways that are thought anew by the Left as a political movement. However, even a thoroughly redesigned politics of freedom and justice will falter without a rethinking of what is understood as "the political" by both the Left and society at large. We want to open new ground on which the Left can flourish, but, to be clear, we do not believe that in a world of multiple practices, there is any single answer or singular practice that can achieve that goal. As a matter of both fact and function, leftist futures have to be understood as more open, more opportunistic (in the best sense of the term), and more democratic in that knowledge and invention are understood as distributed among the population as a whole and not just taken to be the preserve of a few seers and prophets. This stance has implications not just for the official Left and its relationship with publics and social movements, but also for self-appointed visionaries of the good life and their relationship with the urgencies and contradictions of the day.

Let us put this point another way by turning to one of the touchstones of this book, William James. James discovered Utopia in 1896, when he made a visit to the town of Lilydale, in western New York State. Lilydale was a utopian community founded in 1879 in the belief that everyone "has a right to be all that he can be — to know all that he can know." At first, James found the community nearly perfect, with its excellent health facilities, numerous educational institutions, and love of learning. "The ideals of the Assembly's founders coincided fully with those of James and he quickly praised the features of life he discovered there. Nor did he intimate that these particular aspirations are misguided; in fact, he termed Lilydale a success. James initially extended his stay at the grounds from a day to an entire week because he found the atmosphere so salutary; he is given, 'in effect, a foretaste of what human society might be, were it all in the light, with no suffering and no dark corners'" (Ferguson 2007, 2). Yet James found Lilydale disappointing, even enervating. Why? "Instead of elevating the human psyche, he determined, the embodiment of perfection deadens it, primarily because such an existence leaves no place for the dissension and friction that ultimately gives life significance" (Ferguson 2007, 2). In other words, in James's depictions of the polis — and in ours — difference and disagreement are central to existence. Political projects need to "keep the doors and windows open." They cannot stay fixed, or they risk becoming, like Utopia, a passive expression of principle that lacks the essential element of individual or collective courage (Stengers and Goffey 2009). Without this perpetual airing, politics becomes a cipher.

The three political arts of "world making" that we emphasize in this book — the ability to project new habitable environments out of latent injuries and concerns, the ability to alter the means and terms of political conduct so that the latent can emerge with effective and affective energy, and the ability to develop the means of organization to sustain momentum and cement gains—are devoted to this perpetual task of airing the polis and shaping its yearnings in what James called an imperfectly unified and never unitary world. In line with the "pluriversalist" orientation we adopt, in which thinking must be put to the test through its consequences, these arts are, of course, distributed among many constituencies, communities, and ideologies. What we are arguing is that the Left needs to be more skilled at identifying and reinventing these arts if it really wants to succeed. Over the past twenty or thirty years, the Left has not always been willing to take these arts as seriously as it might—to its undoubted detriment—because it has been too concerned about the possibilities of pollution by alien traditions and because of an instinctive feeling that home-grown must be best.

To avoid being misunderstood, we are not interested in a politics of catching up, a Left rebooted to match the Right or any other reactionary political force. Rather, our argument is that without expanding the political field that the forces of conservatism have managed to colonize through mastery of precisely these three arts, but bound either to the service of nostalgic and mythical purities or to the simple opportunism of the retail politics that now holds sway in so many parts of the world, the Left will be unable to build nostalgia for a future unknown. Nor are we interested in the Left as simply an eclectic melange of different communities, although we doubt that it can ever be more than a set of sympathetic acquaintances united by common feelings. Rather, we are interested in the Left because of its potential to offer a set of futures that are different, more enriching, and more caring. Currently, we might argue that the global Left "appears as a battery that functions halfway: it accumulates energy without pause but it does not know how [or] whether to discharge it" (Virno 2009, 1). This is not just a failure of the official Left—parties, trade unions, governments, and other representative bodies—to keep up with the protests and social movements that are clamouring for justice even in the transatlantic West. Rather, nowhere near enough time has been devoted by the official Left, or by erstwhile familiars, to the arts of producing a world in which there is a palpable sense of affront, even of desecration, at blows to equality and justice, a sense that is understood not just as a set of arguments but also as a felt and glistening potential. It is therefore not enough to deploy rational argument, as important as that undoubtedly is.[1] In the best of all possible worlds, these arts would turn certain forms of argument, and their accompanying modes of desire and being, into something that lingers on the skin and in the gut. The momentum for change to other ways of living and engaging might then become unstoppable.

1

the grounds of
POLITICS

POLITICS + THE POLITICAL

Let us make one thing clear right from the start. We take progressive politics to be the domain of practice in which new orientations toward a just society can emerge. This is a wider domain than leftist politics as we know it, since it can also include, for example, what Lauren Berlant (2008) calls the juxtapolitical domain. This is the domain that thrives in proximity to the political; it occasionally crosses over into political alliances of various kinds and even participates in actual concerted political campaigns now and then, but it is not normally organized around specific political goals. Thus, our interest lies, on the one hand, in retaining political aspirations historically associated with the Left, but also, on the other hand, in being open to considering all sorts of other domains as having the potential to be drawn into the political, when issues of common concern are brought to the table of disputation. At these points of inflexion, the Left has to invent new stances, which cannot simply be extrapolated from previous concerns, forms of attachment, and means of gaining emotional sustenance. The Left cannot simply assume "the positional safety associated with the arrow of emancipation" (Stengers 2011a, 139). It has to venture outside the circle.

Times are often awkward for progressive political forces, but the current conjuncture seems to be a particularly awkward moment. The pressure of events has compounded some standard political dilemmas while also producing new ones. According to one familiar lament, the Left and other progressive forces have been disarmed by many of these developments. They have lost their grip, at the same time as losing certainty over what they stand for. But since the same forces are apparently gathered — capitalism and imperialism, for example — while the environment seems to be going to hell and high water, all we need to do is sing the same old refrains, suitably adjusted for modern times: the same song of class struggle, the same song of the need to recover old values, the same song of adulation of subversive politics, the same song of suspicion of all commerce, and the same song of pristine political clarity. Rather unkindly, Michael Bérubé (2009) calls this kind of attitude Great Leap Backward thinking. Whatever it is, it isn't helpful.

It would, of course, be difficult for anyone to argue that the world is in a state of perfection. But what we want to argue emphatically in this book is that songs of nostalgic and often Manichean militancy cannot be the way forward. Instead, the Left needs to redefine itself so it can both face up to issues that are longstanding and understand that many of the issues the world now faces have no immediate solutions, for what we might call the "Left" or the "Right," a distinction that, after all, was originally based on the seating arrangements of the French Legislative Assembly of 1791 (Bérubé 2009). This will not be an easy task. To begin with, the Left as conventionally understood has splintered and in some cases sundered. As Albena Azmanova (2011) has argued, globalization has brought about new political cleavages that challenge a simple left–right divide and mean that the structure of political contestation and the nature of political mobilization are less easily correlated than before. The shift has resulted partly from the addition of new concerns (whether they are identity politics or ecological issues) and partly from the results of a series of continuing economic and cultural tendencies, such as the diminishing political relevance of class, the growing salience of post-material values and risks (often summed up by the term "lifestyle"), and a general tendency toward individualization, as well as from the concrete economic results of globalization, which has produced very definite losers and winners (most notably through the widening of the gap between low-skilled and highly skilled workers). In turn, patterns of political mobilization have altered so that collective action is no longer the exclusive preserve of the typical social constituencies of the Left and the paramount political debates have increasingly hinged on issues such as insecurity of income and sheer physical safety—or what Azmanova (2011) calls the order-and-safety agenda.

Issues that were originally clearly the preserve of the Left have been taken up by the Right, too. Look at how in Britain, for example, an issue such as social empowerment, which traditionally has been championed by the Left, has become a matter of concern to the Right. Look at how in Europe identity politics has become a concern of both Left and Right, although often in very different ways. Or look at how, in the United States, following the first victory of President Barack Obama, what counts as the Left has often returned to traditional social-democratic concerns such as market regulation, social welfare, and global peace, while some parts of the Republican Right have turned to greater regulation of the economy in the wake of the financial meltdown. More broadly, look at how the historical opposition between secularism and religiosity has become blurred in many places around the world.

So simply extending the left brand will not suffice. But looking forward is no easy matter, either; it is by no means clear what historically defined political movements such as social democracy, socialism, and environmentalism should stand for; how they should take a stand (that delivers); what political tools they will need—or, indeed, on whose behalf they now speak in a time of considerable political heterodoxy. In this book, we therefore try to provide the beginnings of a map of what a new leftist politics might look like. When we say beginnings, we mean that in two ways. First, this is a map with no strongly defined destination. In a sense, it is a map of continual beginnings. Second, it is a map in which the journey is open-ended. In politics, the goal and the means are never entirely clear, and they very often need to be created as the process unfolds. We are aiming to produce a sense of the world in which politics has a grip in situations that are ill-defined and do not always make clear what the stakes are. So this means that we are not seeking out notions of transcendence or immanence that can act to stabilize what is and what is not regarded as political action. Political actors normally have to work within situations that are themselves powerful determinants of what is possible and how it may be understood and acted on.

An important task of political thought is to be able to read the situation and mobilize publics that will want to think in a particular way about it. Mobilization here is a matter of key words and phrases, resonant images, affective interest in what is on offer, and thereby an inkling of the kind of world that might produce both satisfaction and voice. That means that we have to be clear that the way forward lies in a combination of vision and a commitment to an open-ended, democratic politics in which others are able to feed into the political process without being dismissed out of hand. Walking this fine line requires the ability to offer attractive futures that really call out to people and that allow them some role in their achievement. But it also requires openness to changing direction, as the momentum of democratic debate and involvement grows, not just as a deviation from some set line but, in the spirit of a contribution, to a politics that is able to expand worlds and their orientations.

Most important, there may be more things vying for the Left's attention in the world than have been countenanced as occupying the political sphere, and some of them may well pull the Left in unexpected directions, some of which will prove to have potential and some of which will prove to be dead ends. The challenge is to articulate a "mid-range" politics that is able to recognize and talk about this sometimes forgotten world that is continually producing pressures in all our lives, steer a course across such diversity, and make appropriate connections. We are, of course, well aware that such a depiction of leftist politics might seem akin to simply going with the flow as defined by the polls at any given moment. But a large part of the political consists of knowing precisely when and when not to go with the flow. It requires *judgment,* and this is not a secondary matter automatically following on from a political program. Rather, it is a key part of the arsenal of political skills and crafts that the Left needs to develop. It has long been attractive for the Left to think in terms of a program that can be burnished and kept pure, but the price is stepping out of life. So the kind of political judgment we have in mind is a political art that can open up situations so the possibilities become clearer, that can invent instruments that allow leverage to be applied, and that can generate new feelings of commitment and solidarity.

Lest it sound as though we stand for a Left without a project — or, worse, that stands for a project that unfolds opportunistically, simply following the twists and turns of changing popular sentiment — this is absolutely not the case. Rather, we believe that the project can only become clear in the unfolding: circumstance is a powerful tutor. So for us, being on the Left is about mobilizing world-making capacity that we recognize can come only from a combination of fidelity to some basic principles and an understanding of the circumstances, a cultivation of political arts that can bring these two together, and a permanent commitment that arises from the fact that world making can never be complete.

In other words, there is always more there to come, and if there is a consistency of cause that allows us to claim the Left as Left, this has to be the historical commitment to contest oppression and exploitation through struggles by many that have made the world more than the preserve of the gilded few. As Adolfo Gilly (2010, 33) notes, it is generally the case that "one is led to rebellion by sentiments, not by thoughts," and historically the line of leftist thought that has grasped this particular point has "in common a concern with the preoccupations of the people, based on the impulse to understand their world and what motivates them. The reasons why people rise up in rebellion are not incidental. They are substantive."

To be clear, what we mean by world-making capacity is the ability to produce what Peter Sloterdijk has called "atmospheres," that is, spaces of resonance in which the oxygen of certain kinds of thought and practice seems natural and desirable. Such world-making requires an arsenal of methods, dispositions, and motilities. At certain times in its history, the Left has understood this point about constructing what Sloterdijk (2011) has also called "sounding chambers," but then, too often, it has tended to opt for command and control as a simpler and more efficient way of proceeding, thereby producing movement but without consent. Alternatively, the Left has offered world visions that have no sensory grip and therefore appear to large parts of the population as nothing more than fairy tales. What we have in mind instead is not the construction of a total world in which everything runs in lock-step, but rather a series of worlds that act as glimpses of a better future, worlds that are worth fighting for, and that strongly resonate with actual and real concerns and needs. These are worlds that, quite literally, are attractive in two senses: they both articulate a practical necessity and, at the same time, they are sufficiently glamorous to draw in new proponents.

Any leftist politics, in other words, has to be willing to take risks to invent new worlds. It has to experiment without certitude. What should mark leftist politics is not just its allegiances, but this experimental stance, which understands the world as an opportunity even in the most difficult circumstances. This is not to duck the question of content or canonical principles historically associated with the Left, but it is to say that these principles must be continually adapted and reinvented and that these adaptations and reinventions will themselves be formative. There is no set manifesto that can simply be adjusted to suit all times and circumstances, and there is nothing necessarily wrong with mutation. A prevalent tendency on the Left has been to try to legislate the nature of the political field by restricting it to class, revolutionary subject, or the clamorous public, to give three examples. Our view is that this is a politically disabling way to proceed, because it ignores the continual reinvention of the political that occurs as a result of political action, as well as the fact that no emancipation comes without new attachments.[1]

An alternative way to proceed adds to the range of what we might consider the political by recognizing that through history, different kinds of politics have been formed that have manifested openness to what the political can consist of in any moment in time. To put it differently, many books about politics are written as though it is a defined field that, while changing in form, consists of roughly the same activity over many centuries. They hold political practice to be an invariant entity. But another way to look at politics conceives it not as a stable field but as a field whose form and content are continually redefined. It is this view that we attempt to push in new directions in this book in the belief that this is the shifting ground on which the Left must operate. Once we are willing to admit that the political field is complex and mutable, we in turn are able to highlight certain aspects of the conduct of politics that remain relatively neglected. So, for example, we want to take what is now becoming a familiar view that places all human, nonhuman, natural, and artificial objects on the same footing (Latour 1999) and expands the realm of the political according to the dictum that "all reality is political, but not all politics is human" (Harman 2009, 23).

Like the pragmatist theorists, we do not believe that theory can be used as if it were a well-defended base from which it is possible to foray out and righteously pronounce about how the world is and what it does, secure in this judgment because the theory has already dictated what is there, has already yielded abstractions which require no need to pay attention to what might escape them, or even the desire to do so. Such a stance of cleansing the world of doubt in which "we sort between the good (reasonable, objective, progressive) and the bad (irrational, subjective, backwards-looking)" (Goffey 2011, xviii) is the road so often taken by writers "who have an enemy, who array themselves in some kind of intellectual battle . . . and for them there is no true theory, but only an encampment discourse. Every morning marks the issuing of an order, a briefing and the observation of hostile operations" (Sloterdijk, cited in Van Tuinen 2007, 303). Critique, in other words, is too often a way to make your mind up before an event. You know what is there: all that needs to be done is to confirm the existence of the bloody entrails and make the prophecy. "Is it not the case," writes Isabelle Stengers (2011b, 380), "that conveniently escaping a confrontation with the messy world of practices through clean conceptual dilemmas or eliminativist judgments has left us with a theatre of concepts the power of which . . . is matched only by their powerlessness to transform?"

Insofar as this book is a work of political theory, we want to moderate the tendency to critique in four ways. First, we want to strengthen the hands of those who believe that politics is important in its own right. Whatever one thinks of Lenin, he knew one thing well: politics counts for and in itself. It is not an epiphenomenon that arises out of other forces. Second, we want to inject a note of uncertainty about what the political is. The field we often rather glibly call the political is constantly being redefined: new struggles come into existence, and others fall away as relations shift shape. At the same time, we do not want to appeal to the political simply for its own sake as though the very utterance of the word provides a promissory note. Third, we are keen to understand the whole of the political field. There is a tendency among some on the Left to argue that the only political game worth the candle is transgression. Although transgressive hideouts may provide a sense of security, they also tend to limit what can be regarded as political action in a way that can be counterproductive (Read 2008).

Fourth, we want to inject an ethic of generosity into the often fractious field of left politics. As Graham Harman (2009, 120) notes, "The books that stir us most are not those containing the fewest errors, but those that throw most light on the unknown portions of the map." So we are interested in "promoting the gambler who uncovers new worlds" over the author who is the strictly accurate legislator who has nothing to say. After all, we want to create an appetite "for an effective type of hold, and not a taste for voracious denunciation" (Pignarre and Stengers 2011, 22). Sometimes that will mean flashes of inspiration. Sometimes that will mean sheer hard slog. Sometimes that may mean reconsidering unpalatable moments in politics and political theory on the grounds that there might be redemptive moments that get lost in the rush to outright rejection (Žižek 2008). But whatever it might mean, it is not about converting lost souls; nor is it about the sacrificial militancy that so often accompanies that practice. Rather, it is about encountering and working with mutually interested parties according to a pragmatics that suits a world that is irremediably hybrid and can therefore respond to the questions that are put to it in unforeseen ways. It is, in other words, about cultivating the power to activate thought and practice and so transform the urgent cry of the misfit into worlds that require "the affirmation that exposes, not the prudence that reassures" (Pignarre and Stengers 2011, 9).

To summarize, this book is akin to a political primer, but of a specific nature. It is interested in privileging the sheer hard work of multiplication but without falling back into a completely open field. The book is resolutely materialist in that it not only understands politics as being able to exist within the particular circumstances of the time, but it also understands those circumstances as new material that can be forged into fresh movements and alliances and into new inventions of what the political itself consists of. We come to this stance within an ever more complicated and entangled political field — a field that consists of many more organizations that regard themselves as political, many more forms of possible political organization, and many more notions of what can be included within the political domain. To repeat, to see the political as a field whose form and content are other than constantly shifting strikes us as a categorical mistake.

For some of our readers, this will be an uncomfortable vision in which political views do not hold stable, and neither do matters of concerns or direction of travel. But our view is quite straightforward. It is that any other view forecloses forms of political action and thought that may prove to be decisive. We believe that the place to start is with an expanded understanding of the political itself as an active field that cannot be reduced to the expression of other forces, though it is inevitably influenced by them. We believe that such a stance is particularly necessary for the Left, for when it has worked best in the past, it has done so by inventing new worlds out of the present, disclosing that which lies latent, bringing together that which has been dispersed, making explicit that which has lacked form or representation, finding the right openings, and working with a map of the future whose cardinal is rather like the magnetic North Pole in that it is a fixed point but one that constantly moves.

To anticipate an argument developed through the rest of the book that the success of world-making projects depends on the mastery of particular political arts, in the next chapter we illustrate how the European and American Left in its formative years some one hundred years ago — caught in a struggle to compose a vocabulary, a constituency, and a political forum while operating in an extremely hostile environment — managed to make considerable gains precisely by fashioning such a politics of invention. It did so out of necessity rather than design, to avoid being choked by the closures of political thought and action of the time. Movements campaigning for the rights of women, the working class, and other neglected and downtrodden subjects managed to turn engrained orthodoxies on their head in the quarter-century before the First World War by building mass support and accompanying socio-political reform. Although these movements applied particular principles and practices, the record shows that their acts of redefinition went far beyond what was originally intended. These movements freed up new imaginations, invented new political tools, pointed to elements of existence that had been neglected or concealed, and created a constituency that, once constructed, longed for another world. In other words, these movements produced a new sense of the political and of political potential. The emerging Left both opened the doors of perception and provided the tools with which to do something about these new perceptions. This is what was common, in our view, in the disparate examples we consider, from the American Progressive Movement and British feminism to German Marxism and Swedish social democracy. In their own way, each of these movements disclosed new desires.

The thesis that drives this book is that progressive movements should pay more attention to such world-making capacity, understood as the ability not just to produce a program in the future but also to open up new notions of what the future might consist of. The most important political movements, in our estimation, are those that are able to invent a world of possibility and hope that then results in multiple interventions in the economic, social, and cultural, as well as the political, sphere. They free thought and practice and make it clear what values are being adhered to, often in quite unexpected ways. It is the to and fro between the invitation to think in new ways provided by the actual process of construction and the ability to construct practices that makes those inventions incarnate rather than prematurely banishing them as error, which seems to us to be key to opening the lock on any process of transformation.

Invention, Organization, and Affect

The approach we take is to consider political arts that have often been implicit in leftist politics and make them the subject of representation so they can be worked on. We focus on three political arts that seem particularly important at this time, not only because they have become tools that the Right has learned to master much better than the Left, but more important, because they are the means by which a radical alterity can become not so much domesticated as felt as an urgent desire for and a reasonable expectation of how the world should be. These are political arts that have been quite central in times past, when the Left has managed to gain ascendance more often than not against the grain of particular circumstances.

The first is *invention*, or the capacity to disclose the new—understanding, however, that this disclosure has to take place within a world in which many traditions of political thought and practice now coexist. A useful analogy might be with art or music. In both cases, the field of possibility is now crowded, which makes invention both more and less easy. There are more resources available that can be combined in new ways; however, originality is probably harder to achieve. Accordingly, a political art is the ability to generate publics, bring them together, and make them see and long for a different future. In the third chapter, we therefore consider recent writing that seeks to reframe what the political might consist of in terms not just of actors but also of spaces, political content and style, and affective fields of action, which come together as the achievement of sentiments that add up to concern. In particular, in thinking about how to align political programs with the often everyday concerns of the public, we consider the issues of affect and of objects (nature *and* things) as a means by which to both mark and talk about aspects of the world heretofore neglected and bring them into political discourse and the art of constructing publics. These considerations show

how actors are produced and co-involved in making actions that count as the new staples of politics in a given age.

That means making worlds. But by using this phrase, we do not mean to restrict our orbit to the construction of spatially bounded communities in which so-called socialist principles abide that are well understood and adhered to. Rather, we mean the ability to bring together often only half-intuited explanations of the world in such a way as to produce atmospheres of momentum and commitment. This stance can be seen as in line with a more general move away from conceptualizing space as bounded toward understanding space as a set of multiple overlapping territories, each of which represents a different political opportunity and a different form of political agency and subject position and a different kind of opening on to dreamed-of futures. Of course, it would be naïve to suggest that these developments are just an independent manifestation of contemporary leftist thinking. They arise from a definite moment in political economy, which increasingly privileges the whole register of the senses and an ability to produce worlds (Thrift 2011). But what can be made out of this moment depends on the emerging capacity to build on this recognition of new registers in inventive ways.

Chapter 4 surveys the adequacy of contemporary leftist thought, from anti-capitalist and post-capitalist thought to work on humanist ethics and social-democratic control of capitalism. Our intent in chapter 4 is not to play one strand off against another, for we genuinely believe that these currents of thought can be together rather than at odds with each other. Our interest lies instead with how contemporary leftist thought can inform new modes of political conduct. Our argument is that these currents exist in a wider world than their proponents acknowledge and could draw strength from that world, especially in creating publics around issues of concern, in the way that the Left found itself doing one hundred years ago. Such a politics of interests and concerns—latent or disclosed—has to be seen, however, as only a first step in a fuller leftist politics of invention and world making if it is to work with the openings outlined in chapter 3. The different strands of the contemporary Left fall far short in this regard.

The second political art we focus on is *organization*. This book takes it as self-evident that organization is more than a passive vehicle for the expression of political will. It has its own agency, which is not always malevolent and can at times be extremely creative, changing the course of political agendas as particular forms of political will are instituted. State institutions, parties, movements, the media, books, pamphlets, and other kinds of political technology all count and all require methods of circulation and reinforcement. They form the stuff of politics. And they are not incidental. Let us be clear. Political organization is often aligned with a Kafkaesque vision of bureaucratic practice. Although some organizations may take on this form, just as many come with positive outcomes. For example, who would not want to have a bureaucracy that protects children or the environment or particular states of peace? We therefore take political organization to be fundamental, not incidental, and in this book we look for various ways in which organization can underpin invention and mobilization as it produces its own political agendas. The ultimate interest is in searching for organizational forms that can sustain the democratic impulse.

One of the central issues confronting politics today is the pragmatics of advancing a cause. In the past, this was often seen as a matter of simply providing a stentorian campaign call and an appropriate organizational structure, which would then result in the desired objectives being achieved. So the state could be either reused or overturned, old political technology could be reworked or cleared away, and the core choice was therefore between reform and revolution. Matters of process were often left to one side (although this is clearly something of a caricature when the detail of individual cause making is considered, as in chapter 2). Such an approach, as we will try to show, is both a simplification of what happens in practice and a distortion of how progressive causes are advanced. We argue that a politics attentive to organizational concerns needs to respect some principles. One of these is to build disagreement into the political machinery. It should be possible to belong to the club without signing on for every facet of a common cause, while simultaneously recognizing that an alliance brings with it inevitable obligations. Another principle is to understand that the political process is always a diplomatic task. This will often mean a more disaggregated means of going forward, valuing the skills of diplomacy in bringing together positions that are not merely heterogeneous but often antagonistic, stemming from different worlds that can only ever have some degree of understanding of each other (Stengers 2010a). The third principle follows from the previous two. It is that a good deal of attention needs to be paid to producing organizational forms that can have latitude, redundancy, and creativity and that are able to sustain these qualities and harvest any specific gains.

All of these principles need to be brought together to produce the final principle, which is that a functioning political field is often best achieved through the design of particular spaces that act as arenas for managing disagreement, as partial models of process, and even as glimpses of a hopeful future. Chapter 5 thus illustrates how the concept of political organization defined this way can help to identify new tools of transformation and change that the Left ought to recognize. These include a consideration of "resonating spaces" in which the medium provides a message, the redefinition of inanimate objects as animate, bureaucratic routines that are self-examining in productive ways, modes of aesthetic conduct than can be threaded into action and produce a different style of proceeding, and styles of deliberative democracy that allow open outcomes rather than consensus or a choice of pre-given alternatives.

Chapter 6 focuses on the case of the European Union (EU), understood as a laboratory for the kinds of organizational and procedural practices we have been trying to conjure up. The formation of the EU provided the opportunity for a set of experiments with democracy in large, dispersed, and diverse polities. Our aim, especially at this time of EU-wide crisis, is not to eulogize each of the structures of the EU, but instead to chart how new organizational forms can change the possibilities of the political field for the better. Europe is not a unitary state, and many of the states that compose it are themselves non-unitary. Yet in some areas of policy and social life, the EU has been able to make significant progress in a multiply contested field, brokering a consensus and bringing about major social-democratic gains. This achievement, we argue, is the result of technologies of organization that allow the process of negotiation and compromise to become an end in itself and that provide room for bureaucrats to become political actors in their own right, without being able to break free from the political constituencies that surround them.

The EU's frequent focus on directives, which require considerable deliberation and negotiation before they can be passed, can be seen as a process of simultaneously creating an issue-based public where all interests can be revealed at the same time that they demand the formation of new political actors. Moreover, it requires that modes of diplomacy be invented that both inform the process and take it forward, rendering it a practice marked by continuous creation and experimentation. In turn, the rules of diplomacy are such that many gaps are opened that constitute an array of political opportunities for the Left and a means of generating new issues. Europe has given many opportunities to various social and extraparliamentary movements, offering them the chance, for example, to become involved in the policymaking process and in defining new objects of political attention.

The third and final political art that we take seriously in this book is the mobilization of *affect*. This is the topic of chapter 7. The animation provided by affect is crucial in the practice of world making. If there is one thing that we know about political mobilization, even more in our age than formerly, it is that affect counts. Political judgments are not made in rational or deliberative ways; they follow the ley lines of emotion. Many political impulses are contagious and require only momentary thought, which can lead to decisions that, in aggregate, can be momentous. The science of influencing these momentary decisions has become more and more exact, and in most cases that has required more and more political-aesthetic knowledge to press the right emotional buttons and, in the notorious vocabulary of contemporary policymakers, "nudge" them toward a desired outcome (Connolly 2008; Protevi 2009). The Left has often been dismissive about this form of deliberation, yet any moment of reflection will make it clear that affect is part and parcel of any political decision—many a past revolutionary or reformist movement, for example, has depended on mobilizing affect as a political opportunity, as shown in chapter 2. However briefly they may consider an issue, people have to be engaged; they have to care if they are to act on it or give consent to be acted on. There is a pre-political political realm that depends on the black arts of what we might call pre-mediation. Thus, in the first half of chapter 7, we tackle thinking the aesthetic/affective and the political together, an issue that holds the most promise and also causes some of the most violent disagreement in modern political discussion.[2] This agenda has particular resonance with the present in that it tries to understand and work through some of the stupefying aspects of modern media-saturated democracies in which what Sianne Ngai (2005) calls "stuplimity" (the admixture of boredom and shock) and paranoia often seems to reign supreme. Indeed, we begin the chapter by addressing the issue of how it is possible to have political communities under these conditions. In particular, we consider the whole phenomenon of what Walter Lippmann (1961) called the manufacture of consent: how it is being bent to the needs of the Right and how it could be mobilized more effectively by the Left. At the same time, we attend to how the consideration of affect brings space into the frame. A whole array of spatial technologies has become available that operate on, and with, feeling to produce new forms of activism, which literally map out politics and give actors the resources to kick up more and across more places.[3] In other words, the practical mechanics of space must be part of the politics of the Left. There is now a flowering of new knowledges and practices of space on which the Left can draw, all the way from new developments in the economy that increasingly are framing people as creatures of affect through new means of organizing routine human practices such as work and child care (e.g., emotions of care, loyalty, and responsibility, but now as part of the world of work) to numerous experiments in the arts and humanities, which are trying to make the world manifest itself in ways that have rarely been considered before (e.g., poetry and techno-visualization as the material of political invention).

In the last part of chapter 7, we return to the question of what makes the Left left in light of our analysis of affect. Our argument is consistent with the rest of the book in that we are concerned with showing that leftist politics is about not just formal modes of solidarity but also the way in which solidarity can be built through shared structures of feeling, to use Raymond Williams's (1977) now famous term. We outline the structures of feeling that the Left needs to cultivate.

So what difference does adding these three political arts make? To begin with, they enrich our account of what politics is. Then they provide us with the means to spot new political opportunities and agendas. In turn, they allow us to better understand when and where pragmatism is necessary to channel the conduct of idealism. They guard against the idea that political agendas can be simply and unproblematically translated into practice, with practice acting as a kind of blotting paper that has no function other than to soak up what others have derived. Every action produces a reaction, and the Left has to stop thinking that in a complex world these reactions can be controlled. Instead, it needs to aim for an art of modulation that allows the possibility that new ideas can be generated from the swash of politics. Finally, they allow us to define democracy as a plural field in which "matters of concern" are both brought to the fore and potentially resolved through the vigor of publics, peoples, institutions, bureaucracies, experts, laypeople, and more constantly jostling with each other.

We close the book by listing some of the major challenges of our times that need to be addressed by the Left—challenges that constrain freedom and possibility in new ways. We illustrate what the Left might gain by addressing anew known challenges such as "financialization" and market organization or rising inequality and technologies of the self as opportunities to change conduct and political alignment through the expanded political arts presented in this book. We explore the openings created by working on affective desire—and organizational preparation—for futures that can harness markets and money to meet needs and develop capabilities; that can allow more complete forms of human being to flourish; and that kick back instinctively against inequality and injustice.

We want to make clear what this book is not, as well as what it is. Most obviously, there are lots of things missing. Of course there are. In a sense, that is our point. The world is very full. Even within the realm of political conduct, we cannot claim to be touching on every issue that might claim to be relevant. This, then, is not a work of political theory. That does not mean that there are no elements of political theory in it. But our firm intent is to intervene in practical political issues, which requires more than just the broad theoretical canvas that political theory offers. But neither is this a "how to do politics" book. It is, quite literally, a *primer* in that our intention is to prime new kinds of political thinking and practice. We will be satisfied if we set off in the reader new thoughts about how particular political goals might be achieved and even thoughts about the kind of politics in which they are engaged. In other words, the kind of politics we espouse is not grandiose. Big steps often begin with small steps that slowly gather momentum, and it is those small steps with big intent that most interest us.[4]

2

leftist
BEGINNINGS

In the late nineteenth century, the orders of aristocracy, industrial capitalism, and empire left little room for a politics of justice for the oppressed and downtrodden. For such a politics to arise in ways that were more than the passing concern of liberal reformers or other types of concessionary interest, new worlds would have to be invented, with their own protagonists, desires, and rules, forcing the established orders not only to engage, but also to concede ground in an expanded field of political representation and struggle. The fervor and sometimes the furies unleashed by the women's movement, communist and social-democratic thought, anti-imperialist struggle, labor organization, and a host of imaginations of freedom beyond the strictures of feudalism and capitalism succeeded in achieving just this.

The historiography of this experimental burst of activity between 1880 and 1914, first in Europe and later in North America, is vast and varied. Our interest here, however, lies in presenting a relatively well known account of effective mass political mobilization by an emergent Left as an exercise in world making that was successful in forcing change because of such inventiveness. Our claim, central to the thesis developed in the book, is that if a fervor for mass human emancipation and social justice spread across society—and in some instances, secured tangible outcomes—it did so because the forces seeking to break from tradition managed to animate a radically redesigned political arena. Through experiment rather than design, these forces invented new political subjects, tools, and goals out of suppressed life, exposed the existing field of political representation and validation as wanting and deformed, and developed an art of futurity involving imagination, yearning, and organization to give promised orders tangibility.

The rise and subsequent rapid ascendance of a politics of mass emancipation during this period was clearly emblematic of the times, not simply a matter of inventing new worlds and new historical subjects. For one, this was an extraordinarily uncertain and turbulent period—a time of hegemonic instability trapped between the death throes of feudal or mercantile society and the disruptions of an emergent industrial, urban, and imperial order. Amid the gaps created by systemic disruption and the tears produced by the jagged edges that marked the juxtaposition of orders, amid the misery born out of the materialities of the old and the materialities of the new, the case for a "third order" could be made. The disruptions of feudal decline, mass industrialization, and imperial expansionism—from the agonies and torments of factory life, urban poverty, and rural dislocation to the humiliations and exploitations of colonial rule—threw up their own grievances and related demands. And, sure enough, the promise of change in a new century spawned many new movements: anarchists, communists, and socialists seeking to overthrow or tame capitalism; progressives, workers' unions, and republicans fighting against industrial and political corporatism; suffragists struggling for women's rights; social reformers of various hues and ethical persuasions campaigning against child labor, poverty, malnutrition, disease, and appalling working and housing conditions; utopians and visionaries promising human solidarity and spiritual or ecological harmony in a new transcendental or social order; and the beginnings of organization against imperial and racial subjugation.

Given this book's concern with how grievances and interests can be swept into a coherent and sustained politics of emancipation that forces its way into the public imaginary and established political practice, it is not the fervor of political struggle or the pluralism of cause or idea of one hundred years ago that is of prime interest. The world abounds with both today. Instead, what we consider significant and relevant is the efficacy of a certain kind of futurity and, more precisely, the invention of a pragmatic utopianism—a politics of joining the unthinkable to the fabric of experience. In contrast to our times, in which too often the Left shows an inability to envelop latent injuries and concerns in models of future being and belonging, in the 1880–1914 period, against the grain and against the odds, some nascent revolutionary and reformist movements managed to propose a new world that made sense to, gave hope to, and endowed the masses with social and political subjectivity.

This was the genius — in different ways and with varying degrees of intentionality but with a similar measure of success — of the four movements we consider in this chapter. They were not emblematic of the time, for there were many other nascent progressive movements that were crushed or ignored. In turn, each of the four was different in its ambitions and tactics, and in its impact and legacy. No equivalence is implied in their selection. However, like other modern emancipatory projects in other periods that combined clear leadership with unenforced popular involvement (e.g., the anticolonial struggles of the twentieth century, the antiauthoritarian movements of 1968, the politics of social welfare after the Second World War), all four had a clear understanding — tacit or explicit — of the arts of political invention that were needed to make lasting cause for a new world. Each managed to fashion a new utopia out of lived experience, to change and charge public sentiment and desire, to transform the tools and subjects of political action, and to build the means to make a difference. Each intuited the arts of invention, affect, and organization needed to fashion and deliver a program of radical reform by working on the very nature of what it meant to be political. In its formative years, parts of the Left discovered a world-making capacity that the Left today seems to have lost.

We turn to the nature of this capacity in the four examples selected to foreground the case that the future of the Left rests on its ability to imagine and fashion hitherto unknown ways of being, made apprehensible through arts that altered the landscape of desire and political possibility. We begin with the German socialist movement led by August Bebel and Karl Kautsky, a movement that grew rapidly to dominate antiestablishment politics in Germany and elsewhere in Europe in the early twentieth century, aided by its ability to make tangible an impossible utopian ideal of the good society. We then turn to the origins of Swedish social democracy. Although it was late to arise and formed out of a dispersed and heterogeneous working mass, it had established itself as a significant political force by 1919 through its ability to make the case for a social and civic state carried by the industrial worker and extensive welfare reform. Next, we consider the successes of the British women's movement, traced to arts of tactical inventiveness, organization, and affective persuasion that radically altered understanding of women as human and political subjects. The final example is the Progressive Movement in the United States that, also against the odds in a rapidly transforming and fragmented society, managed to mobilize a politics of support for a "Social America" to expose and combat a corrosive corporatism ushered in by the new century.

Pragmatic Marxism: The German Socialist Party

The history of modern German socialism dates from May 1863, when Ferdinand Lassalle, the shrewd tactician who campaigned for universal suffrage under an imperial and authoritarian Germany governed by Bismarck, founded the German Workers' Association. The movement's emergence as a popular force coincides with the formation of the German Socialist Party (SPD) at Gotha in 1875, which brought together Lassallians and Marxists. Under the towering leadership of Bebel and Kautsky, who could claim the support of Karl Marx and Friedrich Engels in their commitment to displace the consolidating bourgeois state by a proletarian republic, the SPD rose to prominence in Germany and within the international socialist movement. Bismarck's attempts to distance the masses from socialism through welfare concessions introduced during the Anti-Socialist period (1878–90), when all forms of socialist and labor organization were outlawed, failed to dampen the rapid progress of the SPD. After 1890, as David Caute (1966, 61) notes, "The Party moved from strength to strength on a wave of rapid industrialization, emerging, in terms of members, candidates elected, organization and intellectual caliber, as the dominant force in the Second International."

While active SPD maneuvers to lead the Second International played their part, aided by favorable interventions from Engels, the party's real success lay in its efforts to become a mass political force within Germany standing for a very different kind of society. The overthrow of the imperial order and of capitalism was planned through the ballot box and the support of a new and organized industrial working class. By 1912, with nearly 1 million members, the SPD commanded 35 percent of the vote (universal men's suffrage was introduced in 1875), to emerge as the first party in the Reichstag. Its votes came from the rapidly grow-ing industrial working class, which by 1907 accounted for 39 percent of the German workforce. This was a unionizing workforce, especially in the fast growing building, coalmining, manufacturing, and steel indus-tries. From modest beginnings in the late 1870s, the membership of the SPD-sympathetic "free" unions had grown to 680,000 by 1900 (com-pared with the 77,000 members of the "Christian" unions) and then to more than 2.5 million by 1913 (and only 340,000 members of the "Chris-tian" unions). The "free" unions were popular because, in addition to protecting workers' interests in the trades they represented, they also ventured into providing welfare support — for example, insurance to workers against sickness, disability, or loss of income during strikes.

That the SPD's emergence as a major political force formed around an imaginary with no antecedents was quite extraordinary. It was all the more so because it occurred in a context marked by fervent national-ist agitation in the newly unified state, early-stage industrial and urban growth, large-scale attachment to agriculture and the church (especially in the southern regions), and authoritarian responses from an ancien regime clinging to power. Perhaps the fragile balance of power created an opening for the SPD and its vision of a better future. The German bourgeoisie was weak and fragmented, lacking — unlike elsewhere in Europe — a progressive and modernizing ideology such as liberalism to galvanize mass opposition to imperial autocracy. The German situa-tion did make space for an alternative vision of modernity. It would be a mistake, however, to assume that the historical conjuncture explains the success of the SPD, for it was not at all clear that the doctrine of scien-tific socialism pushed by the SPD (speaking of the misery of wage labor under capitalism, the inner contradictions of capitalism, the inevitability of socialism, the classless and repression-free society) was the doctrine of change that either the oppressed or those most desiring change were ready to endorse (Bartolini 2000).

What explains the success of the SPD was the ability of its leaders and organizations to name a new political subject and to present this subject as the force for change for the good of the many. As Donald Sassoon (1996, 7) explains:

In today's language we could say that the great intuition of the first socialist activists was that they had identified a "new political subject" with definite potential aspirations, able to produce a coherent set of political demands for both the short and the long term. If politics is an art, then this was one of its masterpieces. Socialist politics and the socialist movement could comprehend the most varied issues: short-term demands such as improvements in working conditions; national reforms such as pension schemes; comprehensive schemes such as economic planning and a new legal system; major political changes such as the expansion of the suffrage; utopian projects such as the abolition of the state, etc. All these demands could be embodied into a single overarching project.

The project required the invention of a vanguard subject, something that the new socialist leadership grasped clearly. The prevailing circumstances offered no obvious political protagonist. Everyday working-class culture continued to be shaped by the sheer needs of survival, propped up by rituals and religious superstitions remote from any culture of class pride and hope. The working masses were desperate, downtrodden, and fragmented, and so the SPD and the "free" unions looked to the young and aspiring skilled male worker employed in new urban trades such as printing, building, or metalworking to bear the torch of progress and possibility (Berger 1995, 73). These were individuals enjoying relatively stable work in the emerging large firms of Germany's new industrial conurbations, and they were receptive to ideas of workplace or trade solidarity, craft respectability, and their social power and worth beyond the punishments of everyday toil. This receptivity was enhanced by the tangible gains the socialists managed to secure on their behalf, from negotiating better wage and working conditions to providing welfare support to members and their families and access to educational and leisure activities. Visualized in the form of this kind of model worker, and "by thinking of the working class as a political class, ascribing to it a specific politics and rejecting the vaguer categories ('the poor') of earlier reformers, the pioneers of socialism thus virtually 'invented' the working class" (Sassoon 1996, 7).

But the new invented subject had to be given popular credibility, and this required another art: the mastery of tactical politics. For example, despite the rhetoric of abolishing capitalism, most of the victories of the "free unions" were secured through collective agreements

with employers, without strike activity. By 1913, two-thirds of all industrial conflicts had been settled peacefully through negotiations between
employers and the unions (Berger 1995). A movement committed to
the overthrow of feudalism and capitalism made its progress though
coalition-building, electoral campaigning, and pragmatic compromise.[1]
This included participation by the SPD in elections, understanding the
daily lives and desires of workers (including the primacy of supersti-
tion and faith), recognizing new kinds of organization such as cooperatives to provide "living demonstration of an economic system superior
to capitalism" (Landauer 1959, 315), and collaborating with Catholic and
conservative organizations in the agricultural south to gain a foothold
among the rural poor.

The pragmatic concessions were necessary in a newly unified, still
fragmented, and deeply traditional nation, yet they did not divert the
SPD from its socialist program. This is what makes the SPD interesting compared with an official Left today that is easily derailed by the
exigencies of political opportunism. The party managed to bridge the
pragmatic and programmatic by making the latter affectively present.
Although it remained a movement fashioned by urban intellectuals, professionals, and skilled workers, the SPD managed to portray socialism as
a future "clothed with the beauty of a thousand stars," a "millennium of
peace, democratic fellowship and material abundance," in the words of
Julius Braunthal, the leader of the Austrian social democrats, soon after
the First World War (as quoted in Rabinbach 1985, 126). Beyond the
pragmatic accommodations, the leadership worked at maintaining and
popularizing a clear utopian project, with the help of varied affective
technologies. Books played their part. Bebel's *Woman and Socialism* was
reprinted more than fifty times between 1879 and 1914; it was widely read
because it argued with conviction that the rights of all women would
improve in a future of common ownership, scientific advancement, cooperation, and collective governance. Pamphlets, newspapers, and public gatherings proliferated as new media for the "popular" classes, along
with many cultural and recreational societies after the 1890s living out
the socialist dream beyond the harsh realities of work and home. As Carl
Landauer (1959, 316) observes: "In the 1880's national organizations were
founded for the workers' athletic societies, the workers' cyclist clubs, and
the workers' hiking clubs. Eventually the workers' recreational movements extended to many other activities from chess to theatre, and, in

the latter field, through the *volksbühne* (People's Stage), it exerted a considerable cultural influence. The philosophical interests of the workers were pursued by the Proletarian Freethinker's League, which had for its program the most determined opposition to the churches."

Very quickly after its formation, the SPD developed an authoritative capability that drew on ideological clarity, strong leadership, international influence, ground-level organization, and effective communication. This is what helped the party to become the symbol of socialist success in Europe and to stitch together a web of interests at home and within the Second International. The party worked hard to develop an independent communicative space. Kaustky's and Bebel's books were translated into many European languages and soon became blueprints of socialist vision and practice. The leaders wrote pamphlets, edited newspapers, communicated tirelessly with other socialists in Europe, and led the Socialist International, all of which enhanced the political authority and reach of the party. In turn, the many reading and discussion groups that proliferated (spontaneously in the workplace or organized by the "free" unions and recreational societies) acted not only as the forum in which the party disseminated its influence, but also as part of the socialist "community," widening the chain of interest, responsibility, feedback, and organization. As Stefan Berger (1995, 72) explains: "The SPD [developed] its own organisational world consisting of party, trade union, cooperative and cultural, educational, sport, youth, women's and other ancillary organisations, which . . . provided every possible service for members 'from the cradle to the grave'. 'Organisational patriotism' came to characterise the 'community of solidarity' formed by the labor movement in many proletarian neighborhoods in Imperial Germany." This was not an achievement of cold or cumbersome organization but, rather, an experiment of authorization that allowed the SPD to extend its influence while also gathering new worker identities and interests. By 1914, the SPD had developed a structure of influence that was both efficient and empowering, but one that would be shaken by the war that followed.

Welfare Utopia: Swedish Social Democracy

Swedish social democracy, by contrast, drew on the power of nondoctrinaire ideas of communal well-being. It developed another idea of the good society, and it managed to make something of it through a different politics of public formation and persuasion. Shortly into the twentieth century, a new model of social emancipation and collective being emerged, to dominate Swedish political life from the 1930s until recently, playing on the hopes of a fair, equal, and providing society. Such hopes, it is important to note, arose without precedent in a far from "ready" society. Sweden in the late nineteenth century, like Germany, was socially and politically fragmented. Both countries were late to industrialize and did so rapidly, but in Sweden the process was essentially rural, involving small artisan enterprises in the primary industries. Fifty percent of the industrial workforce in 1913 was based in the countryside, and enterprises with more than 500 workers accounted for only 19 percent of the industrial workforce (Tilton 1974).

The bourgeoisie was dispersed and politically weak. Urban professionals and intellectuals were not an inventive or political force, while the industrial workforce was fragmented by geography, size of enterprise, and craft or skill. In the countryside, where half the population lived in 1900—largely in abject misery—the historical failure of the landed aristocracy to develop commercial agriculture had created a disjointed farming system of variable economic potential. In the late nineteenth century, therefore, Sweden possessed a weak capitalist class and weak liberal opposition to conservative rule by the old landed aristocracy and powerful commercial families, the Protestant church, and a Parliament dominated by farming interests (propped up by voting rights offered to only the propertied adult male population).

Sweden, like Germany, was open to change because of the weaknesses of the ancien regime and the emerging commercial bourgeoisie, but there was no reason that social democracy should have emerged as the "natural" alternative in a country with a small, variegated, and dispersed industrial working class.[2] The tide had to be created, forged out of diverse forms of subjugation and social need, an opportunity that was grasped by the Social Democratic Workers Party (SDAP), formed in 1889, and the national union organization (LO), formed in 1898. Together, the two movements managed to shift an ingrained culture of craft solidarity toward one of class recognition (Fulcher 1991) through efforts to unite the different fractions of labor and invest a brand of socialism with popular appeal. The process began with the SDAP's moves to form general trade unions—first locally and then as national bodies—that brought together craft, skilled, and semiskilled workers in related industries under one roof.[3] Building labor solidarity through a new form of unionism became a key tool of the SDAP in a context of limited suffrage and an absent mass industrial proletariat. The LO's arrival helped to convince different unions to join together in industry-wide campaigns, which started to yield improvements in wages and working conditions as employers felt the opposition of an organized labor movement. The combined strength of the LO and the SDAP resulted in the passage of a law by the Parliament in 1906 permitting state mediation of industrial conflict.

Organization and pragmatic reform were important aspects of early Swedish social democracy. So, too, was the fashioning of a unique vision of future social justice and freedom.[4] Ernst Wigforss, who served in Parliament from 1919 to 1953, played a vital role in the process. He reworked the definition of socialism as a "provisional utopia" that should guide policy practice but also should be reviewed on the basis of evolving experience. Accordingly, the SDAP's case for socialism in Sweden swung toward practical reforms consistent with the principle of a fair, equal, and just society, in the process building widespread cross-sectional appeal (Tilton 1979). In 1919, Wigforss also wrote the "Gothenburg Programme," which anticipated reforms that would dominate social-democratic policy for years to come, relating to the workplace (e.g., the right to employment, shorter working hours, statutory holidays), social welfare (e.g., old-age pensions, maternity allowances, public housing, universal educational, progressive income tax), and public ownership and control (e.g., public banking and insurance, worker participation, consumer cooperatives, and collective control of the economy).

Six enduring tenets of social democracy were drafted, which eventually settled as the moral compass of reform and achievement in Sweden (and beyond). One was the elimination of social sources of inequality in wealth, income, and education. Another was the inviolability of civil and political rights, collective ownership of the means of production, and state-led redistribution. The third was the indispensability of parliamentary and participatory democracy, spreading from the universal franchise to workplace participation and public involvement. Fourth was the provision of social security through work, well-being, and state insurance against hazard and risk. The fifth tenet was the importance of controlling the capitalist economy through state ownership and effective planning, progressive taxation, financial and market regulation, and the encouragement of cooperatives and worker enterprises.[5] And the sixth, and final, tenet was the need for social cooperation, solidarity, and mutuality to make for the new collective society.

After a century of leftist causes around the world based on such tenets, it is difficult to appreciate how novel and prescient they were for their time—all the more so in a conservative, rural, and fragmented society. Nascent Swedish social democracy had to work hard at building popular momentum behind its core tenets, and it did so by managing to engineer hope around a program—ideological and pragmatic—of welfare reform. The tenets, continually discussed and refined in the party, Parliament, labor movement, publications and public meetings, gave shape, meaning, and direction to manifold practical struggles. Welfare universalism became the means by which a new commons and a new public were constructed out of Sweden's many subaltern communities and many dispersed ills, a way to reimagine social power and historical possibility.

Here, too, a vanguard subject was imagined—the responsible, disciplined, socialized, and industrious worker—as the nemesis of the idle, superstitious, ignorant, and wretched worker or peasant. But it was also clearly understood that the making of one collective out of such stark dualisms required the formation of new common habits and feelings, new subjectivities of welfare society shared by all of its protagonists and beneficiaries. For example, temperance appeared at the center of the new politics of transformation (Hurd 1996). In 1900, the metalworkers' union in Stockholm banned its members from drinking alcohol, recognizing that the struggle for a new society required altered subjective states. More widely, along with qualities such as thrift and mutuality, temperance came to be understood as the means by which Swedes could free themselves from the bonds and miseries of both the old order and raw capitalism as habits of the welfare society. As Madeleine Hurd (1996, 631) explains, "To be involved in temperance was to forge links with men's and women's suffrage, charities, and housing-reform groups; organizations for alcohol-free harbor workers' waiting-rooms, 'reading-rooms,' and 'warmth rooms'; the Study Circle adult education networks; penal reform and World Peace organizations. Here again, temperance, while not necessarily converting workers to individualistic reformism, helped integrate social democrats into a larger social and political network." In short, Swedish social democracy grew and lasted as a radical political force because of its ability to place a "provisional" utopia within reach by constantly reviewing the balance between principle and pragmatic reform and by working on the sentimental structure of the society to come.

Reinventing the Political: The British Women's Movement

While the preceding two examples illustrate the power in particular of the art of utopian preparedness, something more was at work behind the success of the British women's movement in the first two decades of the twentieth century. Here we see a wholesale reinvention of the political — its spaces, purposes, technologies, and subjects. The women's cause turned assumptions about womanhood and femininity on their head, forced the acceptance of women as political subjects, expanded the sites and technologies of political action, and altered the very meaning of political life and its ends. The gains achieved for women came from a displacement of the political from itself. We illustrate this claim by returning to three significant inventions. The first is the campaign for the "New Woman," which redefined femininity and brought hidden injuries of sexuality, marriage, and family life into the public and political arena. The second is the introduction of new subjects — working-class women — into the women's cause, which altered the course of women's demands and opened new political alliances. The third is the invention of new forms of protest by the Women's Social and Political Union (wspu), which jolted the rules of political conduct in remarkably effective ways.

We will turn first to the politics of the New Woman. While the women's campaign had focused largely on the vote (avoiding scrutiny of Victorian norms of marriage and femininity), attention in the 1910s shifted to the private lives and social roles of women. Novels and new women's magazines such as *Shafts* and *Freewoman* questioned old shibboleths such as the place of the woman in the home. Dora Marsden, the editor of *Freewoman*, reputed to have coined the term "feminist," urged women to fight for their own personal, sexual, and economic independence (Caine 1997). The New Woman campaign shattered convention by calling marriage an enslavement that atrophied women's intellectual abilities and personal identities. While some feminists urged women to leave husbands and homes, others pressed for recognition of marriage as an equal relation, allowing women the right to privacy, freedom, and divorce.

Letters and articles in magazines such as *Shafts* asked women to demand a life true to their real needs by joining the campaign for birth control, equal moral and sexual rights, and economic independence. Alongside the private, the New Woman was asked to take active part in public life, not only through the acquisition of voting rights, but also by participating in diverse cultural and social associations. For the time, these were unimaginably subversive demands because they promoted an entirely new idea of womanhood. The campaign was met with ridicule or anger from the press and the political mainstream, condemnation from the majority of men, mute support from the emerging labor and socialist movements, and anxious nervousness from women who wanted the vote but not so comprehensive a call on, and for, women. However, the campaign was supported by many young, literate, and educated women, and most important, it developed an idea of womanhood that shaped feminist politics and social understanding in the course of the twentieth century.

The second great invention was the integration of working women into the feminist cause, which immediately altered the nature and scope of gender and class politics. After the 1880s, women began to join the factory labor force in large numbers. The working woman's problems, from poor wages and working conditions to the balancing of work and domestic life, kept her away from the almost exclusively middle-class women's movement, with its focus on the vote and femininity. She became the figure of a new kind of politics, with different resonances and connections with other struggles for emancipation at the time. For example, the 1880s and 1890s saw the rise of the Women's Trade Union League, which focused on workplace reform and the participation of women in the wider labor movement; the Fabian Women's Group, which campaigned for the economic independence of women and equal rights with men; the Women's Co-operative Guild, which tried to bring working women into the cooperative movement; and other organizations such as the Women's Trade Union Association, the Women's Labour League, the Women's Industrial Council.

The "social feminists" often clashed with the suffragette movement, condemning its neglect of the problems faced by working women, its belief that suffrage would lead to other gains for women, and its assumption that the married woman should stay at home. While many middle-class feminists opposed women giving up their traditional duties as carers, new organizations, such as the Women's Industrial Council, the Fabian Women's Group (which included Beatrice Webb), and the Women's Co-operative Guild led by Margaret Llewellyn Davies, actively campaigned for paid employment for married women as a source of extra income for poor working-class families and as an opportunity for women to realize their potential. The response of the labor and socialist movements was equally mixed. Organizations such as the Fabian Women's Group and the Women's Co-operative Guild were unusual in campaigning for women in both the workplace and at home. So while the guild succeeded after fifteen years in getting the co-operative union to accept a minimum wage for both men and women in 1912, most other unions and leftist political groups continued to think of politics as a men's affair. The Trades Union Congress resolutely opposed campaigning for women's voting rights, as did the newly formed Labour Party and the Social Democratic Federation, while more sympathetic socialist organizations such as the Independent Labour Party and the Fabians waxed and waned on the issue until well after the First World War.

But such opposition simply stirred new energies, and hardened the resolve to extend the women's struggle beyond more established channels. For example, the "radical suffragists" — working-class women who started out in the factories and mills of Lancashire and Cheshire as union activists — eventually left the unions, disillusioned by the lack of attention paid to women's rights, to join feisty new women's organizations such as the wspu and the National Union of Women's Suffrage Societies (nuwss). Despite the obstacles put up from within and beyond the women's movement, a fervor was maintained and organized in shifting ways, yielding a twentieth-century politics of emancipation that could no longer ignore the presence and needs of the working woman.

Turning to the invention of new political means, the years between 1890 and 1914 saw the women's movement transformed into a force of extraordinary energy and guile, sparked by a campaign of public disorder and militancy led by the wspu. It was a campaign that introduced new political weapons and tactics that not only disarmed established political practice to the advantage of the women's cause, but also redefined women as public subjects.[6] The wspu, formed in Manchester in 1903 by the Pankhursts, catapulted to national prominence two years later, when Christabel Pankhurst and Annie Kenney launched a campaign of direct action by interrupting a Liberal Party election meeting. Following their arrest and imprisonment, which sparked vituperative public and political commentary, the WSPU scaled up its campaign of disruptions. It organized clamorous demonstrations inside and outside Parliament; hectored politicians; distributed suffrage literature; and staged dramatic protests that included women chaining themselves to the railings outside Parliament, throwing acid at polling booths, breaking windows, and setting buildings on fire. The result was more violence, more arrests, and more media and political attention.

While the WSPU remained a small and controversial organization, rejected by many women who disapproved of its tactics and military discipline, other women's organizations expanded and developed effective tools of direct action. For example, the number of societies affiliated with the NUWSS increased by more than 400 between 1907 and 1910, adding more than 50,000 new members (Caine 1997). The NUWSS attracted a younger generation of women, many from working backgrounds, who were fearful of losing their jobs and respectability if they were linked to the WSPU. Under the leadership of Millicent Fawcett, the NUWSS too began to organize "suffrage stalls" in marketplaces, culminating in the "mud march" of February 1907, when 3,000 women marched in central London. Whether it was the WSPU or the NUWSS,

> This was the start of many outdoor marches, pageants, and demonstrations featuring the banners and costumes through which militants and constitutionalists served to transform the suffrage movement, making its public demonstrations eye-catching and memorable. Women artists and writers were drawn into the movement as exhibitions were mounted to draw further attention to the movement and its activities, while suffrage songs were sung and plays staged. The pageantry and sheer scale of suffrage demonstrations now brought excessive news coverage even to the older societies, which were increasingly coming to be called "constitutionalist" in contrast with the militants. (Caine 1997, 161)

The combined impact of the militant and constitutional feminists was to redefine the meaning of human emancipation by questioning patriarchy, articulating new notions of womanhood, extending the class base of the women's cause, and bringing women from different backgrounds to a common cause. At the start of the twentieth century, British feminism stood at the vanguard of the international women's movement. This achievement was no doubt the result of effective organization around certain women's concerns and causes, but none of this could have been achieved without inventions that redefined political subjectivity and agency (Mayhall 2000), as well as the content and conduct of politics.

Inventing Social America

Our final example to illustrate the arts involved in wresting space for a new commons is the Progressive Movement in the United States and its campaign for a "Social America." The great depression of 1893–97 had left millions of workers unemployed, underemployed, and exploited as company after company collapsed, reduced activity, or extracted more from its workers.[7] Americans who remained in jobs were split by location, skill, trade, gender, race, and ethnicity. Unions, where they existed, were largely local, fragmented, under-resourced, disorganized, weak, and in competition with one another. Or, like the American Federation of Labor led by Samuel Gompers, they decided to mimic corporatism by standing for only particular sections of the skilled working class, against other sections of labor, and in cahoots with emerging political forces scrambling for control in the new corporatist America (Greene 1998; Wiebe 1967). The business shakeup initiated a large-scale merger movement, leaving America with 200 massive corporate trusts in the new century that would dominate its economic and political life for a very long time (Chandler 1977; Lamoreaux 1985).

In this context arose socialist tendencies with varying but largely hapless fortunes.[8] But another reformist movement also arose with wider reach and appeal that chose to address the infringements of "Corporate America" through a politics of "common America." This was the Progressive Movement, which rose in prominence after 1910 and was led by pragmatist philosophers such as John Dewey, social reformers such as Jane Addams, and reform politicians such as Theodore Roosevelt. The Progressives opposed a politics of self-interest and corporate organization, campaigned for the rights of the common American and for social justice, and proposed a nation led by the people. What makes the Progressives so interesting for current discussions on leftist renewal is that precisely at a time of constrained citizenship, centralizing power and authority, and ill-formed publics, a movement should have attracted popular attention and support by focusing on the idea of democracy itself and its constituents (Kann 1982).

John Dewey and Herbert Croly were two prominent exponents of this idea. According to Richard Rorty, Dewey maintained that democracy should mean "nothing save freely achieved consensus among human beings," a "matter of forgetting about eternity" and building, instead, "social hope for what might become real" (Rorty 1998, 18). This meant dispensing with "a theoretical frame of reference within which to evaluate proposals for the human future" (Rorty 1998, 20) in preference for a pragmatism of collective effort to shape the future (Dewey 1954). In *The Promise of American Life* (1963 [1909]), which became a manifesto of the Progressive era, Herbert Croly extended Dewey's critique of transcendentalism, ideology, and centered authority by also tackling liberal individualism.[9] The American future, for Croly, required extensive democratization, putting the national purpose before individual advancement, pushing the state toward the social redistribution of wealth, and introducing institutional reforms to give citizens the means to shape the American future.

For the Progressives, thus, the steps toward a social America could be open and pluralist as long as they extended social power. "In a hectic round of activity," Alan Dawley (2003, 2) observes, the Progressives "set out to regulate big business, rid money-driven politics of corruption, secure a place for industrial workers in American life, and give the New Woman time to grow. As if dealing with issues of class and gender was not enough, they also tried to improve relations among ethnic groups."[10] What defined the movement, and public support for it, was the commitment to social America. This meant leading the fight against market power in the name of a new kind of "mastery" over the economy (Lippmann 1961 [1914]). The Progressives became involved in campaigns to ensure tighter regulation of the market, to break up or control the trusts, to restrict monopoly practices, to establish multi-partner government commissions, and to spread job opportunities.

It also meant developing a politics of "social conscience," which Dawley (2003, 43) judges to have been the movement's most "most enduring contribution . . . to American reform." The Progressives worked hard at highlighting the social ills of America—from poverty and unemployment to immorality and ill health — as the consequences of corrupted power, individualism, and the unregulated market, and they worked hard to build the social capacity to tackle these ills. Social reformers like Addams and Robert La Follette joined with religious groups, suffrage campaigners, radical unions, socialists and republicans, temperance organizations, minority ethnic groups, and reform-minded local administrations to fight deprivation and desperation in the rapidly expanding cities of the North, West, and Midwest. They helped to improve housing quality; combat malnutrition, disease, and illness; fight for women's rights; provide facilities for child care, education, and recreation; curb child labor and limit working hours; build community support networks; and tackle drinking, prostitution, idleness, and depravity. These local initiatives linked into national campaigns led by the Progressives for improved welfare legislation.

Moreover, the campaign for social America involved the invention of a politics of public interest that aimed to change prevailing sentiments. For the Progressives, this certainly meant government freed from private interests, especially those of big business. One success they engineered with the support of Woodrow Wilson, who led with a Democrat majority in Congress, was a suite of anti-corporatist reforms passed in 1913–14, including the creation of the Federal Reserve System (a first step toward collective regulation of the financial system) and the Clayton Act (which outlawed interlocking directorates and brought in a new Federal Trade Commission to regulate monopoly practices). It also meant a greater say for citizens in public affairs, with Progressives joining the campaign for universal suffrage, worker participation, consumer organizations, neighborhood committees, and other public interest or grassroots movements springing up in America at the time.

Any campaign for a new America that was based on reinventing the idea of democracy itself was never going to be easy in a land heading fast toward corporate capitalism. Indeed, the balance sheet of reform in the pre-1914 period tipped in favor of big business and corporatist interests in general. However, the period sowed the seeds of a public-interest politics that would slowly be assimilated into Americans' understanding of a desirable democracy. An idea of social power as the counterweight to unregulated expansion and centered authority began to mature, yielding a politics of civic intervention between state and market. This was a very different kind of politics of reform from the moves in Europe to look beyond feudalism and capitalism, but it was one that resonated with the new continent's situation of massive social mixture and churn, spatial enormity and fragmentation, and rapid economic transformation, along with the principles of civic opportunity and freedom enshrined in the American constitution. The Progressive Movement made space for a Social America by counterposing, if not wresting, the meaning of democracy and being democratic out of their corporatist corruptions at the start of the twentieth century.

Conclusion

We close this chapter by summarizing the propensities that characterized the movements that we have covered as an indication of the kind of invention needed if the Left is to reclaim its place at the head of a politics of transformation. In all cases, progress depended on prizing open new political ground and filling it with real hope and desire. Appeal and effectiveness—at a time heavily laden with the weight of tradition, vested power, restricted social force, and new capitalist imperative—had to come from an ability to imagine and build community around the yet to come or the yet to be revealed. This meant inventing new historical subjects, new technologies of organization and resistance, new visions of the good life and social possibility, new definitions of human subjectivity and fulfillment, and new spaces of the political (such as "direct action," "voting," "public involvement," "class struggle," "welfare reform," "government for the people," "women's rights"). A possible world had to be fashioned to render the old unacceptable and the new more desirable and possible. The Left today seems to have less desire or ability to stand outside the given to disclose and make way for a new world.

World making in the movements we have considered relied on particular inventions of togetherness and desire. One was the organization of hope, with the help of core ideas, disciplinary capacity, techniques of persuasion and influence, and institutional efficacy. All of the movements examined, whether ideological or pragmatic, possessed a clear sense of cause, vision, and journey. They offered a politics of enchantment, sustained by inspiring leadership, literature and propaganda, solidarity born out of collective action, and, in some instances, a foretaste of the life to come provided through the material, recreational, cultural, and aesthetic initiatives of the movement. Perhaps the ground of possibility today has become too colonized or corrupted by the corporate manipulation of information, knowledge, and desire by powerful vested interests, leaving space only for limited outbursts of popular anger and revulsion (Castells 2009). The organization of hope around a clear diagram of future being might help to break this deadlock and spawn new and independent means of realization.

Then, the movements we have considered in this chapter developed the means to make tangible a future society, and as a freedom for the all. Even the most revolutionary and ideological of the movements — German socialism — worked for tangible reforms in the labor market and workplace, in the arena of social welfare, in domestic and recreational life, and in the public arena. Even the most focused campaign — the women's movement — was able to draw the many into the cause or to make the cause relevant to the many. This was achieved in different ways, from powerful imaginaries of the commons to deliberate efforts to bridge differences. Today's Left sometimes seems to have given up on idealistic pragmatism, on gathering difference around common cause. Perhaps this is due in part to the sacrifice of principled intent and of principled opposition in favor of opportunistic gain. All of the movements tell a story of immense tenacity and courage, sustained by ethical zeal, indignation, a sense of right, and the desire for a better world. They went against the grain, posed great risk to those who participated, and were roundly attacked; without moral commitment, they would have collapsed.

It is also clear that the success of the movements depended on developing organizational durability and reach. This involved clear leadership and effective institutionalization so that a consistency of representative and participatory effort could be maintained. But other modes of organization were also involved, often on the margins of mainstream modes of representation, so that new forms of gathering and maintenance could arise with the help of associations, societies, rituals, propaganda, and affective participation. Organization took on a new meaning. Today, there is no shortage of organizational variety (think of only the many spaces of union opened up by the software society), and the social movements that proliferate typically make the most of these opportunities (Castells 2009). But the Left's aspiration for power often seems to have lost its sense of finding ways to make gains amplify, resonate, count.

What can be learned from this brief historical journey into the years of the rise of modern emancipatory politics in the West is that success came from reinventing political practice and the meaning of the political, in the process creating a space for new principles of human purpose and fellowship. Into that space flowed imaginaries of emancipation and organization that were simultaneously without precedent and yet feasible. Whether the Left in its formative years was conscious that its historical mission lay in imagining the impossible and anticipating it by altering the terms of political engagement is a moot point. Today, the Left needs to return to a similar program of radical inventiveness more consciously if it is to prepare the ground for new ways of thinking and feeling the good life. But to do that requires thinking anew about the political arts of how to make worlds and, indeed, about what we mean by the political itself. That task commences in the next chapter and stretches through the rest of the book.

3

reinventing the
POLITICAL

I will not say . . . how the new reality we desire should be constituted
as a whole. I offer no depiction of an ideal, no description of a utopia.
— CARL LANDAUER (quoted in Jacoby 2005, 112)

To set out to write about "the political," we first need to have some sense
of what we mean by the term. There is, of course, a narrow definition
of the political as relations between governments and other governments and between governments and people. A slightly broader definition might work off particular goals. For example, the political might be
understood as the question of how to distribute a scarce quantity of resources in a just fashion or how to distribute and achieve power through
a social contract of some kind.

But notice one thing: nearly every political theory tends to assume
that the subject of politics is human being unfolding in time. But what if
we no longer take this as a given, not only in the obvious sense that we
no longer assume that there is such a thing as "progress" (which does
not mean, of course, that we can no longer be progressive) but also in
the sense that a determinate object called "the human" exists that can
be worked on? What if we then start to have doubts that the "human" in
human being can be captured by a model that thinks of humanity as so
many bodies intersubjectively linked in groups?[1] What if, then, we allow

other forces to enter the political fray that do not measure up to this conception?

What if, at exactly the same time, we were to think about the being in human being as a constant process of becoming in the style of thought pioneered by Edmund Husserl, Martin Heidegger, Henri Bergson, William James, and Alfred North Whitehead? That would mean that we would see politics itself as an unfolding in space and time, constantly creating new worlds — a pluriversal experiment rather than a universalist statement of fact, as William James might have had it. At the same time we would have to clearly trace the outlines of the political ground, since this kind of speculative philosophy has often been accused of having no political theory of any import so that such a theory has to be constructed from the ground up (Harman 2005).[2]

What if, consequently, we were to consider politics as a repertoire of practices that run far outside the usual writ of what is regarded as "political"? What if we were to allow practices to move into and out of political attention, from what Lauren Berlant (2008) calls the "juxtapolitical" sphere into the political sphere and back again, as has happened, for example, when understandings of womanhood have changed? What if we were to take relational practices like art as not mere trivialities, clearly outside the orbit of serious political discourse and practice, but as having something real to say about politics — and not least the need to redefine the political? What if we were to admit actors who traditionally have been regarded as objects of political attention but rarely as subjects? Animals, plants, bacteria, the climate — all manner of objects might become part of a much expanded notion of a "sociable life" that extends those whom we meet with and care about, and, by implication, the political sphere (Hird 2009).

This chapter is about precisely these possibilities of political relocation so that the Left can begin to stake out a new and profoundly hybrid world and fashion appropriate practices and modes of occupancy instead of finding itself perpetually on the back foot in territory marked out by the fixities of tradition and the dubious purities of the last stand. This book takes up what is now becoming a familiar view that places all human, nonhuman, natural, and artificial objects on the same footing (Latour 1999) and expands the realm of the political accordingly so that, to use that phrase again, "All reality is political, but not all politics is human" (Harman 2009, 89). In other words, this chapter's goal is to try to describe, and then begin to work with for progressive ends, a political landscape that no longer excludes the many players that might be thought to have political import once the political is no longer restricted to human beings understood in a particular way—as, in some sense, rational—and once the actions and decisions of these rational beings are no longer understood as unproblematically following on, like arrows from a bow. We want to take up Bruno Latour's (1999) call for a new parliament and constitution that can accommodate the myriad beings that populate the world, a call that entails acts of definition and redefinition of "actor" so that many humans and nonhumans can jostle for position, gradually expanding the scope and meaning of "collective" politics.

The chapter is structured in four parts. We start by describing certain aspects of human being that are often left on the shelf when the political sphere is understood as so many rational interchanges and, in particular, the pre personal domain of affect. We then move on to the issue of other beings and existences, which we will illustrate through the three groups of entities: "animals," a problematic term in itself in that it groups all manner of beings with all kinds of affects into just one category in a way that could itself be deemed political, and "plants" and "objects"—both of them equally problematic terms in that they ascribe a passive homogeneity to entities that are often very far from passively homogeneous (Harman 2005). We will then move on to the issue of space, but understood as a "psychotopical" atmosphere, which is a key determinant of the content and conduct of the political. Finally, we consider the kinds of leftist politics that can arise from expanding the domain of the political in the way we are espousing.

Human Being

Politics is often assumed to be based on *rational* decisions made by free-thinking and sovereign people. Liberal political theory has conventionally relied on some version of political contract theory, in which human beings are essentially individual, self-sufficient entities; they are rational agents who generate politics through different patterns of civil association. In making this assumption, political theory, as many feminist political theorists have long noted (e.g., Jaggar 1983), ignores the simple facts of biology that dictate that human beings are always interdependent, reliant each on the other for sustenance and survival. Although most recent currents of political thought track away from the assumption of rationality, most particularly in continental philosophy, it is still difficult to argue that they have been entirely successful in replacing the powerful liberal paradigm, which looks to establish set rules by which a society can act, striving to negotiate difference and incommensurability in a way that treats each and every one with impartiality and aims to produce human subjects to suit. This matters, since it circumscribes not only what is political but also what is politically possible—or, indeed, legitimate or even thinkable.

Take just the impact on a notion such as political skepticism. Political skepticism is a condition that liberal political theorists persistently invoke, but what they mean by the term varies. For Michael Oakeshott (1991), for example, it involves a claim about the limitations of technical expertise in politics. For Isaiah Berlin (1979), it is the insistence that we cannot assume that there will be any natural harmony between the plurality of political values that we pursue. But it is a condition that has been espoused by a number of continental theorists, too. Take the case of Nietzsche. His basic argument, according to Tamsin Shaw (2007, 9), is that "even if we can assume that there are knowable normative truths, secular societies will still have a tremendous problem in making these truths effective in public life. Even objective normative truth would not be able to provide a basis for genuine political legitimacy because the majority of people would have no means of recognising it as such."

Given these kinds of reservations, how might we think about rationality? Rationality can be thought of as having a series of components. They include intelligence, normativity, some form of reflective consciousness, and the related qualities that follow from these components: language, certain kinds of conceptual ability (e.g., the ability to recognize higher-order mental states that make it possible to generalize from the here and now), means of recognizing causality, and some degree of instrumentality (recognizing that the classical distinction between means and end can never be other than a relative affair). But, as has become clear, there are problems with picking out each and every one of these qualities. To begin with, it is not clear that language is a necessary accompaniment to rationality. Recent work on body "language," and more generally on the senses, suggests that there are all kinds of registers in which it is possible to think. There is also an enormous debate about higher-order thinking and what it consists of—a proto-empathic capacity; an ability to simulate others' behavior; an ability to lie, deceive, or dissimulate; an ability to invent tools and memory routines that allow thinking to be retained, worked on, and distributed.

The position is even more complicated as far as causality is concerned. Recent work in the history of science shows just how radically what might be called the epistemic virtues can change over time. For example, Lorraine Daston and Peter Galison (2007) argue that "objectivity" is a nineteenth-century invention arising out of the rejection of the idealization of representation. Likewise, instrumentality is a quality that has been debated for many centuries, but one thing now seems clear: the heuristics that link means and ends are imperfect. The norms of behavioral rationality are constantly and systematically violated. This is partly due to the nature of the environments with which agents are interactively coupled, but even here, the opacity of many situations makes it hard to see what would actually be "rational," given uncertainties about human sociality. Kim Sterelny (2003) and others have argued, for example, that the sheer complexity of social life, with its numerous opportunities for deception and manipulation of information, has forced the development of advanced cognitive capacities: what we might identify as Machiavellian intelligence has driven intelligence, thus placing the conduct of politics right at the heart of evolution. In contrast, Michael Tomasello (2008, 2009), Sarah Blaffer Hrdy (2009), and others argue that the driving force of social life is cooperation, driven by the communicative bidding that is possible because of shared intentionality and by the need to care for offspring, placing another kind of politics at the heart of evolution.

What all of this shows is that the best we can do is work with a notion of what might be called process rationality, which recognizes that reasoning is often an inefficient way to negotiate the world that at best meets only weaker requirements of normativity and generality. There is also the issue of people and personhood. Western societies work with an idea of personhood that is quite specific and occupies only one of many possibilities of how one might think of cases. The work of Philippe Descola and Eduardo Viveiros de Castro in anthropology; of Ralph Ellison, and Valentin Groebner in history; and of Berlant in cultural studies all shows how it is possible to think of, and with, quite different models of personhood. Each of these models brings with it different consequences for what counts as political thinkability and rationality, not least through what is allowed to count as exteriority or interiority. After all, to take but one example, if a person thinks of an animal as a person with animal "clothing" (Lloyd 2007), that is likely to produce political results different from those for a person who thinks of an animal as convenient natural furniture. And this has, after all, been the worldview of many people:

> Social roles and cultural life are not limited to human beings, but are (in this view) widely shared by other animals and spirits. By the same token . . . there is no operational notion of "nature" that describes a domain of animals and creatures other than humans as a distinct, non-social category. Originally, indeed, animals and humans were undifferentiated, though it was not humans who then became separated off from other animals, so much as they who lost some of their human traits. Moreover the boundaries between one species and another, and those that mark individual membership of a species, are and remain unstable and subject to transformation. Shamans, especially, are thought to be able to cross these boundaries more or less at will. (Lloyd 2007, 146)

Finally, there is the issue of political ontologies. Our view is straightforward here: there are plural and often incommensurate modes of existence (Latour 2012), which are much more than just different worldviews—mere matters of different perceptions of a common object—since their idioms cannot necessarily be rendered in each other's terms.[3] The modern world provides plenty of evidence for this pluriversalistic proposition, and not least in its contrary political framings of what exists as what James called "genuine options." But because of the epistemological bias of Western thinking, we tend to have a sparse and unforgiving vocabulary for thinking through variation in basic commitments to what counts as reality and often tend to consign such plural thoughts to the basket of relativism, even though what is being advanced is "not a relativity of truth but, on the contrary, a truth of the relative" (Deleuze and Guattari 1994, 130). As Viveiros de Castro (1998, 92) puts it:

> The Cartesian rupture with medieval scholastics produced a radical simplification of our ontology, by positing only two principles or substances: unextended thought and extended matter. Such simplification is still with us. Modernity started with it:

with the massive conversion of ontological into epistemological questions—that is, questions of representation—a conversion prompted by the fact that every mode of being not assimilable to obdurate "matter" had to be swallowed by "thought." The simplification of ontology accordingly led to an enormous complication of epistemology. After objects or things were pacified, retreating to an exterior, silent and uniform world of "Nature," subjects began to proliferate and chatter endlessly: transcendental Egos, legislative Understandings, philosophies of language, theories of mind, social representations, logic of the signifier, webs of signification, discursive practices, politics of knowledge—you name it.

Yet we can see the production of sensuous certainties as a political act in its own right. Many political movements are intent on making new worlds in which new forms of the obvious can thrive. In the twentieth century, movements such as fascism and communism are probably best interpreted precisely as attempts to produce new ontologies in which world and attitude to the world combine as one. But even in the most straitjacketed of cultures in which conformity to a particular ontology is strictly enforced, it is worth remembering the sheer range of interpretations of what exists that are on offer, each of which engenders the opportunity to produce new inventive associations. For example, as Geoffrey Lloyd (2007) points out, there never was one ancient Greek worldview, as is commonly supposed. Rather, a cacophony of competing interpretations existed, united only by a very few commonplaces—for example, that gods and spirits could be found in the world. Thus, in talking about ontologies, it is important to understand that we are not talking about utterly stable entities: everyday practices can and do change. Just recently in the West, women have become understood as equal citizens with men, gay and lesbian couples have been able to become gay and lesbian couples, smoking has gone from being seen as a sign of sophistication to the sign of those consigned to the outer darkness of the world, and the healthy body has become a moral imperative to be constantly worked on in the same way that used to be reserved for the soul.

So we are thrown into a rather different kind of world from the one so fondly imagined by many political theorists. It is one in which the more we know, the more peculiar things get. In particular, the idea that "people" simply pick up political "ideas" (whatever those are) and behavior, calmly examine them, and then act on them contains elements of fantasy. It questions three models of political ideas and behavior that account for a large part of political theory. One is to make an appeal to the social. "Social" groups make facts, and this process of fact making is what politics is. This kind of model is typical of Marxist and other structural approaches. A second model fixes on a particular form to which the world must measure up — for example, justice or freedom — and measures the waywardness of the world from these ideals. A third model is concerned with the social contract in all of its forms and often works alongside discussions of sovereignty and the state, expecting governments and their people, for example, to behave in certain ways.

But we want to move in another direction, toward a fourth model, and talk ontologically about "affect." Affect has been a key moment in a number of political theories, if only by proxy. For example, think of the pivotal role of fear in the theories of sovereignty and the state in the work of Thomas Hobbes or Niccolò Machiavelli. But it is in the discourse of philosophical aesthetics, rather than that of political philosophy or economy, where affect plays a key role. Think only of the work of Immanuel Kant on the sublime. In taking this turn to political aesthetics, we are shoving off from a fugitive form of political philosophy that can legitimately be understood as passing through Spinoza, Leibniz, and Whitehead.[4] For Whitehead, there is no stable and essential distinction between mind and matter or subject and object or human and nonhuman or living and non-living. Such distinctions are always situational: they are differences of degree, not kind.[5] For Whitehead (1933, 47), "The basis of experience is emotional" — even a plant or an inorganic object has "feelings" or "satisfactions"[6] — so he puts aesthetics (the mark of what Whitehead calls concern for the world) at the heart of his system and experience of the world as the reflexive process by which the world is constituted. These emotions are what we would now call, after the work of Gilles Deleuze, "affects."

Moving toward the constituency of vitalist philosophy, our attention moves to Deleuze, who took a particular view of affect — a view popularized by authors such as Brian Massumi that has become a currently influential one. In this interpretation, affect is sharply distinguished from emotion. Emotion is a culture's way to talk about the content of the feelings of a subject. It has function and meaning, therefore. In contrast, affect does not require a subject. As Lawrence Grossberg (2009, 183) puts it, "Unlike emotions, affective states are neither structured narratively nor organized in response to our interpretations of situations." Instead, following the Deleuzian interpretation for practical political purposes, affect can therefore be defined as:

> Public feelings that begin and end in broad circulation, but they're also the stuff that seemingly intimate lives are made of. They give circuits and flows the forms of a life. They can be experienced as a pleasure and as a shock, as an empty pause or a dragging undertow, as a sensibility that snaps into place or a profound disorientation. They can be funny, perturbing, or traumatic. Rooted not in fixed conditions of possibility but in the actual lines of potential that a *something* coming together calls to mind and sets in motion, they can be seen as both the pressure points of events or banalities and the trajectories that forces might take if they were to go unchecked. . . . They work not through "meanings" per se, but rather in the way that they pick up density and texture as they move through the bodies, dreams, dramas and social worldings of all kinds. Their significance lies in the intensities they build and in what thoughts and feelings they make possible. The question they beg is not what they might mean in an order of representations, or whether they are good or bad in an overarching scheme of things, but where they might go and what potential modes of knowing, relating, and attending to things are already somehow present in them in a state of potentiality and resonance. (Stewart 2007, 2–3)

However, notice straightaway that this "definition" remains determinedly indeterminate: we are pushed this way and that by the ebb and flow of affect; affect provides a perpetual refueling of the situation and all the more so because human and other bodies themselves depend in large part on a pre-personal realm in which they are situated and from which they gain sustenance.

Welcome to the World of the Pre-personal

Politics and political theory have often referred to the pre-personal field, even if indirectly, as an element of the business of persuasion. So, for example, work in political communication has often acknowledged the way in which politicians make appeals at the so-called subliminal level, especially as modern media — from posters to television — have become regnant. Perhaps the most potent example of the invention of a world in which media and environment mingle comes from Nazi Germany. Jeffrey Herf (2006, 274) notes how the Nazi Party attempted to design environments that would produce a total political experience by using radio, mass meetings, print media, and especially wall newspapers that "stared out at the German public for a week at a time in tens of thousands of places German pedestrians were likely to pass in the course of the day."[7] Similarly, work on liberal capitalism shows how political subjectivity is worked on in a marketplace of affects, filled with values, images, analogies, stirring narratives, and moral sentiments in which logic plays only a walk-on role or acts as a thin veneer (Western 2008). In turn, work on political violence can hardly ignore how violence relies on brushfires of affect, as well as on the marshaling of affects so that they focus energy and commitment on to a particular political program. Work on racial hatred shows how the other is "othered" at levels outside pure cognition by judgments made without much cognitive articulation at all (Amin 2012).

But note something here: in nearly every case, the pre-personal is considered a problem. It is the field of instinct, of animal spirits, of irrational desires, of random antagonisms, and of glib emotions. It is easily swayed, and it is associated with mobs and crowds. It needs to be controlled, or it will get out of hand. Indeed, fear of the mob or the crowd has classically been considered a motivation for the writings of a number of conservative political theorists. But what if the pre-personal cannot be passed by; what if it can only be formatted in various ways, as a vital element of the conduct of politics that no force seeking influence, progressive or conservative, can ignore?

Following from and extending the work of Tarde and Deleuze, Maurizio Lazzarato (2006) argues that there are two planes of subjectivity: what he calls the plane of subjection and (rather too dramatically) the plane of machinic enslavement. For Lazzarato, the subject is constituted through language and communication. The subject is an effect of the semiotics of the machine of communication: "believing itself to be a subject of enunciation, feeling itself to be the absolute, individual cause and origin of statements, whereas in reality it is the result of a machinery, no more than the end point of the process. Your words are folded over statements and modes of expression that are imposed on you and expected of you." But the "pre-individual, pre-cognitive and pre-verbal components of subjectivity," which access affects, percepts, and sensations, must also be pulled into the account (Lazzarato 2006, 2–3). In common with Giorgio Agamben (and his account of bare life), Deleuze (and his account of a molecular economy of desire), Félix Guattari (and his account of territories of existence), and Nigel Thrift (and his account of the nonrepresentational), Lazzarato, in considering this plane of existence, wants to make no distinction between the human and the non-human, the subject and the object, and the sentient and the intelligible. Rather, individuals and all manner of machines become open multiplicities.[8] They are sets of elements, affects, organs, flux, and functions, all of which operate on the same level. Thus, subjectivity

> finds itself simultaneously on the side of the subject and on the side of the object. Capitalism derives its great power from these two devices, which operate as two sides of the same coin. But it is machinic enslavement which endows capitalism with a sort of omnipotence, since it permeates the roles, functions and meanings by which individuals both recognise each other and are alienated from each other. It is through machinic enslavement that capital succeeds in activating the perceptual functions, the affects, the unconscious behaviours, the pre-verbal, pre-individual dynamic and its intensive, atemporal, aspatial, asignificant components. It is through these mechanisms that capital assumes control of the charge of desire carried by humanity. This aspect of the reality of capitalist "production" remains invisible for the most part. (Lazzarato 2006, 4)

What can we therefore understand about the pre-personal realm that Lazzarato and others are so keen to bring to our attention? To get some sense of what this realm is like, it is useful to go back to the classic psychological experiments of Benjamin Libet in the 1960s. Libet found that reactions to events started to happen sometime before cognition took place, in some cases up to a second in advance. In other words, we are aware of intentions to act only after the area of the brain responsible for initiating action has already been activated. But, as has been pointed out since, Libet's finding is actually quite conservative. It relies on a narrow definition of free will in which agency must involve self-awareness: "The suggestion underpinning Libet's claim is that unless the initiation of the action is something we are aware of, the action itself is not under the kind of control we think we have as agents, the kind of control in virtue of which we speak of freedom of the will" (Roessler and Eilan 2003, 1). In fact, all the evidence suggests that we have only very limited freedom of will—at least, in the sense that we act as individual cognizing agents. But that is not a counsel of despair. Rather, we need to see human being in a different way that dispenses with a series of comforting nostrums. First of all, we need to stop seeing human beings as being bounded by their skin. Instead, we need to grasp them as "dividuals" who for most of the time are simply part of a combination of bodies or parts of bodies, resonating around a particular matter of concern. At other times, usually for a brief moment of time, the adhesive friction that we call individuality can be achieved, but it is an achievement, not a natural state. We need to think of that part of human being that operates outside the cognitive realm as not irrational but as a part of how decisions are thought and made. Take the example of morality. Marc Hauser (2006) has argued that morality actually has biological origins. It is wired in as a universal grammar, on Chomskian lines, as an unconscious set of principles dictating what is right and wrong that are then perverted by our emotional reactions to groups we count as "other."

Moreover, we need to understand that human being does not just consist of the body. Human being is fundamentally prosthetic, what is often called "tool-being." We are surrounded by a cloud of all manner of objects that provide us with the wherewithal to think. Much of what we regard as cognition is actually the result of the tools we have evolved that allow us to describe, record, and store experience. Take just the example of the craft of memory. This has extended its domain mightily since the time paintings were made on the walls of caves, and as a result, a whole new means of thought has come into being. This craft has an intellectual history. Thus, Mary Carruthers (1998) has shown that Francis Yates's notion of the rhetorical mnemotechnics of the Middle Ages having as its goal the cultivation of prodigious memory was mistaken. The actual goal was to give an orator the means and wherewithal to *invent* material, beforehand and, just as crucially, on the spot. Memory is a compositional art depending on the cultivation of images for the mind to work with. This state of affairs has continued but has been boosted by modern media technology and its ability to produce communal rhetorics that would have been impossible before and that are inevitably heavily political, especially in their ability to keep inventing new variants of themselves that can be adapted to new situations. For example, consider the modern notion of thinking in terms of "nation," which has evolved from its early meaning connoting a birth group to revolve around issues of sovereignty and state, heavily influenced by the imaginary of an imagined community that is a mantle taken on as a result of state institutions (such as schools) and the modern media.

Human being is practice-oriented. What is distinctive about human being is its ability to build practices — grooves or refrains of concerned being — that are, in effect and quite literally, matters of oriented concern, backed up by particular spatial settings, linguistic formulas, distinctive emotional signatures, all manner of bodily cues, and all sorts of objects that form a corona that is part and parcel of their existence. Finally, thought itself is bound up with aesthetics. Aesthetics is not an incidental of human life. It is central to it. This applies particularly to its political manifestations. Aesthetics has been a staple of the political arts since the invention of something we might understand as recognizably political, whether that might be the grand expression of imperial ambition bound up in a Roman triumph or the Nuremberg Olympics or the less imposing but still important arts of political advertising or television performances. *Homo aestheticus* is not some feeble-minded cipher. S(he) is central to modern politics.

Thus, we can argue that very large amounts of human activity lie outside what we consider "our" direct control. They reside in a layer of thinking that is not open to conscious inspection, away from the "internal conversation" that Margaret Archer (2007) argues is the mark of reflexivity. This is hardly a new insight. It was central to German psychophysics and was already an important theme in psychology in the mid-nineteenth century (Sloterdijk 2007). It fueled much of the work of James and other North American luminaries. And, of course, the continent of the unconscious was the territory that the psychoanalytic tradition made its own.

But equally, this depiction produces a problem. In the scholarly tradition, the social and the psyche are traditionally split apart from each other. In one realm dwell all kinds of social forces that constitute facts in themselves. In the other dwell individuals who run to psychological demands that constitute their own set of facts. Of course, it has never been quite that simple. Thus, Freud and others were happy to stray over into social explanation, as in *Civilization and Its Discontents*. Equally, even the most diehard exponents of the social fact, such as Émile Durkheim have proved quite willing to make psychological generalizations, as in his work on suicide. But in this book, we will not allow this divide to get in our way, not least because, with the advent of technology such as the Internet, it is becoming an untenable division as the range of traces that each person leaves behind is compounded in ways that routinely defeat the distinction. Like Tarde, we will deny the capacity of this division to make sense of the world. And we will want to complicate things still further by adding to the brew of being the object world and all manner of living beings that may not have been given the status of human but certainly do more than act as a passive background to the political. Think only of the ship or barbed wire or the horse. These are not infinitely malleable entities, but in combination with human bodies working to set routines that themselves are key elements of the story, they have been quite literally the stuff through which empires have been built.

What we are moving toward, then, is a world of human being that resembles nothing so much as vortices of influence pulling all manner of entities into their field—some small, some large, all of them constantly on the move, forming and reforming like so many weather systems. And here, too, the circulation of affect is crucial.[9] We are beginning to understand more and more from the grounded work of feminist political theorists such as Lauren Berlant, Jane Gallop, Sianne Ngai, Kathy Stewart, Jane Thrailkill, and Jane Bennett how any political conclusion will include a particular affective palette, not as an incidental moment, but as a fundamental part of how a conclusion was drawn. Take two of the most iniquitous but widespread of the minor feelings that infest everyday life—namely, the supposedly positive feeling of competition and the supposedly negative feeling of envy (Gallop 2006). Competition and envy have become interesting to feminist political theorists precisely because of their political connotations. At first ignored because of their association with outdated Freudian concepts such as penis envy, and difficult to negotiate because feminism was thought to be concerned with a solidary sisterhood that in turn found it hard to discuss such unseemly emotions, competition and envy are now a focus of attention because of their immanence. As Ngai (2005, 111–12) puts it:

> In everyday life as well as theory, it remains difficult to pry competitiveness apart from envy entirely. Both affects are fundamen-

tally social, arising only in groups and highly determinative of their formation. Although sufficient in the case of an emotion like fear, a single self pitted against a single other does not suffice to generate either competitiveness or envy. Interestingly, competitiveness and envy do not exist outside a condition of numerousness: a field of many others for the self to interact with the singled-out other in. Both have unusually abstract objects (unlike the very concrete object of, say, lust or anger) that are, and encode and generate, social relations. In other words, while envy and competitiveness are often directed at specific persons, she or he is not technically speaking either feeling's "object." Indeed, among our culture's current spectrum of negative affects, envy stands out as the only one articulated explicitly in response to a perceived inequality: a relative state of affairs that can be assessed only by comparison. Competitiveness's object is likewise positioned: more specifically, the subject's position, relative and contingent upon the position of many others, in a larger hierarchical order. There is thus a sense in which competitiveness and envy both tend to call up some idea or mental representation, however fleeting, of the social field as an articulated and differentiated totality. Both are responses to the positionally unequal distribution of a limited resource across this field: whether it be affect, capital, rights, or other symbolic goods.

To summarize the argument so far, we now understand that what we fondly count as human being comes jam-packed with uncertainty. The rational, political citizen only ever fitfully reaches the surface of action. Most of the time, political agency of this kind is far removed from what occurs, offset by all manner of pre-personal currents. As Ngai (2005, 2) points out, what we need to do is to meld together Hannah Arendt's claim that "what makes a man a political being is his faculty of action" with Spinoza's description of affects as "waverings of the mind" that can either increase or diminish one's power to act. The political citizen is then shown to be a knotted or condensed set of predicaments that can only rarely produce the kind of critical productivity that "cold" political theory wants and needs for its argument to function.

Even at its most effective, that critical productivity is constantly being engaged in a series of changing modes. For example, Paolo Virno (1996, as cited in Ngai 2005, 5) has made much of the power of minor affects such as opportunism in modern societies, not least because opportunism offers a "relation with the world [that] tends to articulate itself through possibilities, opportunities, and chances, instead of according to linear and univocal directions." It enables a new kind of fleeting politics:

> Indeed one could extrapolate from Virno's claim to argue that in the transnational stage of capitalism that defines our contemporary moment, our emotions no longer link up securely as they once did with the models of social action and transformation theorized by Aristotle, Thomas Hobbes, and others under the sign of relatively unambiguous emotions like anger or fear. In other words, the nature of the socio-political itself has changed in a manner that both calls forth and calls upon a new set of feelings—ones less powerful than the classical political passions, though perhaps more suited, in their ambient . . . but still diagnostic nature, for models of subjectivity, collectivity, and agency not entirely foreseen by past theorists of the commonwealth. This is why, for Virno, even an unattractive feeling like opportunism can provide the "kernel" from which to shape "transformative behaviour." For all its pettiness, the feeling calls attention to a real social experience and a certain kind of historical truth. (Ngai 2005, 5)

It is therefore worth thinking about models of political agency that exist outside the political mainstream that might be able to take up and work with this experience. Such models do exist: models in which the pre-personal realm is given a much more dignified political role than that of simple ataxia by virtue of the kind of intention that is recognized to have agency. One example is the early modern non-identitarian model of political agency that consciously blurred the boundary between mover and moved, which is so crucial to prevailing models of active political agency, in its desire to produce "new creatures."[10] In particular, this seventeenth-century model makes it possible to talk about the virtues of *passivity*. Amid the cut and thrust of current world events, this will no doubt sound a discordant note, but passivity points to a different way of doing things that relies on a very different idea of political agency and a very different rhetoric of passions, both of which are dependent on understanding subjects as transmitters and receivers of infectious relationships. As far as the idea of political agency is concerned, it is crucial to understand that, for new creatures,

agency admits of more positions than "autonomous agent." . . .
In addition to the autonomous agent undermined by recent discourses, an "agent" can also refer to one who acts for another. . . .
This deputized "agent" is not a "sovereign ruler" but a subject li-
censed by another authority to perform predetermined actions.
The gap between "agent" and "autonomous agent" is crucial to
seventeenth-century writers, who often deny "autonomy" but insist on "agency," both descriptively (each individual has agency)
and prescriptively (all individuals must act in the world). As
"agents" or "instruments" of another, individuals are simultaneously "acted by another," in Thomas Hooker's phrase, and en-
abled to act in the world. "Acted upon, we act," summarizes John
Cotton. These writers desire agency only insofar as it differs from
autonomy: they desire not "shaping power" over their identities
and actions but to be shaped by another power. (Gordon 2002, 23)

As far as the rhetoric of passions goes, what is important in the early
modern period was the mobilization of particular passions, "with the
apparently 'active' vice of pride condemned for its ineffectiveness and
the 'passive' virtue of humility serving the most dramatic revolutionary
ends" (Gross 2006, 110). Why? Because the religious model of a radical
that was prevalent was connected to the practice of a feminized humility.
The agent was an instrument, "the product of humiliation, anxiety, and
soulful, feminine passivity, in the best sense of the word" (Gross 2006,
93), an agent "humiliated for collective sins past and reformed for the
time to come." This is a "feminine" passivity, but not, we hasten to add,
in any pejorative sense. Rather, this is fragility as a precondition of grace,
passivity as a precondition of change. Such a model persists in certain
nonviolent traditions. In our opinion, though it may need reworking,
it could still act as one possible model for a new form of left politics of
sentiments.

Welcome to the World of Non-Humans

While mainstream thought worries about whether things exist inde-
pendently or are constructed by the mind, we subscribe to the non-
correlationist view that there is no interplay between a so-called natural
and a so-called social world. All that exists is a legion of actants, which

have no interior kernel or essence but are defined by and through their often ramshackle and quarrelsome alliances with others that need work to achieve. There is no center, in other words, and relations have to be made; they are a result, not a starting point. Take the actant "Bruno Latour" as a case in point:

> The impact of Bruno Latour as a thinker is deployed in the bookstores that carry his works, the admirers who recommend them to others, and the careers that are altered by contact with his writings. If we meet Latour in person in the Latin Quarter, we will surely have a good conversation, but we may learn just as much from taking one of his books on vacation in Peru and discussing it with a random stranger. When we encounter Latour himself, trumpet blasts do not sound; trains of devotees do not follow him shaking tambourines in the street as we approach a glittering interior compound at Sciences-Po, from which a new philosophy would emanate like radiation from Chernobyl. There is no central point in the network where we encounter the very heart of Latour and his philosophy. There is no inner essence wrapped in transient wool or chaff, but only a network of allies mobilized by his philosophy. Most of the network remains outside Latour's personal control, and much of it is unknown to him. (Harman 2009, 20)

For our purposes, there are two consequences of this radically decentered stance. One is that the role of politics and the politician is valued in and for itself as a vital worker toiling in the field of coalition and compromise. It is important not simply to sneer at the supposedly venal compromises of the politician or the diplomat: "contempt for politicians is a deadly pitfall" (Pignarre and Stengers 2011, 15). There is often a value to politicians' supposed mendacity (Jay 2010). As Latour (1993, 210) puts it, "What we despise as political mediocrity is simply the collection of compromises that we force politicians to make on our behalf." Indeed, "It takes something like courage to admit that we will never do better than a politician. . . . [Others] simply have somewhere to hide when they have made their mistakes. They can go back and try again. Only the politician is limited to a single shot and has to shoot in public." The politician forever has to balance "information, funding, threats, kindness, politeness, loyalty, disloyalty, and the perpetual search for ways and means. In this respect, the politician is the model for every kind of actor. To declare oneself untainted by strife between conflicting forces is to deny that one is an actant" (Harman 2009, 21). Isabelle Stengers (2010b) argues something similar in the case of the diplomat, despised by everyone but absolutely necessary if opposed and incommensurable worlds are to be brought into some kind of alignment. One consequence is that what counts as a materialist approach, a common goal in so much work that claims to be materialist, is radically refigured. If we accept that reality is reducible to material factors, we make an a priori and dogmatic decision about what the primary qualities of "material" really are. In other words, a one-dimensional *idea* of what actors must be replaces what they might be. Seen this way, materialism looks not like a hardheaded realist doctrine at all but like a form of idealism put there to damp down surprise.[11] The problem is that no one really knows what an actor is. To define materialism solely in terms of hard physical matter is to allow us to laugh at the naïve dupes who still believe in ghosts and spirits, but the laughter is hollow. Surely it is better to say with Latour (2007b) that all objects are real, but not all are strong.

The second consequence, and the one that we will dwell on in the rest of this section, is that "we" are in constant interaction with all manner of other beings as we make our way through life. All of them are essential to "our" existence—plants and animals, landscapes, all manner of objects, some of which were constructed by human hand, some but not all of which have their own forms of *concerted agency* with which they can resist as well as aid human fabrication.[12] In other words, the world is chock full of objects that allow us to live in particular ways but that have their own existence, too, that is not necessarily bound up with the wants, needs, and general consciousness of humanity (Bryant et al. 2011). To ignore their influence in any political equation is to ignore much of what we might count as the means by which the political gains traction, yet again posing a whole series of challenges to prevailing notions of the political as being exclusively human.

Let us start by thinking of just one form of concerted agency, "animals,"[13] at a time that all kinds of dividing lines between humans and animals are being shown to be chimerical. Timothy Morton (2010, 71) overdoes it, but his view is not merely rhetorical: "Do nonhumans possess language? Yes. How about imagination? Check. Reason? Copy that. A sense of mind? No doubt. Can they use tools? Indeed. Do they display improved skills and learning over time? Absolutely. Can nonhumans feel compassion? Of course. Do they have a sense of humor? Why not? How about wonder? Yes. Choice? Also yes. Humans are fairly good at throwing and sweating: not much of a portfolio." Indeed, as Pat Shipman (2011) demonstrates, it might be argued that a defining characteristic of being human is an intensified connection with animals. Indeed, much of our capacity for empathy, tolerance, and communication may have come from animals as much as from other humans. So how can we bring animals back into politics? Perhaps the political history of how animals have been approached can help. In the West, for a long time, animals were seen, following Descartes, as something like machines. But as Keith Thomas (1983) reminded us some years ago now, that was never a commonly held view. Even when animals were subjected to the most horrendous ill treatment in society as a whole, certain animals—dogs, horses, cats, for example—were often valued through emotional relationships that were more than incidental. Others were valued for their worth and their ability to act as elements of practices that could be considered ennobling, as in the importing of more than two hundred Oriental horses into the British Isles between 1650 and 1750, which would have an influence on horse breeding and riding styles out of proportion to their numbers (Landry 2009). In time, these horses would produce the English thoroughbred and with it the gentlemanly ideal of free movement over the countryside as an enactment of certain political liberties (and privileged masculinities, as captured in Jane Austen's novels). Since then, of course, animals have become politically charged in all manner of other ways, as they have increasingly become included in the mechanism of political calculation by Western societies, as in the case of the growth of vegetarianism and of active animal rights movements.

It is the political incarnation of becoming "with those with whom we are not yet" that lies somewhere between the original meaning of politics as both polis and polite, showing good manners to others, and the "invitation to speculate, imagine, feel, build something better." This means that fewer and fewer beings fall "below the radar of sentience" (Haraway 2008, 89, 92–93). In other cultures, the political history of animals is very different. Consider India, where some sects have routinely espoused kindness to animals since the Harappan culture. They continue to do so, sometimes to a degree that in the West would still be regarded as extreme. For example, orthodox Jains wear face masks in case they inadvertently breathe in and kill an insect.[14] Furthermore, in India animals can be the subject of fierce religious passions and political differentiations: the treatment of cows is an important moment in some forms of Hindu political identity and caste politics, able to spark passion and communal violence in ways that can only be considered a relict form by the most determined rationalists.

It is also worth considering how history itself is being redrawn to include animals. For example, some forms of Marxist theory insisted that the successful peasant was doing better than the poor peasant through exploitation of the poor peasant's labor, with terrible consequences. Now it is clear that what in reality made the kulak able to do better was access to animal labor. The successful peasant made a living not from the surplus value extracted from other peasants but from the work of horses and other animals (Netz 2009). Equally, the books that are systematically writing animals into history and philosophy can be seen as part of political labor, moving animals from the juxtapolitical to the political sphere.

Then there is the plant. Again, plants can produce all manner of political struggles. Whole books have been written about the political adventures of particular plants—most notably, spices and various stimulants, but equally beans or citrus—and such plants have been understood as having political import because of the attractiveness of their particular properties. Take just caffeine, distilled from plants like coffee.[15] Daniel Smail (2008) shows how coffee was the precursor to the modern psychotropic economy—that is, an economy based on the alteration of mood through chemical means. Artificial affect, in other words. Coffee was produced almost exclusively in what is now Yemen from the fourteenth century to the sixteenth century, and it was widely consumed in the Islamic world. Among Europeans, in contrast, it was treated early on as a curiosity or as a medicine. Only in the decades after 1660 did coffee take off as an item of luxury consumption. Coffeehouses and cafés sprouted up across Europe, the very heart of the emergent public sphere. By 1739, coffeehouses in London outnumbered taverns. Coffee was seen as the preferred stimulant for the affluent and leisured classes. In contrast, among the working classes, alcohol held sway. However,

there was a limit to how much the European economy could afford to devote to alcohol . . . once the production of beer and wine necessarily reduced the amount of land available for food. Yet in the early modern era, the production of sugar on the slave plantations of the Caribbean and Brazil allowed for the distillation of rum, imports of which, in England at least, soared between 1720 and 1750. During the so-called gin craze of the mid-eighteenth century, cheap grain was converted into gin, which was consumed in vast quantities by the lower classes. In this way, the two status groups were each tightly associated with a single, mildly psychoactive commodity, the leisure class with caffeine, the lower classes with alcohol. By the very late eighteenth century in England, however, caffeine had made its way into the working-class diet in the form of sweetened tea. Tea imports to the British Isles, which had been steadily increasing over the eighteenth century, soared in the first decade of the nineteenth century as a result. (Smail 2008, 180–81)

Equally, plants have increasingly come to be understood as having qualities that run for election representing "environment." Think only of two modest examples. The first is the increase in various forms of ecologically minded gardening in recent years—a movement that has had a significant impact, given the popularity of gardening in so many countries. This movement mixes the undoubted sensual pleasures of gardening (Tilley 2008) with a practical environmental awareness and a large market infrastructure to produce undoubted environmental gains that stand against, for example, the kind of environmentally damaging gardening represented by the lawn (Robbins 2007). The second is the longstanding history of vegetarianism, a movement now gaining an increasing hold in the West, with all sorts of economic and cultural—and political—consequences. But note in the cases of both animals and plants how we tend to think of them almost automatically in terms of their relationship with human being. We have done the same here. But this makes no sense. These animals and plants have their own worlds on which humans often encroach but with which they are not therefore coincident.

This point becomes even clearer if we move to another set of crucial agents—namely, objects. Recently, the status of objects has been overhauled. Rather than being seen as entities that have to be chaperoned by human beings to gain agency and meaning, they are coming to be understood as having their own active private lives that do not have to go through human access points to have impact. As Graham Harman (2009, 103) notes, there is a whole roll call of concrete entities going about their work that conform to two laws. One is Whitehead's: everything that happens is a consequence of the reality of specific entities. The other is Latour's: all entities have consequences. Or, as Harman sums up, "grass can do things in the world, just as atoms and Popeye can do things."

It is worth expanding on this point. It is not required that we see objects only as passive, inanimate companions to thinking subjects. Harman (2005) has argued that part of the reason we think this way lies in the hands of phenomenologists, who fenced off two "wild borderlands," one the question of the object's independent physical existence that science had laid bare; the other the realm of raw sensation, the side of sensation that is "sheer formless enjoyment, quality without substance" (Harman 2005, 32). In other words, objects can never reveal all of their qualities when they are restricted to the homeland of human perception: "rooted in the world, we depend on a surplus of reality that comes from beyond the sphere of intelligible meaning" (Harman 2005, 36). So we link up with objects rather than take them over; we neither coincide with them nor fully take them over in thought. Instead, we participate in overlapping negotiations that are conducted through the whole sensual range of the body and not just its cognitive aspects in a kind of "machinic animism" (Melitopoulos and Lazzarato 2011) that produces a trans-individual form of subjectivity.

To illustrate, we will take just one potent political object—barbed wire—to illustrate the need to understand objects as players and not just as mute receptacles for human impulses. Barbed wire was invented in 1874 to be used on the North American Great Plains to prevent cows from straying. Its invention resulted from the needs of a special kind of colonization that, as Reviel Netz (2009) points out, was new in terms of space (in that an entire landmass was to be exploited rather than points on it) and of time (the colonization needed to take place very rapidly). Massive space and rapid time demanded a special kind of technology of control. Barbed wire provided the answer by allowing new and cheap ways to control land that produced the opportunity for new entanglements. What was thought of as a cheap agrarian tool for the enslavement of animals quickly became something else—something that had not been predicted. It became a means of containing men as well as bovines. New kinds of victims became possible as the ratio between violence and motion was decisively changed. Wire had been used as an obstacle in battle for quite some time, so the evolution toward barbed wire should have come as no surprise. But with its barbs, barbed wire was simply more effective, producing an artificial terrain that one could pass through only with the greatest difficulty. Barbed wire was used fitfully in the Boer War and in the Russo-Japanese War but came into its own in the First World War when, in combination with the trench and the machine gun, it produced a new space of battle that favored defense as never before: it cost 15–140 times more to cut barbed wire than to replace it. No-man's land became what Netz (2009, 109) has called a "river of steel, 475 miles long (though usually no more than half a mile wide), flowing all the way down from the Swiss Jura to the North Sea." The wire itself transmuted: barbs were placed closer together and were made longer to prevent motion. Even attack became a generally static operation, spawning new innovations, such as poison gas and the tank, that could overcome the newly enforced immobility.

But barbed wire's history gets worse. There is its reprehensible prominence in the construction of concentration camps, in a long roll call of colonial wars as a means of concentrating population, in warfare at vast prisoner-of-war camps, in many countries as a means of internal colonization and, of course, as means of calculated genocide and extermination. Teaming it with other actors, including dogs and electricity — and with slave labor — meant that islands of internment and terror could be constructed rapidly, not just as camps, but also as corralled spaces within cities. In the case of the Nazis, the camps became a ghastly exercise in logistics premised on working from the corpse backward (Netz 2009). Violence was both reduced and made more extensive.

It would be possible to see developments like these as episodes in the social construction of a particularly unpleasant tool. But this would be too simple a move, as we have already seen from the references to Harman's writings. We can use Gilbert Simondon's work to show how the tool itself plays a part that we might term "political" in its effects and influence. Simondon (1992) conducts a war on the tradition of thought he calls "hylomorphism," the dualism of form and matter in which it is assumed that materiality is passive and can only be given shape by an intelligence imposed from outside. Hylomorphism ignores all of the intermediaries at work in any process of formation and the fact that matter is never entirely passive but always contains incipient form. He proposes to give tools their own presence by bringing out their "transductive" aspects, showing not just that what appear to be stable entities are worked out over long periods of time through a series of transformations that transmit energy but also that this process often arises from the way in which over time two or more dissimilar entities can be brought together as one: "For the process of transduction to occur, there must be some disparity, discontinuity or mismatch within a domain; two different forms or potentials whose disparity can be modulated. Transduction is a process whereby a disparity or a difference is topologically and temporally restructured across some interface. It mediates different organizations of energy" (Mackenzie 2002, 25). Thus, as Simondon (1992, 315) writes:

> The transduction that resolves things *effects the reversal of the negative into the positive*: meaning, that which makes the terms fail to be identical with each other, and that which makes them *disparate* (in the sense in which this expression is understood in the theory of vision), is integrated with the system that resolves things and becomes a condition of meaning. There is no impoverishment in the information contained in the terms: transduction is characterized by the fact that the result of this process is a concrete network including all the original terms. The resulting system is made up of the concrete, and it comprehends all of the concrete. The transductive order retains all the concrete and is characterized by the *conservation of information*, whereas induction requires a loss of information. Following the same path as the dialectic, transduction conserves and integrates the opposed aspects. Unlike the dialectic, transduction does not presuppose the existence of a previous time period to act as a framework in which the genesis unfolds, time itself being the solution and dimension of the discovered systematic: *time comes from the preindividual just like the other dimensions that determine individuation.*

As important, Simondon is pointing to the need to see the tool in this way as part of nature, not set off from it, as the result of a systemic or recursive ontogenetic process that correlates, in the philosophical register, to what Simondon has conceptualized as "mediation" or "individuation" and, in the biological register, to what Lynn Margulis (1998) has theorized as symbiogenesis, the formation of a new phenotype through a symbiotic relationship. Such an ontogenetic process throws down a number of challenges. To take one example, "The promise of Marxism — the essence of the promise of modernism — was to enslave nature so as to free humanity. But what if humanity itself is part of nature? Modernity, indeed, brought everything under control — the world with all its species — and humans, naturally, shared the same fate. In this particular case, at least, it turned out like this: a species that enslaves another forges its own chains" (Netz 2009, 230).

But Simondon and Margulis also point to something else: the way in which tools and other symbiotes can produce environments that are lively in their own right, that prompt new actants to come into existence. To illustrate this point, we need to look no further than the types of digital technology that have become a perpetual overlay to so many practices and the way in which they are changing political practices. Here we find a domain that has gained a grip only over the past ten years but is now being used as part of an attempt to mass-produce "ontological strangeness" (Rodowick 2007) based on semiautomatic responses designed into everyday life through a combination of information technology-based tools and the practices associated with them (from implants and molecular interventions to software-based perception and action). In particular, these automatisms are concerned with the design and prototyping of new kinds of space that can produce different affective vibrations. It is to these spaces that we turn next.

The Space of Being-Together

The case of barbed wire has already given us some insights into space, showing how new landscapes can be created, sometimes without exact direction. What we want to do in this section is argue why space is so important in the schema we are presenting. Space intervenes in politics in numerous ways. There is the obvious issue of boundaries, which we have already touched on. There is the issue of how communications of various forms allow political organization to take place in new ways, as in the way in which the telegraph produced new possibilities for both working-class and government action, a story that is currently being retold through the medium of the mobile phone and the Internet. There is the issue of state space—both the way in which bureaucracy is able to impose new grids on space and the allied issue of governmentality, to which we will return in a later chapter. There is the issue of events and how they can be framed as spaces (Badiou 2001).

But in this section we point to another issue: space as the flow of being itself. Specifically, we use the word "terrain" to indicate a sensory and knowing field—in other words, to mean more than the environment in which humans dwell. We argue that terrain is itself an actor, not just a background or a resource. This is a different interpretation from the one often found in traditional accounts of being in that the "environment" (itself a nineteenth-century term) is not just a term in a human equation but a part of what it is to be human. The two are inseparably joined in a sphere or envelope in which one term implies the other. Thus, we move on from Heidegger to Peter Sloterdijk. This may seem to be a trivial move. It is not.

To begin with, it presages a different view of human being, understood as "co-existential and sympathetic" (Van Tuinen 2007, 280). Thus, in the trilogy *Sphären* (Spheres), Sloterdijk (2005) takes Heidegger on dwelling as a root point of reference, especially the qualities of nearness and being-in, but then spatializes his thinking by posing the question of being as the question of being-together; with other people, with things and circumstances in an environment. "Being-a-pair" or a couple precedes all encounters. In other words, Spheres is concerned with the dynamic of spaces of coexistence, spaces that are commonly overlooked, for the simple reason that "human existence . . . is anchored in an insurmountable spatiality" (Sloterdijk 2005, 229), an insight that is itself so often passed by.[16] For Sloterdijk, humans are first and foremost inhabitants of "spheres," spacings that are always already implied by oppositions such as inside–outside, subject–object, and friend–enemy and thus often fall outside any discussion based on the usual representational logics. The task that Sloterdijk faces is to coax these spheres into the representational limelight (that Sloterdijk understands the work that has to go into this process is made clear by his use of the term "explicitate" to name this process) using a whole series of devices, including "the mother's womb, theories of angels, twins, and doubles, early modern magnetism, ancient macro-spherical cosmopolitism, the mediological strategies of the apostles, the nautical ecstasies of Columbus and Magellan, and our

'egotechnical interior designs' in the age of globalization and information technology" (Van Tuinen 2007, 280). The method of spheres is a bit
like psychoanalysis in that the aim is to get at unconscious truths but, in
this case, by explicitating the truths about our atmospheric places of existence and without using the analytical means of representational reason.
Equally, Sloterdijk uses a psychoanalytical model to suggest that before
the oral stage, there are all kinds of other pre-personal stages through
which we learn to communicate.[17]

Such a viewpoint immediately produces a very different stance to the
world, since what constitutes "inside" has to be rethought. People and
things and circumstances become intermixed in an interior community
that offers some degree of immunity to its members and so produces
a kind of skin. The "environment" in which "we" are situated becomes
much more fluid. Context becomes all-important since it is no longer
that which surrounds action but is a part of the action. The questions
become: With what does each culture surround itself? What is each culture's equivalent of the womb (what Sloterdijk calls the social uterus)?
How does each culture attain communion? This is why, in the second
and third volumes of Spheres, Sloterdijk tries to give a history of how we
have moved from little dyadic bubbles through the "primary animism" of
walls, arches, and temples through the globalizations of Greek rationalism and capitalist imperialism to the current situation in which the great
age of global holisms has been replaced by a networked world in which
spheres of various forms exist in a hybrid complexity, a plural ontology,
just like "foam." Sloterdijk uses the metaphor of the apart-ment, among
others, to illustrate the kind of world he is thinking of: "Everybody is
everybody else's neighbour, but nonetheless still lives in the luxurious
position of excluding the Other from the privacy of his apartment" (Van
Tuinen 2007, 283). If this is the case, then

> the concept of the society is no longer of any use to describe social
> scenes where social cohesion is constituted. Instead of established
> sociological categories, or theories of the social contract or the so-
> cial organism, [Sloterdijk] prefers Gabriel Tarde's recently redis-
> covered . . . micro-sociology, a neo-Leibnizean attempt to general-
> ize the concept of imitation in terms of monadological associations
> so as to describe all empirical facts as states of co-existence. Ac-
> cordingly, the scene of modern representative democracy—the

"social" was never more than an "autogenous illusion," a society in the mirror, and should at least be supplemented by a monadological understanding of "agglomerations and conglomerations of foams" according to which "everything is a society. Even if there is no symbolically mediated communication." (Van Tuinen 2007, 283)

Sloterdijk is gesturing to a new kind of political sphere, what he calls the politics of "psychotopical tuning." It is not entirely clear what this politics of terrain might be, but that is no reason not to set out in pursuit of it. Some encouragement can be gained from the fact that others are trying to do something that has at least some similarities to Sloterdijk's project. Lazzarato's account of "worlding" draws on some of the same sources as Sloterdijk—most notably, Deleuze and Tarde—to produce a similar sense of a psychotopical dynamic. It also comes to not-dissimilar conclusions about the modern world and where it is heading, though it makes more of elements such as the power of minor affects such as envy to be used as political tools.[18]

So What?

We can take some of the bare bones of psychotopical projects like Sloterdijk's and Lazzarato's and ask what they might mean in broadening our sense of what is political and thus in instituting new kinds of leftist politics. We want to argue that there are five main directions in which it is possible to go and that this book will follow—directions that identify new spaces, with their own possibilities of forming immunities and, in time, atmospheres that might constitute the kernels of new practices and meanings of the political. What unites them is a sense that old ways of thinking that depended on grandiose notions of once-and-for-all change resulting from analyses provided by equally grandiose theoretical frameworks need to be replaced with something more modest. One might see this move as akin to replacing some of the grandiose urban plans of Robert Moses with the more human scale of the writings of Jane Jacobs. This is not to deny the urgency of the problems we face—not least, a planet battered by a humanity that has only recently realized what a fragile spacecraft the Earth actually is. Nor is it to argue against hyperbolic theoretical accounts, so long as one realizes that these accounts are not solutions. Rather, it is to say that there is no one path out of our woes. The modernist messiah needs to be, quite literally, re-placed by a host of different paths, each of which tracks a course away from perdition.

The first direction is the most obvious, given the preceding discussion: to turn to what John Protevi (2009) calls "political physiology" to understand more broadly the affective palette that we currently acquire and think about how it might be used in different ways and in different places to produce an enhanced critical productivity, especially in instances where subjectivity is bypassed in favor of a direct link between the social and the somatic. We have already discussed envy and competitiveness as particular forms of proto-political analysis and have touched on love, rage, and fear (see Protevi 2009). But there are many others. Think only of the supposedly dysphoric affects that cluster around anxiety, irritation, and paranoia, as well as what Ngai (2005) calls "stuplimity," or the stupefaction of the repetitive static that arises from a mixture of shock and boredom. Although the negativity of these affects is algorithmic and operational rather than value- or meaning-based, we are starting to produce a new political vocabulary that can link these affects to particular controversies and causes in productive ways. Part of the procedure of producing that vocabulary will surely have to include the process of cultural translation of affects into nameable emotions so that they can "acquire the semantic density and narrative complexity" (Ngai 2005, 27) that will allow them to be used as a political resource that can be owned by particular first-person feelings. Conversely, some emotions need to be denatured into affects so they can again become third-person feelings that can be generally circulated. Another part of the procedure will be the production of spaces in which these affects can, quite literally, make sense. A large amount of work in modern art and film is exactly bent to this project in that it is concerned with producing affective achievements that demand naming.

Another direction requires bringing out what Smail (2008) calls the psychotropic dimension of long-run human history. What is clear is that cultures increasingly have delivered goods and devices that allow human beings to influence their own body states. Some of these goods and devices are, in effect, chemical:

Some of these practices and mechanisms constitute highly exaggerated forms of mechanisms that existed in Paleolithic societies.

These same mechanisms exist in our own societies: facial expressions, somatic reactions, body postures and gestures, tones of voice, grooming, sex—the list goes on. All of these forms of expression make known such things as patterns of dominance and control, feelings of sympathy and altruism, states of insecurity and confidence. They are felt in the body by means of chemical messengers. Civilizations did not, could not, invent new forms of body chemistry. Instead, civilizations found new devices for exaggerating existing neurochemical states. Persisting patterns could even embed themselves in our synapses, where they underlay relatively durable behavioural forms that have the look and feel of being "biological" without being genetic. (Smail 2008, 200)

Increasingly, as we have already shown through the example of caffeine, these exaggerated states are being induced through various chemical devices. A whole biosocial politics has grown up around the efficacy and fitness of these devices. Think only of the controversies around alcohol, which is, after all, a staple of daily life in many countries, or the new staples that are appearing based somewhere on the dividing line between "medicine" and "drugs"—for example, Ritalin, dispensed for attention deficit disorder syndrome, or Prozac, dispensed for depressive conditions. These controversies are leading to the creation of new political zones that have their own dynamic, the result of the growth of all manner of interested parties whose interests do not coincide. Spaces are currently being produced that attempt to simulate some of the effects of psychotropic states in that they provide an enhanced stimulus to the body but through immersive spaces designed to transfigure viewers by bringing them into intimate relation with these spaces. A series of these simulated spaces (Castronova 2007; Turkle 2009) have been created out of the confluence of polyglot computing and a series of practical spatial arts—stage practice, film set-ups, choreography, landscape design, software design, to name just a few—underline Marshall McLuhan's famous saying that "the effects of technology do not occur at the level of opinions or concepts, but alter sense ratios or patterns of perception" (McLuhan 1964, 33). These spaces instruct bodies as much as the other way round. What is different about these new spatial psychotropics is that it is not just demand and supply that are political; the medium itself is political. All manner of values and orientations can be smuggled in, producing a lively political field. One thinks of the efforts to produce computer games that do not reflect masculine values; the burgeoning field of ethno-computing, intent on producing worlds appropriate to indigenous cultures; the war over redefining notions of property going on in domains like Second Life; and so on (Fuller 2008).

The third direction is a broadening of our understanding of politics as a mimetic canvas. The idea that imitation is a key determinant of human behavior is an old one. Consider just the words of one of our touchstones, William James (Richardson 2010, 139): "Some of us are in more favourable positions than others to set new fashions. Some of us are much more striking personally and imitable, so to speak. But no living person is sunk so low as not to be imitated by somebody." In turn, James wanted to "inoculate" the population of the United States with new political standards. But let us follow instead the lead provided by one of James's contemporaries, Gabriel Tarde. Through the work of Tarde, we can understand politics as the art of generating affective fields, as an art of sympathetic vibration (Barry and Thrift 2007). Tarde's work seems to prefigure a modern political landscape in its commitment to an epidemiological model based on processes of imitative contagion in which imitation and invention are the key forms of the "universal repetition" that Tarde conceived as at the base of all action (Beirne 1987; Rogers 2003). Such models provide a much better sense of how specific kinds of affective phenomena do their work, in particular, because the spread of feelings (through gesticulation, bodily movements, and motor coordination and repetition, as well as all of the technologies of the body that now exist) is such fertile ground for thinking about mental contagion. At this point in time, Tarde can seem like a very modern thinker for three reasons. To begin with, and notoriously, Tarde questioned the idea of society. Insofar as he was willing to countenance the use of the word at all, it was to refer to the complete range of entities that exist in association: "Tarde's sociology is not a science of the social according to the categories of sociology. It is an understanding of 'associations', of co-operation, with no distinction made between Nature and Society. It is the sociology of atoms, of cells, and of man. Tarde takes Durkheim's premise that the social is a fact and must be analyzed as such and turns it on its head. 'All phenomena is social phenomena, all things a society'" (Lazzarato 2004, 187).

Tarde's work is exactly concerned with passions—passions transmitted, most particularly, through a semiconscious process of mimesis (Leys 1993). Feeling becomes a propensity to engage in conduct considered "automatic" and "involuntary." In other words, Tarde was a part of a long tradition of work on imitation-suggestion, which would subsequently take in Freud, Morton Prince, and Sándor Ferenczi, among others, as the very ground and origin of psychic experience (Leys 2000). For example, in *Économie psychologique*, Tarde produces a model of the economy in which bodies of passion multiply as so many animations (Barry and Thrift 2007). Finally, it follows that for Tarde, space is key. But this is a particular kind of space that continually questions itself by generating new forms of interrelation. It is a space that is as likely to value the indirect as the direct; it therefore bears some relation to models of action-at-a-distance like those found in theology, spiritualism, mesmerism, hypnosis, telepathy, immunology, epidemiology, and so on, as well as to so-called cultural genetic models that examine waves of stress and their consequences, recently revived by Heiner Mühlmann (1996, 2005). Such viral spaces have, of course, been present for a long time — consider only the spaces generated by the transgenerational imitative behavior of culturally organized extreme emotions such as those found in religion (Trüby 2008) — but lately they have been invented in profusion because of the advent of the Internet. They are providing a new political resource that runs to the dictates of Tarde's model but uses it in new ways. Take political blogging since the late 1990s as but one instance of this tendency. This new medium has complex ancestry but has created a new and more decentered geography from which political information, comment, and gossip flow in continuous ways through spaces that often conform to Tarde's viral tenets (Boehlert 2009; Wasik 2009). Group sites such as Talking Points Memo and individual sites such as Andrew Sullivan's are the tip of a political blogging universe that reflects both the decline of the conventional newspaper industry and the rise of new forms of political communication. These developments are part of an unsettling but well advanced process of decentralization and democratization in which power is shifting away from the individual journalist and journalistic institutions to the work of aggregators and individual writers.

The fourth direction is the most explicitly concerned with the psychotopical. There is ever increasing evidence that one of the most intensely fought-over political fields of the future will be designed environments that are able to communicate wants and needs in ever more intensive ways by exciting and intensifying various kinds of passion. These environments represent a number of different things, all of which are open to "explicitation" and, therefore, political momentum. Thus, they represent new, non-discursive technology that allows these environments to communicate without much in the way of text or as new forms of text. Born out of diverse non-discursive traditions, from brands to cause marketing, and from all manner of art (installation art, participatory art, site-specific art) to the enhanced capacities that have become possible as a result of information technology, these environments are based on tapping into the pre-personal plane through a powerful combination of a reworked phenomenology, knowledges of performance, and new technology to move what Maurice Merleau-Ponty called "perceptual faith." They represent the advent of a new consumer sensibility that puts much more emphasis on understanding these environments as in some way "authentic" with all of the economic and cultural stakes that word has now acquired (Gilmore and Pine 2007). Finally, they represent means of "signifying the real" that are a part of a powerful ontological politics. We can argue about what reality consists of across the full register of the senses and in full knowledge of the arts of construction that are so often hidden from us, because the power of these designed environments comes precisely from the fact that they are knowingly constructed, often in ways that are intended to be reflexive, since feedback from consumers is a powerful element in their dynamic. A powerful leftist politics of space functions here, too, involved in the mounting of staged political interventions that can redefine media publics just as the state uses all of the arts of political theater to assert its sovereignty (Foucault 2007). These interventions are based on the creation of "image-events" that are based on building "image ecologies" that can intervene in conventional acts of representation, showing their manner of construction, questioning authenticity, producing various forms of avatar, and producing feedback loops (Joselit 2007). The explicit aim is to form counter-publics that can find their own voice by creating spatial manifestations of noise and interference.

In tune with the case we have made that not all history is human history, the fifth direction is that we need to understand environment and ecology differently as a politics of a terrain in which many actors are involved in all manner of shifting alliances. It could be argued that work on environment and ecology has already begun to make a transition to this sort of vision. Think, for example, not only of some of the results of the interdisciplinarity now being forced between the sciences, social sciences, and humanities but also of the exigencies of the post-phenomenological turn, full to bursting with the need to see the world from other viewpoints (Ihde 2008), or the performative turn, replete with actual performances that mix actors in all manner of combinations and often do attempt to produce something like a parliament in their attempts to act out "nature" (Szerszynski 2005), or the general interest in the works of Jakob von Uexkull, evinced not just by Sloterdijk but by a whole host of authors. This activity points to the need for what Latour calls an "earthly" politics that understands certain things very well. It understands that the world is an assemblage of heterogeneous threads, none of which can be explained by the other. It equally understands that it is not possible to form a collective made only of social ties. Finally, it understands that *politics is not a domain but a relation*. In turn, this earthly politics understands the sheer scale of the task that now faces us—and the corresponding need for the kind of hyperbolic thinking (Sloterdijk 2007) that is so often assumed to be passé because it has become associated with prescription rather than imagination. In other words, we need a kind of science fiction, but of the present. Latour's version of this scramble to make the present strange is a lively one:

> Think of it: what was the storming of the Winter Palace, compared to the total transformation of our landscape, cities, factories, transportation systems for which we will have to gird ourselves after the Oil Peak? How ridiculously timid does Karl Marx's preoccupation with the mere appropriation of the means of production seem, when compared against the total metamorphosis of all of the very means of production necessary to adjust 9 billion people on a liveable planet Earth. Every product, every biological species, every packaging, every consumer in excruciating detail is concerned in this, together with every river, every glacier, and every bug—even the earthworms have to be brought in according to a recent article in *New Scientist*. We knew about Darwin's work on earthworms, but where could you find, before today, a Marxist view of earthworms! . . .
> It's now painfully clear that communism was never more than

capitalism's abundance pushed to the limit. How unimaginative was such an idea, compared to the modification of all the sinews and corridors of what abundance and wealth should be. . . . Which communist could think that the day would come when they would have to devise a politics for the Gulf Stream. The Gulf Stream, for goodness sake! . . . Yet this is just the time when activists, pundits, and intellectuals complain about the "the ends of utopias" and the disappearance of "les maîtres penseurs."

No wonder that the travails of explicitation have nothing in common with the naïve dreams of emancipation. But they are radical nonetheless, they are our future nonetheless. Don't fool yourselves: explicitation is a much tougher task than the "business as usual" of the modernizing revolutionaries. (Latour 2007a, 9)

But it hardly needs saying that Latour's work is short on what all of this might mean for the practical conduct of politics and the formation of political coalitions.

This is where space is again important, and on a set of levels, in that contemporary work on space questions the ethic of proximity that bedevils the field of environmental politics, an ethic that puts into close association factors such as spatial closeness, cognitive understandings, emotional attachment, and a sense of responsibility or care, often to produce a kind of phenomenology of spiritual immersion. This is surely the wrong kind of worlding, reducing the planet to something like the enclosed bubbles of Sloterdijk's apartment block. What is needed instead is a leftist politics that stresses interconnection as opposed to the "local," however that is understood. What is needed is "not so much a sense of place as a sense of planet" (Heise 2008, 55) that is often (and sometimes rather suspectly) called "eco-cosmopolitanism." Thus, to begin with, the experience of place needs to be re-engineered so that its interlocking ecological dimensions again become clear. This work of reconnection is already being done on many levels and forms a vital element in the contemporary repertoire of leftist politics: slow food, fair trade, consumer boycotts, and so on. Each of these activities connects different places, and it is this work of connection that is probably their most important outcome. Environmental justice then needs to be brought into the equation. The privileges of encounters with certain ecologies, as well as the risks associated with some branches of industry and agribusiness, are clearly unevenly distributed, and it may well be that certain environmentally unsound practices have been perpetuated because their effects go unnoticed by the middle class. Again, environmental justice movements have to refigure spaces, both practically and symbolically, so that interconnection becomes translucent. Finally, we need new ways to sense and envisage global crowds that are dynamic. The attempts to produce people's mapping and geographic information systems, to engage in various forms of mash-up, and to initiate new forms of search are all part and parcel of a growing tendency to produce new kinds of concerned and concernful "Where are we?" Politics starts from this question.

4

contemporary leftist
THOUGHT

The measure of the Left when it was struggling to emerge as a mass force one hundred years ago was its ability to invent a new language and new practices for addressing the challenges of its times. As we have argued, it was not enough to identify the mainsprings of oppression and inequity and then organize to tackle them. The most imaginative and successful movements managed to redefine politics and the political, intuiting, expansions, connections, and resonances of the sort outlined in the preceding chapter. They managed to harness collective and popular energy to unlock a new world of being out of the latencies of the present. In tackling the challenges, they made new things public out of the contingencies of history and context, projecting a vision of the future that the many could identify with or want badly enough to judge the present unacceptable. They unlocked new worlds, but in ways that resonated with an emergent or plural public and brought that public into being as a coherent force.

This chapter scans the body of available leftist thought to examine the resources available now. Against a Right that sometimes seem to revel in the status quo, and a nostalgic Left that frequently harks back to a time when it was sure of the arc of socialist inevitability, we show that the Left remains alive and kicking and has plenty to say. Much of this is about a less grandiose, more realistic, and plural Left, one that is not "vulnerable to the temptation of embedding [its] predicament into some epic logic, as if 'we' were somehow what must resist if there is to be a future" (Stengers 2011a, 148). That does not mean that this Left is anything other than fired by the desire for a less oppressive and less exploitative world made through the social energies of an empowered public. But this is the world of a plural Left gathering many forces — communist, socialist, anarchist, social-democratic, antiracist, feminist, environmentalist, libertarian, humanist, theological, anticolonial, anti-imperial, and others still struggling to be named. It is a Left animated by various global challenges, anxious about the consequences of individualism, capitalism unconstrained, state authoritarianism, global inequality, rising hazard and risk, and environmental meltdown.[1] With varying degrees of realism and imagination, various Lefts propose a way forward to overcome these dangers. If the question, as often asked by critics of the Left, without and within, is whether the Left has anything to say about the contemporary world, the answer has to be: yes.

However, if the question is whether the contemporary Left comes with the world-making capacity of the movements we selected from the past or sensibility for the post-human and postrational constituent of politics outlined earlier, the answer has to be more circumspect. Measured against the test of an ability to reformulate political space and generate ambitions of futurity played out in new and compelling ways, the Left's tool kit has to be judged as lacking. In what follows, we tackle five contemporary leftist positions with distinctive arguments on the current state of affairs and on a possible future politics.[2] Our evaluation is that most of these positions tend to be too restricted, with those that are clear about the direction of travel (the first three) hampered by unrealistic goals or ideas of delivery that lack grip or compulsion and those with a fertile sense of new publics and political tools (the last two) less convincing on what they deem to be the substantive content of leftist politics.

Our motivation in making this observation is not to diminish the significance and relevance of contemporary leftist politics; nor is it to play off one position against another (although our own preferences are made clear in the course of the discussion). Instead, it is to argue that success — building on our conceptual frame — will come from an ability to make and hold together new worlds. In an age of multiple subjectivity and aspiration guided by diverse logics of organization and association, this ability will not come from uniform and top-down impositions of worth and community. It is far more likely to result, as we conclude in this chapter, from ventilation—diplomacy and learning—between the different communities of the Left so that the radius of invention around each can be amplified. Equally, more can be done to gain succor from the world itself—for example, by identifying new modes of political practice arising out of the continual construction of new publics.

Anti-capitalism

The Left as a project wedded to the overthrow of capitalism may be a much weaker force than it was some years ago, but it has by no means disappeared. Indeed, current economic conditions in some parts of the world may well give it a substantial boost. This Left continues to believe that without the overthrow of capitalism, there can be no prospect of lasting freedom. The anti-capitalist Left tends to regard reformist organization and gain within the confines of capitalist society as corruptible and temporary, failing to address capitalism's reliance on inequality, oppression, and exploitation to secure its own survival and deal with its built-in contradictions (Arrighi 2003; Wallerstein 2006). The system's laws of competitive survival and wealth accumulation, tending toward long-run exhaustion through over-investment, under-consumption, opposition by workers and consumers, or mismatch between the different branches of the economy, are regarded as driving the capitalist impetus (Glyn 2005). It is an impetus seen to be resulting in the growing concentration and centralization of economic power and control; the interpenetration of capitalist and state power; the commodification of everyday life and culture; the destruction of non-capitalist forms of economic and social life; the annexation of new markets and territories; and the destruction of nature, community, legacy, and place as capital continually moves on from old to new.

The protagonists of such thinking are clear that the majority of the world's ills can be related to the rise of an all-powerful capitalism working at a new and more frantic pace set by the race for supremacy between transnational elites, the United States, China, India, and other emergent economies. The literature makes grim reading, aided by a reductive clarity exposing root problems: the hand of multinational corporations in distorting development; the crushing power of corrupt states; the self-serving impositions of global elites; the flaunting incursions of various imperialist projects; the alarming consumption of the world's natural resources; the heightened risk, insecurity, waste, and hazard resulting from market liberalism and technological experimentation; the dependencies forced by global consumerism and individualism; and the general increases in global inequality and division caused by heightened inter-capitalist rivalry and capital mobility (Harvey 2003, 2005; Monbiot 2007; Therborn 2006). The rewards of global capitalism are judged to be based on class oppression. Although they may build global productive forces, they do so at the cost of entrenching an unequal and divisive system.

Projections of utopia have played a central role in the anti-capitalist movement since its inception, as we saw in the preceding chapter. However, this utopian impulse has all but disappeared, for at least four reasons. The first is that poststructuralist accounts of the world as plural, emergent, and always temporary in its settlements have displaced the projections of modernist thinking that set out the promise of a stable and often uniform common weald in the future. In particular, this shift has forced thinking on future community to engage with the quest in contemporary popular culture for fulfillment through the libidinal energy of consumption and self-gratification (Bauman 2003; Jacoby 2005; Stiegler 2010). Thus, and second, the meaning of utopia has changed, with the anti-capitalist Left squeezed between a futurity aligned to the ideological premises of hedonistic capitalism or, at the other extreme, to new forms of post-secular transcendentalism that appeal to religiosity, shared humanness, or planetary preservation. Not surprisingly, leftist utopias have been irredeemably tarnished after the often oppressive and colorless experiments in authoritarian socialism that have taken place around the world, regardless of the link between vision and practice. Finally, the energy for utopian renewal has been sapped by the loss in the socialist movement (in the West especially) of visionary leadership, movement intellectuals, vanguard organizations, international solidarity, and active public debate.

The capacity to visualize a future to come seems to have disappeared from the armory of the anti-capitalist Left, exposing the gap between its clarity on contemporary ills and its hesitancy on a post-capitalist future. Many advocates, as Luc Boltanski (2002) notes, have abandoned the exaggerated notion of political will inherent in total revolution and sided with social movements pressing for radical change in the areas of property relations, work conditions, and labor rights. They no longer really expect the whole capitalist edifice to collapse. Others continue to believe that the mounting internal contradictions of capitalism will destroy the system, citing as evidence of capitalist vulnerability the recurrence of large corporate collapses and financial crises, extreme market volatility and regulatory failure, the rapid spread of contagion in an interdependent economy, and the insurmountable risks and hazards associated with climate change. What will arise from the collapse, or how the world will recover from the destruction caused when markets, institutions, infrastructures, states, and societies fail, is left unspecified, but the inevitability of collapse is left in little doubt.

One significant flaw in this account is that capitalism is as inventive as it is destructive, as resilient as it is vulnerable, and as much an entanglement of parts as it is an assemblage of multiplicity. It is a matter of considerable debate whether capitalism is best described as an integrated system of parts governed by a set of immutable laws or as a collection of relatively autonomous parts whose interactions—which require active effort to be maintained—generate the rules of the system but also new outcomes (DeLanda 2006). The merest acknowledgment of these points would begin to explain why capitalism is able to reinvent itself even when the chips are down, how the powerful are able to mobilize all manner of coalitions to stay in power, why the system can survive (and frequently generate) multiple crises that never add up, and how complex co-dependencies between opposites and antagonists allow the system to stabilize.

The resilience of capitalism lies precisely in its ability to localize crisis and dysfunction, renew itself before tendency can become rule, and accomodate grievances without outright rebellion or collapse. Even in the context of the wholesale collapse of the world financial system and its associated effects, capitalism is still unlikely to collapse under its own weight but will have to be changed through concerted effort, harnessed to a program of deliverance with considerable mass conviction. This is exactly what Marx believed when he argued that socialism could only come about through the combination of systemic capitalist crisis and propitious political conditions. In a world captivated by the promises of capitalism and more reflexive than ever before due to what education, mass media, communication, multiple attachment, popular culture, and individualism provide, the challenge of counter-persuasion has become immense. It has become virtually impossible to gather around one alternative grand vision of the good life. The foundational critiques of capitalism have not led to a credible alternative program for the future.

A counter-argument against a politics of program is that continual agitation, along with popular mobilization behind non-mainstream alternatives of social organization, will eventually add up. One possibility often foreseen is the rise of a "movement of movements" linking the alternatives, spurred by the knowledge that the system will yield under continual and costly disruption. This strand of anti-capitalist politics, following a long tradition of revolutionary, anarchist, and autonomist thought, is rooted in a firmament of destabilization that does not assume programmatic coherence and centered discipline. Indeed, in the view of commentators such as Michael Hardt and Antonio Negri (2001, 2005), the dawning age of power sustained through multiple and diffuse logics irreducible to capital or class requires exactly such a counter-politics of multitude: hydra-like, agile, plural, disruptive, and continually experimental. For others, who are still prepared to name centered sources of destruction and liberation, such as Alain Badiou (2005) and Jacques Rancière (1999), a politics of no compromise with the state and other establishment forces, supported by autonomous organization and an unconstrained demos, is an absolute necessity for a people's republic. Anti-capitalist politics — true politics — will reveal its content when popular energy is liberated from the delusions of capitalism and the oppressions of the state.

There is an appealing ring of popular vitality and direct democracy to this strand of anti-capitalist thinking, but its expectations seem hopelessly optimistic. They romanticize agitation (which remains notoriously fickle and riddled with power inequalities of its own and is seldom fully autonomous), and they neglect the myriad ways in which resistance is often crushed, manipulated, compromised. What concerns us is a kind of mystical invocation of given weapons of change as though this can suffice in mapping a course of prosperity and well-being beyond capitalism. For example, rarely is any explanation given about why and how the many energies of multitude should converge toward a shared post-capitalist future. We readily acknowledge the struggles and victories around the world that have come to be labeled the anti-globalization movement, but we would argue that they need to be seen as a counter-politics of many hues and goals, including demands for human rights;

labor rights; resources; welfare security; gender, racial, and sexual equality; social, environmental, and political justice; local markets and small enterprise; and so on.

These situated mobilizations and achievements do not add up to a total movement or an integrated history of mayday and other machines (Raunig 2010), despite the many efforts and sites of direct democracy today against inequality and oppression, building community and hope. There can be no doubt that individual campaigns find immense strength and learning possibilities from participating in such coalitions, and there can be no doubt that the overlap and contact helps to increase the awareness of common interests and goals. But measured against the power of organized interests and the scale of obdurate the global challenges that need tackling, celebrating a politics of grassroots anti-capitalism without some clarity over how to sustain mutuality and leadership, build a commons that binds, ensure that victories gained are maintained and spread, and fire passion for radical change across many publics (Bull 2006) seems overoptimistic. The analytical clarity of the contemporary anti-capitalist Left is not always matched by the level of practical and propositional competence that might enable it to reach its goals. The task is only made more difficult by the all-encompassing nature of modern capitalism, which means that it is very difficult to locate an outside to the system from which it is possible to build a standpoint.

Capitalism Reformed

This may explain why much of the Left now stands for a politics of reform rather than revolution. The reformist Left reasserts the possibility of social democracy, market regulation, and human development through a combination of national and international reform. Its focus falls on constitutional change, responsible government, and pro-development policies, underpinned by a commitment to distributive justice, social cohesion, and cosmopolitan democracy. This Left seeks, in part, to reinstate Keynesian and redistributive principles swept aside by neoliberalism; in part, to introduce supply-side reforms to unlock human and regional potential; and in part, to institute Third Way compromises between state, market, and civil society in governing economy and society. It also recognizes how globalization—manifest in the rise of world-level processes and institutions and the intensification of international flows and interdependencies—has radically altered the meaning and scope of local possibility. Accordingly, it is interested in global reforms that can address issues that escape national control as well as strengthen the hand of national and subnational social democracy.

We do not assume that the reformist Left is a single or coherent entity. Significant differences in thought and practice can be found over reform priorities and possibilities; the balance of responsibility between local and transnational actors; the spread of power between markets, state, and civil society; and the model of capitalism that might be desirable in the long term. Thus, for example, Third Way thinking in the United Kingdom is less state-centric and more market-driven or growth-oriented than the programs of traditional social-democratic governments and parties in Germany, France, or the Scandinavian countries, which continue to expect more from the state and regulation in general. While not wishing to gloss over such differences, the discussion below is based on a stylized summary of the reformist Left, gathered around the central premise that better regulation and social embedding of the economy can go a long way toward tackling the problems facing our times.

Although the reformist Left has come to accept that markets should not be overregulated and that globalization has blunted many traditional levers of national macroeconomic regulation, it maintains the view that other levers of public intervention are available to reconcile capitalist efficiency and social or environmental justice. As far as markets go, these include incentives to reward fair trade, ethical consumption, and environmental stewardship; tighter regulation of financial markets; public ownership of essential industries and services; resolute action against monopolistic or corrupt market practices; support for small firms and weak economies to compete on a more equal basis in international markets; and interventions to minimize asymmetry of information, knowledge, and communication. The belief is that markets can be tamed through more effective regulation of the terms of trade. More broadly, the Left has begun to think quite seriously about how markets can be created to produce particular social goals—for example, around issues such as climate change (e.g., carbon trading [see MacKenzie 2010] or fairer distributions of water rights without compromising water conservation goals [Castro and Heller 2009; Strang 2004]).

It is recognized, however, that the fruits of competition—even in the most carefully regulated market environment—are not evenly distributed. This is why the reformist Left remains strongly committed to re-distributive justice in some shape or form. While the interventions of Third Way thinking have become much more conditional, tying welfare programs to market re-entry objectives or to strict rules of merit (e.g., welfare-to-work programs, means testing, even vilification of welfare dependence), traditional social-democratic thinking continues to justify redistributive measures on the grounds of social and ethical responsibility or Keynesian justification of welfare as a stimulant to economic demand and future social capability and involvement. Either way, the principle of the social state is reasserted as an antidote to the market state, underpinned by a commitment to progressive taxation, universal welfare, public provision, and infrastructural upgrading (see chapter 6 on the European social state).

Against its critics—especially neoliberal arguments on lack of affordability and general waste and inefficiency—the position of the reformist Left, at least in the rich countries, is that the social state can be funded out of the profits generated by a high-value-added economy. Accordingly, a strong case is made for adequate supply-side reforms, such as investment in education and training and in science and technology, to generate the economic and social creativity, general know-how, and sustained learning required to underpin competitiveness based on trade in information and knowledge, high-value-added products and services, and design-intensive or niche goods. The higher economic returns are expected to generate headroom for welfare expenditure at the same time as providing economic actors with the incentive to improve social and environmental stewardship through actions such as corporate social responsibility, profit sharing, employee participation, and sustainable energy use and cleaner emissions (Dunning 2007; Hutton 2003; Leadbeater 2000; Michie and Smith 1995). The examples of success cited include socially responsible corporations that continue to lead their sectors; regions such as Silicon Valley and Italian craft districts that rely on high levels of social creativity and know-how; dynamic cities that attract talent through inclusive social and cultural policies; and governments that invest in science, technology, education, and progressive social and environmental standards.

The reformist Left's thinking on how to ensure such inclusive growth in the less prosperous countries is less clear. Organizations such as the International Labour Organisation (2009) argue that a new capitalist vanguard with qualities such as those outlined above, with the help of binding international rules preventing super-exploitation and development aid focused on education, science, and technology, will help to raise standards worldwide. The flaw in this argument is illustrated by the experience of the rising economic giants China and India, which have joined the capitalist vanguard without necessarily producing the expected social and environmental upgrading. They show that the rapidly advancing economies—and many global corporations—are able to combine high-value-added and low-cost options to serve markets that are still dependent on the goods of the low-wage, low-cost economy, as well as markets that increasingly demand high-value goods at low prices. Many reasons and incentives to veer from the "gold standard" remain within the emerging (and advanced) economies, working to the advantage of indigenous and global corporations. This is precisely why it is proving so difficult to secure international agreement on upwardly harmonized labor-market standards or environmental regulation.

The reformist Left's argument that growth, equity, and sustainability can be reconciled depends on whether a common set of rules can be enforced at the international level. It is not surprising, therefore, that this Left is calling for increased harmonization at the international or global level in the areas of human rights and social welfare, corporate conduct and terms of trade, citizenship, democratic rights and social justice, and environmental standards. The expectation is that a filigree of international rules and agreements in these areas will gradually guide states, civil societies, corporations, and other institutions around the world away from the norms of a predatory form of capitalism. Prominent in this thinking, as even major development organizations such as the World Bank come to acknowledge the damage and waste caused by neoliberalism, is the desire for a neo-Keynesian global settlement that works to the advantage of the developing nations and the less well-off in general.

Many reforms have been suggested, epitomized by the thinking of Joseph Stiglitz, based on his experience as chief economist at the World Bank. One proposal is to resurrect a pro-South institution out of the World Trade Organization, both to ensure the removal of protectionist practices in the North so that traders from the developing countries are given a fair chance in international markets and to secure an intellectual property rights regime that allows these countries to break the patent-based grip of corporations from the North (Deardorff and Stern 2002; Stiglitz 2003). Another proposal is to nudge the international financial system toward developmental outcomes by restricting short-term capital flight, reducing the debt burden of developing countries, and converting the International Monetary Fund into a development fund. A third proposal is to ensure that developing countries receive better fiscal returns from overseas investors under a stricter system of regulation of transnational corporate and banking behavior. All of these calls accept that a development-oriented international regime has to be accompanied by evidence of concrete reform within the developing nations to eliminate corruption, extend democracy, reorder state priorities, and build human and social capital.

The potential of these proposals should not be underestimated. A socially regulated capitalism that supports plural ways of making and meeting markets can reduce many of the inequalities and oppressions that have emerged under the unholy alliance that has grown up between unregulated capitalism and authoritarian power. The question is whether the proposals will be implemented fairly. For example, there remains often a noticeable silence on the need for tighter regulation of corporate and state practices within developed countries just while developing countries are being put under pressure to introduce bootstrapping reforms. The risk is that a new Keynesian settlement will increase economic expansion in the core at the expense of the periphery. How far such an outcome can be avoided depends on whether an effective system of global regulation can be put into place.

The reformist Left offers two options. Those who believe that societies are becoming globally constituted argue that there is a need for increased world-level governance, while those who see nation-states remaining as the prime political force place the emphasis on interstate diplomacy (while conceding that markets, institutions, and aspects of cultural life are becoming transnational). The latter position is held primarily by national social-democratic forces critical of the Washington Consensus and market capitalism in general (Hirst and Thompson 2002). They propose a strengthening of regional blocs such as the European Union to demonstrate the viability of a model of growth capable of reconciling social cohesion and economic competitiveness or to offer an effective counterweight in military and security affairs to current U.S. and North Atlantic Treaty Organization war philosophy (Kaldor 2007;

Rifkin 2004). Other proposals include reforms to increase the voice of smaller countries in the United Nations Security Council, strengthen multilateral decision making in the world's intergovernmental organizations, and empower the developing countries in various intergovernmental economic policy arenas. The argument is that gradually the world can be returned to a system of negotiated and diplomatic decision making, reversing the unilateral elitism that has come to prevail.

Given the continuing primacy of nation-state politics, an intergovernmentalism along these lines, bolstered by nongovernmental organizations, social movements, and lobbies active at international scale, could help bring about a more inclusive and sustainable model of global capitalism. Whether it can resist attack from other powerful global interests working on the inside or from the outside is another matter. The lobbying power of so-called shadow elites at honeypot sites such as Washington, Brussels, or Davos, striking late-night deals based on trust and confidence between senior civil servants and ministers who have long worked with each other and have ties forged through common educational and career trajectories, reveals that the best intentions — substantive and procedural — of international diplomacy routinely get diverted to favor the most influential states and international interests (Slaughter 2004; Wedel 2009).

Other critics, to come to the second position, argue that new world processes and structures have arisen that surpass intergovernmental politics and require global-level regulation. Their attention falls on evidence of ever-increasing global interdependence and mobility (from interstate connectivity to the flow of people, money, things, and information), the rise of influential planetary formations (such as transnational organizations, virtual networks, global warming), and new patterns of cosmopolitan affiliation (sparked by diaspora links, global consumerism, planetary consciousness, religious attachment). While they disagree over whether such trends will accompany, hybridize, or displace national and regional legacies, or over the precise nature of the new globalism (e.g., the balance between its cultural, economic, and political dimensions), they tend to agree that the world is moving in the direction of requiring action at a planetary scale to tackle both situated and common problems.

Ulrich Beck (2005) and David Held (1999) have been at the forefront of conceptualizing the new political requirements. For Held, the answer lies in putting a rigorous legal framework in place to guide and monitor the basics of business, social, and political conduct around the world. Thus, for example, he proposes a significantly extended bill of rights backed by the United Nations that mandates a worldwide broad range of the basics of human well-being and security, including the right to safety, shelter, food, mobility, employment, education, income, association, legal and social justice, freedom from oppression and discrimination, environmental security, and so on. Such protection of the basics of human life, it is claimed, would ensure that the world's population has access to the means of survival and is protected from the predations of war, famine, violence, terror, risk, and insecurity. It would gradually force — through legal application and changed institutional practice — a better standard of expectation in all parts of the globe with regard to market, state, and corporate practices; an ethic of care toward the weak and vulnerable and among social actors; and guardianship of the global commons. This approach to international reform, situated in a regime of binding rights of personhood and rules of institutional conduct, is claimed capable of immediate global reach.

Yet, the experience to date of United Nations rules and practices has not been encouraging in terms of their universal observation and enforcement. Their implementation is as politically inflected as any other instrument of international governance that overlaps with embedded local, national, and regional systems of governance. And this is the case even when international rules take precedence over others. Assuming that a new regime of global rights and responsibilities can be introduced — and this in itself is a heroic supposition — its implementation will be patchy and open to manipulation. The most obvious factors include opposition by powerful states and organizations when self-interest and vested power are threatened, the absence of international authorities capable of monitoring and enforcing standards, local avoidance or transgression of the rules, and fear or reticence in reporting violations. The gaps between the legal, the institutional, and the everyday are considerable, which is not an argument against the value of a new regime of universal rights. Rather, it is a comment on the low probability of its introduction and enforcement.

That said, some commentators believe that an overarching global order is gradually coming into existence and will demand new forms of global politics. For example, Beck (2005, xvi) argues: "Cosmopolitanism is the next big idea to follow after the historically worn-out ideas of na-tionalism, communism, socialism and neoliberalism, and this idea *might just* make the improbable possible, namely the survival of humanity beyond the twenty-first century without a lapse back into barbarism." His argument is as follows: capitalism has created a single global space, with its topology largely shaped by international business operating as a diffuse meta-power, freed from, and flattening, national geometries of power and organization. One consequence is that politics has become not only de-territorialized, but also constrained; a field of human sub-jugation to markets and their privileged interests, rather than a field of agonistic clashes over the human condition. Since the forces of capital-ist globalization are deeply rooted and irreversible, it is unrealistic to expect a return to a politics of nations and nation-states or a politics of overthrow of capitalism by civic society. The only way forward is to re-politicize politics by gathering momentum around a different kind glob-alism that is pragmatic and responsive to situated particularities but also ventilated by ideals of cosmopolitan society born out of the resistance to business-led globalism. Such a politics requires coalition building at the global scale between states, civic forces, and enlightened sections of business to address the risks associated with capitalist globalism.

Beck's thesis is that a new world movement will arise out of issue-specific organization and the formation of publics that think and act globally. It will survive as a movement of movements bound together by certain common dispositions. One is the desire to reimpose binding col-lective decisions on capital, the democratic process, and the legal system, forcing states to explore alternatives to neoliberalism and "capital to ac-cept the new rules of cultural and political engagement" (Beck 2005, 193). Another is the acceptance of transnational organization, based on the experience of enhanced interstate cooperation and diminished state influence, the growing sophistication and reach of advocacy movements, and the push against business-led internationalism coming from world political interests, international courts of law, and universal human rights. There is a persuasive symmetry to this argument: business-led cosmopolitanism can be reversed only if a widely felt and effective poli-tics of opposition can be put into place at the same spatial scale, mobi-lized around issues of practical and common concern. The crucial ques-tion, however, is whether the time of a cosmopolitanism that is capable of supporting the transnational political organization and public interest that Beck wants or anticipates has come. We do not believe that it has.

This is not simply a matter of noting the continued salience of political force and fervor at other spatial scales, from the local to the national and intergovernmental. It is, above all, a question of how globalization — and its spatial architecture — is understood. Without wishing to ignore the power of transnational organization and interdependence, we would argue that globalization should be understood as an interpenetration of different spatial ontologies. We see this interpenetration to be responsible for the making of a new modernity, not a simple transition from a territorial and national world to a scalar and global world. Accordingly, we would acknowledge the jostle of diverse geographies of formation — for example, the economy of flows, networks, and territories; the politics of local, regional, national, and global organization; presence in virtual, institutional, informal, and symbolic spaces; and attachment to communities of varying spatial stretch and duration. Each has its own powers of organization and capture, and each is transformed but not eliminated by the encounter with other spatial forms.

Consequently, if a new cosmopolitan order is arising, it might not be at the expense of local, national, or interstate processes and politics. This suggests the continuing power and influence of strong nation-states, which are still able to impose their will on global affairs, as well as in various intergovernmental forums. The spaces of the political that Beck places in the past or on the periphery — community and local struggles; state-centered politics; intergovernmental rivalry and diplomacy; hybrids of socialism, liberalism, and social democracy or varieties of cultural and identity politics that remain steadfastly national — have far from disappeared. These continuities will make it very difficult to enact a new politics of radical cosmopolitanism.

Post-capitalism

A third leftist stance on the contemporary world can be described as "poststructuralist," in that it draws on feminist, postcolonial, antiracist, and ecological thinking, much of which heavily influenced by poststructuralist ideas. This Left does away with what it sees as the myth of a capital "C" capitalism and identifies numerous sites for a politics of progressive transformation. This thinking is encapsulated in *A Postcapitalist Politics* (Gibson-Graham 2006). Its central argument is that the economy — its practices of transaction, labor, and enterprise — is an agglomeration of diverse modes of organization and regulation, capitalist and non-capitalist. These modes are seen to exist side by side, sometimes as complementary or linked forms, but most often in asymmetrical relations of power that, however, stop short of eliminating the weaker modes.

A Postcapitalist Politics unveils the economy as a richly heterogeneous and hybrid entity. Its *transactions* are shown to exceed any single "law of the market." Markets are revealed to be more or less regulated, more or less customized, and governed by different rules of exchange, coexisting with transactions of a non-market nature (e.g., gift giving, household exchanges, state quotas, acquisition by "natural" right) and markets guided by principles of mutuality and social reciprocity (e.g., ethical or cooperative trade, time banks, barter). Similarly, *labor* is shown to comprise many forms of wage labor with varied modes of remuneration and protection (e.g., salaried, seasonal, unionized, temporary), forms of unpaid labor that are far from residual (e.g., housework, family care, volunteering, community work, slavery and bondage), and forms of "non-mainstream" remuneration among the self-employed, the indentured, and those involved in cooperative or in-kind wage schemes. In turn, *enterprise* is conceptualized as multiple forms of ownership and organization following diverse rules of appropriating surplus. These include capitalist enterprises governed by different rules of extracting and retaining surplus (e.g., small family firms or large multinational firms); non-capitalist enterprises of a communal, collective, or semi-feudal constitution that respectively share, retain, or return surplus; and hybrid enterprises that combine profit and equitable distribution (e.g., state-owned, green, socially responsible, nonprofit, or cooperative firms).

Grasped in these terms, the economy springs back to life as a field of situated social practice that is open to challenge. The time-spaces of economic evolution can be considered sufficiently heterogeneous and path-dependent to justify an account of "capitalism" that recognizes

> the fruitfulness of more generous definitions of capital and labour,
> of a more plural and less economistic conception of the construc-
> tion of the world market, and a non-teleological conception of the

emergence and transformation of multiple regimes of production and exploitation. The idea that such regimes are not simply the product of the internal workings of relations of production and exchange but simultaneously shaped by forms of domination, accommodation, and resistance at the site of capital/labor relations, analytically locates state, society, and culture as interior to . . . relations of production and exchange. (Chalcraft 2005, 32–33)

In this reading, the economy becomes an object of live political struggle, no longer a surface with a deep structure that must be comprehensively dismantled before new modes of livelihood and fulfillment can be developed. Gibson-Graham goes as far as to suggest that all that the Left should do is provide a broad outline of the normative goals of the desired economy and desist from prescribing its forms and modes of delivery. The model Gibson-Graham proposes is the "community economy," summarized by keywords such as small scale, cooperative, decentered, locally owned and traded, community controlled, environmentally sustainable, ethical, harmonious, and self-reliant. These goals, Gibson-Graham suggests, can be pursued through a variety of means. In the arena of transactions, this might include reforms to alter the market practices of big firms and the general rules of international trade, or campaigns to raise the status of ethical and fair trade, informal and reciprocal exchange, or non-monetary markets. In the arena of labor, this could stretch from ensuring universal access to a basic wage and enhanced profit sharing or joint decision making to campaigning for better rewards for socially oriented work and unpaid domestic labor. In the arena of enterprise, the drive for change might include tighter scrutiny of the ethical, social, and environmental practices of firms, as well as enhanced recognition for social enterprises, cooperatives, nonprofit firms, and mutual endeavor.

This is a post-capitalist politics that values normative and pragmatic experimentation in and beyond capitalism. It is typified by the varied initiatives represented by the World Social Forum that press for ethical trade, socially useful production, local purchasing, slow or organic food, environmental stewardship, sustainable farming, renewable energy, low-waste housing, communal property rights, non-monetary exchange, alternative currencies, fair wages, the social economy, distributive justice, collective decision making, and public ownership and control. It also taps into a rich vein of contemporary leftist thought—Marxist and non-Marxist—on inclusive and participatory economy, with far-reaching consequences for capitalism. This includes proposals for the living wage, birthright endowments, incentives for ethical and social enterprises, global tax levies to fund development in low-income countries, affordable finance and debt relief, shared intellectual property rights, universal access to basic welfare, domestic wages, rewards for environmental stewardship, recognition of time-based transactions, and so on.

This Left is conscious that these experiments could be dismissed as small, dispersed, and fragile developments, forever kept on the margins or crushed by the forces of instituted power. In its defense, however, it argues that the experiments reveal a world that is less closed than is portrayed by the capitalist vanguard or revolutionary Left; that already provides for many of those incapacitated, bypassed, or dissatisfied by the mainstream; and that illustrates the outlines of "another possible world" and new ways to re-enchant the Left (George 2004).

For the anti-capitalist Left, a politics of assemblage of this sort falls short because of its lack of clarity, focus, and grip over the structural sources of (capitalist) violence and inequality (Saldanha 2010). This is a problematic argument, however. In a complex society, injury is the product of immanent forces working interactively in emergent ways and through situated practices (Virno 2004), always beckoning for forensic analysis. Another common criticism is that such a "politics of difference" jettisons the universality of the traditional Left's preference for a "politics of sameness" (Saldanha 2010). But even a glimpse of leftist universalism from our review of the Left one hundred years ago shows that the commons does not disclose itself unaided. It has to be assembled. It arises from the sheer hard work of making a counter-public out of always fragile associations between different forces of change, so that eventually the fixtures that might make a better future can come to light, become accepted, and be made the object of collective aspiration. Even Badiou, who is resolutely universalist, believes that universals have to be constructed out of the worlds of multiplicity. There can be no politics of sameness to conjure up. This is precisely why a leftist politics of general reach might have to begin, once again, with a short list of old and new concepts of progress and emancipation (see the final chapter) that can be harnessed to the varied inventions of post-capitalist thought and practice as what Isabelle Stengers (2011b) calls "operative constructs" that are continually being put back to work as experiments in new stories and practices of intervention.

Central to the success of such a proliferating politics of the commons will be the ability of the Left to rekindle social interest in a just, equal and sustainable society. For Gibson-Graham, that task requires an ethical and emotional shift at the individual and interpersonal level so that a new sense of being in and hope for the world can be kindled. Accordingly, the Left is told to jettison its language of doom or anger for one of grounded optimism, ethical subjectivity, and ventures that meet social needs, build community, and value mutuality. This turn to new subjectivities is not unproblematic. On the one hand, it risks ignoring enduring sources of inequality and oppression and the (un)ethical practices of the comfortable, privileged, and powerful. It offers cold comfort to those devastated or displaced by neoliberalism and a state-military-industrial complex that often seems to be spinning out of control. On the other hand, without it, the Left cannot draw on rooted social desires for another world. In turn, there is a long legacy of leftist inculcation of alternative subjectivities with dubious credentials. On more than one occasion, leftist templates of vanguard subjects, model citizens, and ideal states have crushed human vitality and freedom when put in the hands of an all-controlling and suspicious state.

The interest of post-capitalist thought in subjectivity, however, is very different. It links to an ethic of care and solidarity (Mol et al. 2010) based on the hope, capability, and potential that can be born out of productive engagement and social participation—what Rebecca Solnit (2005) describes as "hope in the dark" cultivated through experience of participation in such activities as participatory budgeting, the communal economy, ethical consumption, and similar collective ventures, guided by social solidarity, and alive to both the ambivalence and multiple modalities of its practices.

Human Recognition

Alongside a politics of hope located in communal practice has been maturing politics of the human ethic. Typified by writing in the feminist or humanist tradition, this politics is troubled by continuing—in some cases, intensified—violence toward women, the vulnerable, the poor, the different, the foreign, the stranger. It is work on recognition and responsibility that draws on the ideas of Jacques Derrida, Julia Kristeva, Luce Irigaray, Bhikhu Parekh, Paul Gilroy, Judith Butler, and Iris Marion Young, to name just a few of the theorists of difference.

The account on offer are richly varied, with some drawing on a philosophy or psychology of self and others on community, with some emphasizing the cultural and institutional dimensions of human conduct and others focusing on the moral aspects of personal and interpersonal behavior. In turn, the accounts are informed by different injuries, including the cruelties of war, genocide, and ethnic conflict; the oppressions of state, class, race, gender, and imperial power; and instincts of aversion located deep in the human psyche. However, a common orientation across these differences seems to be a desire to tackle human violation through an ethic of recognition and care, even if there is little consensus on where the burden should fall (individuals, groups, institutions, publics, or states) or on whether a politics of ethics alone can suffice. The emphasis on the core ontological and ethical question of what it is to be human marks this body of work as distinctly different from the other Lefts discussed in this chapter.

Our aim in this section is not to cover the full spectrum of this Left but to focus on a leftist politics of difference that at times has been carelessly labeled identity politics. In its formative years during and after the late 1960s, the politics of difference, as it developed in the struggles of the feminist, anticolonial, and antiracist movements and in demands by minorities and indigenous peoples for recognition, was a politics that was acutely aware of the oppressions of instituted power. Underpinning campaigns for sexual, expressive, and cultural freedom was the belief that success would come from tackling the embedded sources of injustice and inequality and that the quest for recognition stemmed from a wider desire for progress and emancipation across the social divide. Thus, for example, the women's movement redefined femininity, extended the orbit of women's rights, attacked patriarchy and capitalist inequality, and frequently situated its struggle in a general cause, such as socialist utopia. Similarly, postcolonial politics drew on universal ideas of sameness and unity—Western and non-Western—to press the cause of the poor and vulnerable and to argue for cultural autonomy from the distortions and divisions of colonialism, nationalism, and tradition. In the politics of race, too, the struggle for recognition dug deep to expose the systemic roots of racism and racial categorization, along with attempting to link the iniquities of race with those of class and gender.

This sensitivity has not been lost. It remains strong in postcolonial work, which continues to locate the politics of the subaltern in a critique of capital, hegemony, and entanglements of modernity (Chakrabarty 2002; Chatterjee 2004; Venn 2006). It remains pivotal in reflections on how the practices of state, sovereignty, and nationalism continue to foreclose recognition by reducing some humans to bare life, others to the lower orders of deservingness, and still others to a monstrous status so that inhuman forms of discipline can be imposed (Agamben 2005; Diken and Laustsen 2005). In turn, in some work on race and ethnicity, there remains a concern to reconcile recognition and redistribution in order to ensure that cultural rights come with material security (Fraser and Honneth 2003; Loury et al. 2005), along with an anxiety that the politics of difference — frequently expressed in the language of multiculturalism — could reinforce isolationism or endless commentary by majorities on the rights and duties of minorities. We note these continuities to rebut the aside from the "materialist" Left that the post-1968 "cultural" Left has abandoned a politics of solidarity, structural critique, and total revolution for a politics of identity, separation, and contentment (Badiou 2001; Boltanski 2002; Rancière 1999).

However, the turn to ethics, and of a particular stripe, is undeniable. The focus on ethics is quite different from the postwar Left's effort to replace an ethic of care located in the idiosyncrasies of charities, communities, families, and individuals by one enshrined in the principles of universal welfare, protected by the state and the idea of one society. Today, the focus falls on care toward each other: the rights of personhood, the modalities of interpersonal recognition, the relationship with distant others. It marks a shift from an ethics of political economy largely blind to individual and social behavior to an ethics of human conduct centrally interested in that behavior.

Why this shift has occurred is not entirely clear. Reasons include the displacement of a politics of the collective and the universal by a politics of the particular; to the criticism that institutionalized care has blunted sensitivity and social energy; to reflection on the fundamentals of human association prompted by the continuing barbarisms of genocide, war, and terror; to thinking on community posed by the rise of multicultural and multiethnic society; and to unease over the negation of human empathy by the acquisitive or provisioning society. Perhaps the shift is also symptomatic of a willingness within the Left itself to rethink old assumptions regarding the sources of human solidarity and emancipation, including the role and meaning of personal and interpersonal ethics in the process of social and cultural transformation. Whatever the explanation, there is little doubt that the interest in human ethics has grown exponentially. We illustrate this in the rest of this section by dwelling, first, on a new discourse of togetherness that has arisen around issues of cultural and ethnic diversity, and then one on ethical accountability as a means of dealing with mistreatment of the other.

Writing on diversity—frequently under the banner of multiculturalism—traditionally has drawn on both liberal philosophy and communitarian thought in order to simultaneously defend universal (individual) rights and recognition for ethnic and religious minorities (Kymlicka 1995; Parekh 2005). This model has begun to creak at the seams under the weight of hysteria over incompatible cultures and civilizations fueled by the War on Terror; clashes between Islam, Christianity, and secularism; and national anxiety in the West toward minorities and their claims. Worried by growing mainstream criticism of multiculturalism as—expressed in calls for greater conformity from minorities and immigrants and the isolation of irreconcilable cultures and strangers—some multicultural theorists have argued that a way forward might be to link the formal recognition of minority rights to clearly defined and universally applicable rules of national citizenship (Modood 2007). Others within the Left, looking beyond the balance between rights and responsibilities, have suggested the need to find ways for people from different backgrounds to interact with one another in daily life so a certain conviviality between strangers can emerge to normalize living with difference (Amin 2002; Gilroy 2004; Keith 2005; Parekh 2008; Sennett 2012).

A second strand delves into moral philosophy for new metaphors of reconciliation appealing to a common humanity. Such effort has yielded, famously, Derrida's (2000) insistence on a politics of unconditional hospitality in Europe toward asylum seekers and others "without papers," along with a rediscovery of Hannah Arendt's position on the indivisibility of rights of personhood in the face of state projects of violence and humiliation carried out in the name of sovereign defense. Similarly, definitions in psychoanalytic theory (Irigaray 2000) or pre-Socratic philosophy (Kristeva 1991) of human being and becoming based on recognition of and interdependence with the stranger are being recovered to question ethnocentric and nationalist discourses of belonging and citizenship. Here the language of belonging returns to a pre-societal and pre-cultural understanding of social subjectivity in an attempt, at minimum, to question the naturalized status of ethno-nationalist discourse.

The grim realities of Rwanda, Somalia, the Balkans, and the Middle East have prompted a similar rethinking of the theory and practice of international relations, dominated for too long by a "realist" legacy averse to ethical moorings. The new thinking argues for tying the rules of international diplomacy and military intervention to the essentials of human community, with suggestions drawn, once again, from Derrida or from humanists such as Emmanuel Levinas, asserting that to be properly human is to encounter the other or, following on from Gaston Bachelard and Martin Buber, that human life and language begin with the relation between self and other (Campbell and Shapiro 1999).

Complementing this emphasis on the idea of community before cognition, culture, or nation is a new interest on the Left in the ethics of personal conduct, typified by Butler's *Giving an Account of Oneself* (2005). Butler also draws on the Arendt–Levinas tradition, but now to outline a mode of human responsibility based on explicit consciousness of the other. Thus, for example, she writes of the need to recognize self-opacity and human vulnerability by learning is to reciprocate and accept ethical demands from the other. For Butler, all-too-readily compromised fundamentals of the human relation have to drive an ethical dispensation that

> requires us to risk ourselves precisely at moments of unknowingness, when what forms us diverges from what lies before us, when our willingness to become undone in relation to others constitutes our chance to become human. To be undone by another is a primary necessity, and anguish, to be sure, but also a chance — to be addressed, claimed, bound to what is not me, but also to be moved, to be prompted to act, to address myself elsewhere, and so to vacate the self-sufficient "I" as a kind of possession. If we speak and try to give an account from this place, we will not be irresponsible, or, if we are, we will surely be forgiven." (Butler 2005, 136)

Butler is joined by others wanting the politics of human recognition imbued with an ethic of human vulnerability and incompleteness — for example, Seyla Benhabib, who argues for a "moral cosmopolitanism" to shape institutional and collective culture. Without experiencing "the otherness of others whose ways of being may be deeply threatening to our own," Benhabib (2004, 197) asks: "How else can moral and political learning take place, except through such encounters in civil society? The law provides the framework within which the work of culture and politics go on. The laws, as the ancients knew, are the walls of the city, but the art and passions of politics occur within those walls . . . and very often politics leads to the breaking-down of these barriers or at least to assuring their permeability."

How should this turn to an ethics-based politics be judged? It would be easy to ridicule its naïve idealism, judged against the daily background of embedded state violence, ethical practice compromised by utilitarian or selfish pursuit, and rooted prejudice. This is certainly Badiou's position at the head of the revolutionary Left, mocking the ethical turn as a "self-satisfied egoism of the affluent West" that forgets that "politics as practiced today does not in any way consist of setting objectives inspired by principles" and that is trapped in a fiction of "being-togetherness" blind to how the same language is deployed by oppressors against the other (Badiou 2001, 7). For him, "The whole ethical predication based upon recognition of the other should be purely and simply abandoned" (Badiou 2001, 25). To caricature the ethical Left in this way is to fail to engage seriously with its premises and arguments.

Such engagement might, for example, recognize the risk of a politics of ethics becoming a weapon of the powerful or the hegemonic against the weak and the subaltern. Wendy Brown (2006) argues, for example, that the rise of a public discourse of "aversion" and "tolerance" to regulate cultural difference and conflict in the United States, shared by both state and opposition, has become a tool of liberal rule over particular modes of behavior, carelessly linked to particular peoples and cultures. Brown argues that keywords such as tolerance and "national values" are allowing moral judgment to define good civic and public behavior, in the process rendering the other (non-patriots, fundamentalists, non-secularists, traditionalists) deviant and threatening, somehow underdeveloped, and in need of ethical engineering. A well-intentioned ethical rule is never far from moral condemnation. Tolerance as part of a discourse of cohabitation soon slides into a practice of government that "produces and positions subjects, orchestrates meanings of identity, marks bodies, and conditions political subjectivities" (Brown 2006, 4), ending up associating liberal values with tolerance and everything else with different shades of intolerance and prejudice.

Such criticism should not be taken lightly. The ethical Left would be the first to insist that its proposals are intended as additions to a materially underpinned politics of justice traditionally defined, but the charge that a governmentality based on ethics serves to replicate old cultural binaries is difficult to ignore. Whether this criticism effectively incapacitates a politics of ethics is the key question. Our qualified answer is that it does not, for attending to the ethic of human being and engagement provides some measure of possibility, a reminder of what a leftist politics of justice and equality is for. The just and equal society will not arise out of rules, conventions, and institutions alone. Although after Bosnia, Kosovo, Rwanda, and other holocausts there is cause to doubt appeals to common humanity or a single spine of rights, a politics of recognition of the sort articulated, inter alia, by Derrida, Irigaray, Levinas, and Kristeva begins to reduce the susceptibility of publics to manipulation in the way outlined by Brown. It would squeeze habits of recognition relying on (ethical) difference as a way to discriminate against certain human subjects.

Perhaps the central issue here relates to where the burden of empathy (or any other ethic of care) should be located. The Left, exemplified by Butler's thinking, calls the individual to account in different settings of charged cultural conflict. So Martha Nussbaum (2007), commenting on the resurgence of Hindu violence in India toward Muslims, concludes that no solution can escape from the "Gandhian claim that the real struggle that democracy must wage is a struggle within the individual self, between the urge to dominate and defile the other and a willingness to live respectfully on terms of compassion and equality, with all the vulnerability that such a life entails" (Nussbaum 2007, ix). Our view is that this focus on the individual is an odd place to end up for a Left that historically has emphasized the social—in its various forms—precisely to progress beyond a politics of individual responsibility that will always be compromised, that places too much of the burden of public culture on the ethical individual, and that strays perilously close to a photo-fit ideal of human behavior (despite all of its recognition of imperfectability, vulnerability, undoing).

It is an account that inadequately recognizes other sites of ethical behavior. Echoing contemporary pragmatist thinking (Rorty 1998), we would propose attending to an ethic of care arising from situated social practice (rather more than from self-contemplation). A Left that is interested in the social origins of recognition and empathy might want to look more deeply into the affective and ethical consequences of social participation. This is not automatically an argument for more direct or mediated contact between strangers in the hope that it will magically breed mutuality and trust. Rather, it is an argument for a politics of shared experience of common space so that a tacit reflex of dealing with diversity and difference is stimulated by the situation itself (Amin 2012). Human ethics and situated practice are inseparably interwoven, and it may turn out that the real test of Butler's (2005, 136) desire for a "willingness to become undone in relation to others" lies in what might be achieved through the routines of home, school, work, street, club, shopping, consuming, watching, listening — routines out of which common habits of being in the world might be formed. Participation in these daily worlds shapes social conduct through reflexes of co-habitation, virtual and physical.

Publics to Be Made, Worlds to Be Discovered

This gesture toward an ethic of care based on habits of living in the world — echoing our earlier reflections on the psychotopical — complements writing in the pragmatist tradition on the kind of public sphere that reinforces democratic politics. We illustrate this through the revival of interest in William James's writings on radical pluralism and those of John Dewey on object-oriented publics. We begin by addressing the work of William Connolly, who builds on James in his book *Pluralism* (2005) before going on to consider democracy as *Making Things Public*, as proposed by Bruno Latour and Peter Weibel (2005).

Connolly's proposal for a post-9/11 world of intensified political and cultural conflict within the United States and beyond argues for more — and not less — pluralist recognition; a politics working with the grain of radical difference and strongly felt affective preferences among different communities. Thus, for example, he urges the U.S. Left to accept official recognition and support for diverse faiths and to engage productively with the visceral politics of biological, cultural, religious, and fundamentalist judgments that have come to dominate U.S. public life. Connolly's counterintuitive argument is that if the public arena and politics in general are so pluralized that all claims and claimants come to be minoritized, this will eventually enhance equality as political life becomes reinvigorated, pluralized, and decentered. The surplus of political impulse serving specific needs and specific communities is expected to crowd out centrism, political apathy and majority consensus, as well as challenge isolationism as "layered practices of connection across multiple differences" (Connolly 2005, 66) emerge.

How pluralism might ennoble democracy rests on two readings of the world experienced as plural. The first is a Jamesian "radical empiricism," or recognition of the world unfolding as a universe of random forces, with many more agents than humans alone. It is a world made up of disordered and discordant energies and flows but experienced as a single surface combining consciousness, emotions, "thing-stuff," and "thought-stuff" (James 2003, 72) and a world constantly generating novelty through the clash of bodies in motion. According to James, such an experience of the world requires an instrumentality of provisional ideas, makeshift truths, mediating knowledge, and anti-intellectualism on the part of the pragmatist who "turns away from bad *a priori* reasons, from fixed principles, closed systems, and pretend absolutes and origins . . . toward concreteness and adequacy, toward facts, toward action, and toward power" (James 1995, 20).

The second reading of pluralism as ennobling derives from contemporary thinking on complex and self-organizing systems. This is thinking sensitive to the condition of unstable and partial equilibrium in both the natural and human world resulting from the volatility of initial conditions (Prigogine 1997), randomness produced by the unpredictable interaction of simple rules in nature (Wolfram 2002) and complex regularities in human society, and new causal rules arising from interactions in the vast litter of the world (James 2003). For Connolly, such "rules" of autopoeisis, uncertainty, and emergence demand a "bicameral orientation" to the world, which requires remaining open to mystery, doubt, difference, and critical responsiveness. Connolly is clear, however, that such an orientation cannot assume that radical empiricism will of its own accord steer in the direction of altruism or an end to malice, violence, and inequality. Rather, it should be used to guide an ethics and politics of justice and equality that steps up to the challenge of unstoppable variety, common matter among humans and nonhumans, and virtue and creativity arising from free association in a plural universe.

Ultimately, despite Connolly's acknowledgment of the agency of matter and nature, his politics in *Pluralism* remains deeply humanist in its expectation that pluralism will ennoble human behavior and the quality of politics. He anticipates the "religious virtue of hospitality and the civic virtue of presumptive generosity" (Connolly 2005, 64) to prevail once pluralism is given a chance to flourish. Admittedly, here the burden of responsibility would not be placed on the shoulders of the individual or in the dynamic of interpersonal care, but the expectation is the same as that of the ethical Left: human virtue in the face of multiplicity and difference. More recently, however, in his account of the grip of the fundamentalist Christian Right in the United States, Connolly (2008) has moved more decidedly toward a post-humanist stance not only by acknowledging that a Right "resonance machine" playing on all manner of instituted mobilizations (involving, for example, media, affects, elites, churches, slogans) has kept American politics in a decidedly undemocratic space, but also by arguing that any progressive break from this state of affairs will require assembling a counter-resonance machine from similar sites of material culture, capable of making visible and building public affect around an eco-egalitarian capitalism.

The reference to pragmatist thought in *Making Things Public* (Latour and Weibel 2005) is decidedly post-humanist, reducible neither to human effort alone nor to interhuman reconciliation. In the essay that opens the book (and exhibition), Latour (2005) proposes an object-oriented democracy—a *Dingpolitik*—that involves many forms of political assembly and organization and many human and nonhuman actors, gathered around specific goals. Democracy comes to be redefined in Latour's hands as the politics of creating publics around issues of common concern. As such, it is a more directed and purposeful politics than Connolly's, which ultimately *hopes* that the general good will prevail from active and shared citizenship. Echoing Walter Lippmann's and John Dewey's different efforts to rethink the nature of democratic politics during the 1920s as American society became increasingly plural, technologically mediated, and centrally governed, Latour's answer to a similar contemporary problem of politics mediated and closed down, is to reinvent the political by making issues that affect the public— frequently concealed, ignored, or mismanaged by politics as we know it—visible, comprehensible, and matters of common concern.

Dewey (1954) saw the machine age as leading to a professionalization of politics at the expense of an independent and active public sphere. For him, the machine "age has so enormously expanded, multiplied, intensified and complicated the scope of the indirect consequences, has formed such immense and consolidated unions in action, on an impersonal rather than a community basis, that the resultant public cannot identify and distinguish itself." Publics "too diffuse and too intricate in composition" had come into being, "uncertain and obscure," dependent increasingly on "bosses with their political machines who fill the void between government and the public" and "parties that are not creators of policies to any large extent" (Dewey 1954, 120, 126, 137). The answer for Dewey was for the public to return as the caretaker of issues neglected by the body politic (Marres 2005), reinvigorating democracy in the process by redistributing authority and, most important, conjuring a "phantom" of democracy as "conjoint activity whose consequences are appreciated . . . as a good shared by all" (Dewey 1954, 149).

Similarly, Latour's starting point is that politics as we know it has suppressed democracy. Its established spaces, times, and actors, known problems, goals and means, settled definitions and certitudes of the good life are preventing proper political address of the issues that affect the world. A new approach is needed that is interested in "the material conditions that may render the air breathable again." This means reconstructing "the frail conduits through which truths and proofs are allowed to enter the sphere of politics" (Latour 2005, 18–19) so that the taken for granted becomes a matter of concern, an object of disputed arguments. It also means finding the forms of political assembly that are fit for purpose, responsive to the issues in question and open to all available tools of political persuasion—the treatises of mortals and gods, the weapons of science and technology, the seductions of catwalks and supermarket aisles, and all their affective energies. For Latour (2005, 31), true democracy requires a complete overhaul of the political field along the lines outlined in chapter 2, so that

A) Politics is no longer limited to humans and incorporates the many issues to which they are attached;
B) Objects become things, that is, when matters of fact give way to their complicated entanglements and become matters of concern;
C) Assembling is no longer done under the already existing

globe or dome of some earlier tradition of building virtual
parliaments;

D) The inherent limits imposed by speech impairment, cognitive
weaknesses and all sorts of handicaps are no longer denied but
prostheses are accepted instead;

E) It [is] no longer limited to properly speaking parliaments but
extended to the many other assemblages in search of a rightful
assembly;

F) The assembling is done under the provisional and fragile
Phantom Public, which no longer claims to be equivalent to a
Body, a Leviathan or a State;

G) And, finally, *Dingpolitik* may become possible when politics is
freed from its obsession with the time of Succession.

Dingpolitik is a politics of democratic filling in, of naming many objects of public concern and then ventilating them with new atmospheres
of democracy so that all of the associations and interests surrounding
the objects and all of the offers to tackle them can be brought into play.
This, too, is a politics without guarantees but one that is optimistic of
change in service of the general interest through the recovery and re-
constitution of publics, through agonistic clashes, and through showing
up hidden distortions, oppressions, and injustices — the politicization of
everything in a sense that everything has political potential. This is not a
politics of easy promise, however. It does not assume that pluralism will
automatically crowd out the bad atmospheres of democracy or that it
will open space for the innate sociality of humans and nature to prevail
(as new thinking in biological sociology would have; see Braidotti 2006;
Wheeler 2006). Instead, it is a politics of the hard work spent in making
things public, building momentum around them, persuading suspicious
and uninterested communities, forging unexpected connections and
alliances, and battling it out with powerful vested interests that have the
history of public apathy or assumed truths on their side.

But the hard work need not be seen as incapacitating by a Left interested in a politics of publics to be made and worlds to be discovered,
since much of the challenge lies in recognizing what already exists. A
new awareness, for example, might look to making something out of the
"democracy of mistrust" that has grown in our times among publics disillusioned by formal politics (Rosanvallon 2006). It might learn from the

small victories of a "politics of the governed" over basic rights of settlement and survival, even within societies of hegemonic rule that at face value seem to offer few concessions to the poor and the wretched (Chatterjee 2004). It might reject ideological shorthand that chokes off new possibility (e.g., that the state is intrinsically bad and the untainted mass intrinsically good [Badiou 2005; Rancière 1999]). Above all, it might accept that many potential political technologies and means of assembly exist, as revealed in the collection of essays edited by Latour and Weibel (2005): cosmological imaginaries and communities, musical compositions, laboratory proofs, assemblies of nature and people, voting machines, murals and icons, data plots and cartograms, and the powers of fables, rhetoric, cinema and Internet blogs.

For this kind of Left, much remains to be done through a new politics of *res publica*—things made public in many ways and means—so that the known democracy of rule by government and experts can be replaced by the "reign of excess," the politics of "perpetual bringing into play" (Rancière 2006). Its response to a world of unregulated markets and states, rampant individualism, global inequality, and planetary risk and hazard would be to urge the formation of publics around the challenges and problems generated, without prejudice toward what counts as legitimate practice, space or cause. This is exactly what the nineteenth-century movements discussed in chapter 2 managed to achieve, gathering passionate publics around specific issues of common concern and in the process making leftist cause relevant and necessary.

Conclusion: What Kind of Left?

The Left is alive and kicking and has plenty to say about how the world can become a better place. Notwithstanding our own predilections, which no doubt are clear by now, all of the five Lefts we have considered offer a clear account of what is wrong, and the majority also come with concrete proposals for change. Why, then, has the Left lost grip and momentum? One common set of answers is that the Left has become too fragmented and incoherent, that it travels with the enemy, that it has lost its direction, and that it no longer seeks to tackle the root causes of oppression and inequality (Badiou 2005; Rancière 1999; Žižek 2000). Here, the Left is told to return to a singular and steadfast politics of transformation, clear about the enemy and the goal. We do not share this position. The times have become far too plural, autonomous, and distributed for such a singular politics. They have changed far too much for an old language of the Left to remain unchanged (on how altered a category "labor" has become in post-Fordist capitalism, see, e.g., Virno 2004). Even the fixtures of friend and foe are no longer self-evident under a form of capitalism whose power and reach have become comprehensively diffused, internalized, and hybridized. Which Capital is to be opposed by which Labor?

Our diagnosis, by contrast, is that the Left has lost its ability to imbue the new with power and conviction, displaced by a Right that has come closer to the ground of contemporary publics and their sentiments. It has lost its ability to anticipate and project new and fairer ways of being in the world and to show itself as the natural bearer of the politics — reinvented in its assemblies and its tools — required to move toward these ways of being. It has lost the inventiveness and affective power of its founding movements, and it has forgotten how centrally the politics of transformation relies on intervening in the ecology of life by bringing more and more of its actants into the political domain and by working on the pre-personal, the affective, and the habits of habitation. The problem is one of imagination, resonance, and persuasion, exactly as surmised by Connolly and Latour. The old cultural apparatus of vanguards and dragons, slogans and nirvanas, no longer works. It has lost the capacity to learn (Pignarre and Stengers 2011).

Just as it did one hundred years ago, the Left has to start again from scratch, substantively and procedurally, gathering issues yet to be named; inventing new political technologies; speaking for publics gathered around new disputations of truth, fact, and opinion; and making just cause that many can see and many can support. It is the publics and the issues that will produce the Left — its ambitions, its tools, its aims. Of course, a Left reinvented in this way will be unrecognizable in many ways, and of course, the problem of how the new Left retains its enduring commitment to making a world free from oppression, injustice, and inequality will remain a matter of constant vigilance and reinvention as circumstances change. However, there is no reason why these three principles that have defined the Left from the very beginning should not hold firm, even when specific struggles and actors change.

If the Left can recover its ability to respond to latent concerns, build new publics, and ventilate new sentiments and atmospheres of democracy—to learn, in other words—it can return as a force of future promise. It can rekindle one tradition of its utopian legacy—not the one that sought to "map out the future in inches and minutes" (Jacoby 2005, xiv–xv) but the iconoclastic tradition that "dreamt of a superior society" but "declined to give its precise measurements." This is the approximate utopia of Charles Fourier, Ernest Bloch, Martin Buber, and Isaiah Berlin, who linked the romance of human attainment and emancipation based on practical and material betterment to the wonders of music, community, empathy, poetry, and enchantment with the world. The contemporary Left needs to claim a language of future longing and belonging that is markedly different from the language of narcissism, immediacy, and egoism that the Right has perfected. We turn to the challenge of "creating a great irresistible wave . . . actively, laboriously fabricated by a multitude of local actors who, together, make connections, equipment and operations of translation to hold, maintain and support them" (Pignarre and Stengers, 2011, 28) in the next chapters.

5

organizing
POLITICS

Our purpose in this chapter is to rescue the organization of institutions from a position as the back office of political action and bring it back to the center of attention as a crucial part of what politics is — indeed, must be — when understood as a skilled art.

Not surprisingly, there is a long and involved debate around what is meant by "institution," not least because institutions can be constituted and construed at so many levels. But it is clear that we cannot do without something like the concept to describe a series of practices and associated norms that have grown up over time and that have, in turn, taken on the power to shape perceptions, preferences, and identities. Institutions often grow up as the handmaidens of explicit political policy, but they then take on their own dynamics, often becoming political actors in their own right (Rhodes et al. 2008). Whatever the exact case, any coherent political movement cannot do without them. It must either bend existing institutions to its cause or found resilient new ones. Without that institutional backup, it may be possible to create dissonance and foment dissent, but the Left cannot get a grip, as events after the so-called Arab Spring have shown: protest certainly caused a shift but then often fell back on existing institutions, including the army.

We first consider political institutions of the formal sort, the kind that are organized into collectives of routines and practices that have formal goals. That means tackling the issue of the institutions that go to make up the state. The state has been a key concern of the Left since its inception. For many on the Left, either building up state institutions or taking over existing ones has been the main measure of whether political progress has occurred.

Whatever the political orientation, the state is clearly a key actor in modern politics in its many forms. It is not an entity that can be avoided in any discussion of what constitutes a progressive politics, especially because it continually changes its shape and functions, producing new kinds of resilience — and fragility. For example, who would have thought just a few years ago that so much of the modern state would end up outsourced to the corporate sector, down to and including even the delivery of armed force (Singer 2008)? Who would have thought that the processes of policy layering and policy conversion, in which either new policies are created that alter the operation of older policies or policies are simply reoriented, often in manifestly conservative ways, could become such an important political battleground? Who, again, would have thought that a process of drift would have made so many welfare state policies oblivious to the changes in their environment that have arisen through changing social realities?

Discussions of the state often have gotten bogged down in functional debates of the "What does the state do?" and "What is the state for?" variety. We want to take a different tack, one that is more in tune with the recent work that considers states as entanglements of various policies, each with their own dynamic, remaking connections as they move and, as a result, evolving in form and effect: "mobile policies rarely travel as complete 'packages', they move in bits and pieces — as selective discourses, inchoate ideas, and synthesized models — and they therefore arrive not as replicas but as policies already-in-transformation" (Peck and Theodore 2010a, 170; see also Peck and Theodore 2010b). So in the first substantive section of this chapter, we consider the conduct of state organization itself and its political salience, in terms of both maintenance and invention, as practices. We want to show that any approach to leftist politics must take the state's *practices* into account as part of what brings politics alive by thinking of them as "statecraft" — with the emphasis on "craft." All of those drafts, verbal asides, and moments of inter-institutional warfare driven by the currency of simple gossip add up to something more than a "red tape" mentality simply trying to slow things down in the name of procedure or an attempt to control every lineament of the world. Very often, if we could but see through cultural prejudices, we would notice that they constitute a serried history of political invention in their own right. Think of the recent transfer of models of auditing, and then risk management, from business into state bureaucracies (Power 1997, 2007) and the (often negative) effects that this set of inventions has had. Think of the constant hum of policy formation, with its heterogeneous set of think tanks, academic institutions, and other actors. Or think of the rise of so-called network institutionalism, which concentrates as much attention on the interaction between institutions as on the institutions themselves.

In the second part of this chapter, we will concentrate on just one aspect of the practices of state institutions—namely, the construction of a *bureaucracy*, broadly understood. We have chosen this example because bureaucracy is often criticized as a dead weight on political action. Indeed, commentators have routinely castigated it for offenses ranging from banal interference to Kafkaesque conspiracies to shape the world into a neat set of files. But in line with the theme of worlding that is a constant refrain in this book, we will argue that although modern bureaucracy does indeed construct a world, it is a markedly imperfect one, full of gaps and hesitations that need to be continually filled in. Perhaps the most comprehensive—and contentious—attempt to describe the process whereby states configure the environment is in Pierre Bourdieu's work on state "habitus." But we will argue that this concept only makes sense if habitus is thought of in a more anthropological way than deployed by Bourdieu, which allows more room for the creative side of the habitus to flower. We will use the example of the history of state practices of identification to make our point.

In the third part of the chapter, we will move to a more general discussion of political organization and ask the question, "Does political organization have to be modeled on the state?" There are, we believe, many other, more liquid models of political organization at hand, and we will explore some of them as a prelude to the next chapter on the European Union, a political organization that has some, but by no means all, of the trappings of a state and that, it could be argued, is an attempt to produce an institutionally diverse form of political organization that can be more open and flexible than the standard state form.

Statecraft

As noted, our intention in this chapter is to treat the state rather differently from how it is usually dealt with—that is, as a practical entity rather than as a theoretical monolith. Rather than understanding the state as a set of structures, we want to consider it as a process unrolling in time, as a *tactical* formation that both develops and practices policy and politics at the same time through feedback. We want, in other words, to fix on the notion of the state as a political formation that is proactive and, as a result, constantly redefines both itself and the political landscape (so, for example, the idea that corporate concerns would become key subcontractors of many state functions can move from seeming radical to seeming business-as-usual in a very short span of time).

In particular, we want to play up the craft in statecraft, for we believe that there is a political equivalent of craft. Of course, it does not reside solely in the state, but the state is one of its chief repositories. That craft consists of all manner of things, including not just the ability to make moving speeches but also the ability to set up durable systems that can sort things out, to write in labored "officialese" or with a real flourish, to respond to unexpected events rapidly and with brio—the full range of political skills, in other words.

Recently, Richard Sennett (2008) became the latest in a long line of thinkers to defend craft from its detractors and from its perceived degradation in the modern world. Although we have doubts about Sennett's elegiac tone, we support his appreciation of the importance of the vocation of the practices of craft: it is perhaps no coincidence that one of the chief thinkers about politics, Max Weber, was also keen on emphasizing vocation, particularly as a sustaining narrative.[1] It seems to us that many who populate politics demonstrate this quality, sometimes permanently and sometimes only temporarily—for example, as they find that a particular juxtapolitical concern has moved into a political phase. But we are not naïve. Statecraft also includes all manner of malign arts that date from far before Machiavelli but that are an integral part of politics and political craft. The noble art of compromise can just as often be a shabby deal; coalition building almost inevitably means exclusion; gossip can as easily be a malign leak as it can be a necessary part of oiling the political wheels; the difference between opportunism and a pragmatic change of heart can be small; and the distance between changing horses and back-stabbing is often minimal.

One other writer of recent vintage who has addressed the notion of statecraft is Michel Foucault, whose thought on the *arts* of government is contained in his extensive writings on governmentality. Foucault identifies all kinds of arts of government, pegged to particular rationalities that have sprouted since the end of the eighteenth century:

> In the world we have known since the nineteenth century, a series of governmental rationalities overlap, lean on each other, challenge with each other, and struggle with each other: art of government according to truth, art of government according to the rationality of the sovereign state, and art of government according to the rationality of economic agents, and more generally, according to the rationality of the governed themselves. And it is all these different arts of government, all these different types of ways of calculating, rationalizing, and regulating the art of government which, overlapping each other, broadly speaking constitute the object of political debate from the nineteenth century. What is politics, in the end, if not both the interplay of these different arts of government with their different reference points and the debates to which these different arts of government give rise? (Foucault 2008, 313)

In turn, it may be, as Brian Massumi (2009) has argued, that an "environmental" art of government is coming into existence that allows each of these different arts of government to function as a niche in a wider ecology that reaches across the spectrum of power, mixing and matching as demanded by the event and operating on potential as much as on individuals or populations or even things. This new form of power is capable of combining all of the other forms of power that Foucault theorized, without any of them being able to lay claim to dominance.

But there is a snag with this Foucauldian line of analysis. It could be argued that once Foucault has laid out a programmatic statement on how the state attempts to act out a particular program—for example, in his work on the birth of liberalism (Foucault 2008), which he elaborates to a degree through elementary forms of involvement in every-day life (such as police)—he sometimes loses interest in the apparently duller forms of political and organizational *work* that translate programs into politics, policies, and practices. It can be argued that this is where the real dynamic of these programs comes from. As they meet problems, turn out to be less effective than once thought, and, from these sorts of blockages, are stimulated into reorientation and even reinvention, they reshape desires and apply force in new ways—from compliance to political mobilization, the construction of new solidarities and oppositional identities, and even violent attack—in the manner so brilliantly described by Tania Murray Li (2007) for the case of Indonesia. Foucault's view often seems to be a stratospheric one, the view of the skeptic rejecting all forms of dogma or doctrine or cant. That means that his thought is never monolithic or hectoring, and his politics is never programmatic (although he clearly felt a profound sympathy for those who were excluded or oppressed). But it also means that his excursions into practical politics are often emblematic rather than sustained (Veyne 2010).

Like Li and others (e.g., Agrawal 2005; Tsing 2004), we focus chiefly on what we might call the anthropological character of the state, a tack used by Weber and subsequently taken up in interesting ways by authors as varied as Michael Herzfeld and Michael Taussig. It allows us to highlight the state as a "life order," to use a Weberian term, an attempt to describe a world that brings many different actors together to achieve constantly shifting goals. Focusing on the anthropological character of the state, as we have already argued, means that we must write about what is often thought to be the mere mechanics of politics and, especially the practices of *political organization*; this must, in turn, mean considering the powers and the responsibilities of *bureaucracies*, both small and large. Authors as different as Louis Althusser (2006), Frederic Jameson (2007), and Raymond Geuss (2008) have pointed out that political organization is crucial to political conduct. Anyone who has attempted almost any kind of political action knows how very little of that action is actually concerned with the apparently self-confirming motion of protest marches and other such practices. Most of it is concerned with calling people, stuffing paper into envelopes, sitting in what often seem like endless meetings and sometimes getting a word in, and sending messages. Take Lenin, often cited as the very model of a vanguard activist intent on producing cadres of professional revolutionaries. As his diaries show, Lenin believed in organization—perhaps too much—

as did many of the historical movements considered earlier in this book. Very often, it is clear that political organization is the key to success — as, for example, during Barack Obama's presidential campaign in 2008, with its systematic attention to getting out first-time voters. Yet political organization still often seems like the poor relation of politics: if not inconsequential, then bereft of agency.

The issue of political organization has, if anything, become more important. Why? Because the nature of the ruling order is changing in many countries, often favoring more "informal" means of control (Savoie 2010). Many of what were social democracies for however brief a time are mutating into something else: a turbocharged liberalism "whose objective is its own self-limitation insofar as it is pegged to the specificity of economic processes" (Foucault 2008, 297). An "authoritarian capitalism" has been remorselessly building over the past twenty to thirty years as a post-democratic order in which business and state elites rule the roost through a mixture of control through surveillance and distraction through entertainment. In this order, "The forms of democracy remain fully in place [but] politics and government are slipping back into the control of privileged elites in the manner characteristic of pre-democratic times" (Crouch 2004, 6). Most particularly, corporations have become a crucial part of the political process rather than just a pressure upon it (Crouch 2011). The result is a kind of convergence of state forms around the world based on the premise that it is no longer clear that capitalism and democracy are necessary partners in a world where it is possible to have both the "inverted totalitarianism" (Wolin 2008) of the United States and the machinations of the party in a state like China. In both constituencies, as in many more, politics has become an increasingly managed process geared toward the pursuit of profit, with citizens standing to one side to "welcome change and private pleasures while accepting political passivity" (Wolin 2008, xv). Organization — by elected and corporate bodies — has become the rule of political conduct, bringing the act of crafting space into the center of political life.

Such crafting includes blurring the boundary between the different institutions of the state to underwrite the system. In many countries, state functions have been contracted out to business. In some countries state and business can often be coincident, as in the rise of what Peter Singer (2008, 243, 260) calls the privatized military industry. In states like the United States, the military currently seems to be "on steroids" in its reach and ambition, as "the profit motive enters the battlefield." In China, the state, the party, and business often work in lockstep, to the extent that the People's Liberation Army runs businesses.

Another way to see this confluence of state and business is as a continued weaving together of official and private power and influence as more and more privileged individuals serve in interdependent roles. These networks of individuals co-opt public policy agendas and craft policy with their own purposes in mind by personalizing bureaucracy; privatizing information; juggling roles and representations of those roles; and finessing, circumventing, or rewriting rules at the interstices of official and private institutions (Wedel 2009). They test the time-honored principles of both the canons of accountability of the modern state and the codes of competition of the free market. In so doing, they reorganize relations between bureaucracy and business to their advantage and challenge the walls erected to separate them. As these walls erode, players become better able to use official power and resources without public oversight (Wedel 2009, 7–8).

With political organization hybridized and redefined as multiple arts of government, as a veritable cauldron of powers, civil society has been responsible for making up the democratic deficit that has been produced. And it has. Indeed, so great has been the growth of alternative democratic institutions that, some commentators have argued, a kind of shadow state has been produced that consists of a whole spectrum of institutions that make up a so-called monitory democracy (Keane 2009). It, too—ironically—spreads itself through organizational invention, acting like a shadow state made up of a vast array of institutions and novel field practices:

> Citizen juries, bioregional assemblies, participatory budgeting, advisory boards and focus groups. There are think tanks, consensus conferences, teach-ins, public memorials, local community consultation schemes and open houses . . . [t]hat offer information and advisory and advocacy services, archive and research facilities and opportunities for professional networking. Citizens' assemblies, democratic audits, human rights organizations, brainstorming conferences, conflict-of-interest boards, global associations of parliamentarians against corruption, and constitutional safaris . . . are on the list. So, too, are the inventions of India's *banyan* democracy:

railway courts, *lok adalats* [people's court], public-interest litigation and *satyagraha* [truth insisting] methods of civil resistance. Included as well are activist courts, consumer testing agencies and consumer councils, online petitions and chat rooms, democracy clubs and democracy cafes, public vigils and peaceful sieges, summits and global watchdog organizations set up to bring greater public accountability to business and other civil society bodies. (Keane 2009, 692–93)

The list of new forms of democratic audit is endless:

Deliberative polls, boards of accountancy, independent religious courts, experts councils . . . public "scorecards"—yellow cards and white lists—public consultations, social forums, weblogs, electronic networking and civil disobedience and websites dedicated to monitoring the abuse of power. . . . And the list of new inventions includes self-selected opinion polls ("SLOPS") and unofficial ballots (text-messaged straw polls, for instance), international treaties and criminal courts, global social forums and the tendency of increasing numbers of non-governmental institutions to adopt written constitutions with an elected component. (Keane 2009, 693)

Nearly all of these institutions and procedures have organizational demands—often very heavy demands, indeed. Equally, the sheer diversity of the political field in many countries nowadays throws down an organizational gauntlet to politicians as they make their way around a landscape of institutions that are "less centered on elections, parties, and legislatures; no longer confined to the territorial state; and spatially arranged in ways much messier [than formerly supposed]" (Keane 2009, 697). It is a landscape that, coupled with the demands of the modern media, provides nothing so much as the demand for a state of permanent politicking accompanied by comparatively high levels of scrutiny.

Now, of course, it is possible to look on the growth of monitory democracy simply as a thinly veiled further chapter in the arts of government, a point of transaction between government and the governed resulting from the fact that the notion of civil society is born out of relations of power and everything that eludes them. This might have been Foucault's view—at least, as inferred from his lectures of 1978–79. "Civil society is not a primary and immediate reality; it is something which forms part of modern governmental technology. To say that it belongs to governmental technology does not mean that it is purely and simply its product and that it has no reality" (Foucault 2008, 297). But equally, the growth of monitory democracy can be seen as a complex mix of quasi-government initiatives and real grassroots organization not necessarily hemmed in by the tenets of sovereignty and liberalism or, indeed by the environmental art of government that may have superseded it.

Whatever the case, we would argue that formal modes of institution of the kind found in state bureaucracies and their alter egos in civil society have become indispensable. They are the political field, and they regulate the formation and success of claims as process, constituency, and purpose become blurred and locked into the modalities of conduct. This brings us directly to the topic of the habituations of bureaucracy.

Bureaucracy as Habitus

Think of all of the elements that go into political organization, so many of them lying unlisted in the background because they are supposedly so obvious or inconsequential. Take the various technologies of organization and dissemination as an example. Thus, think of the political history of print and printing and just consider the corrosive and sometimes inflammatory effect of the pamphlet, the news book, and the broadside. Consider the crucial role of the telegraph not just in nineteenth-century government but also in working-class political organization, prefiguring the use of social networking technology today. Reference the history of writing machines: first the typewriter, and now the keyboard and mouse. The advent of the typewriter produced all kinds of new practices—dictation, new disciplines of hand and eye, new forms of filing and archiving, and so on—all of which had political effects (Wershler-Henry 2005). Think of the copier. It revolutionized many political practices because, for the first time, it was possible to quickly mass-produce political material and to tailor it to the moment, foreshadowing the current political uses of the Internet. Then add to this serried history the different ways in which these technologies were taken up to produce a performance of calculation that both convinced and cajoled.

As this still largely untold history of political technology demonstrates, nearly all political movements have to adopt some bureaucratic practices that use the available technology to capitalize on their success, even if it is of a minimal kind. Progressive forces have often viewed this adoption of bureaucratic practices as, at worst, a drag on action and a means of implementing highly political decisions under the disguise of a neutral expertise or, at best, necessary fallout from the pursuit of political goals that will soon become the detritus of history. But following from our discussion of organization, we want to argue that, in many ways, the practices of bureaucratic procedure can themselves constitute political action. Bureaucracies are not just leaden vehicles for others' thoughts and propositions; they are not just collections of "faceless" bureaucrats. They do things. The magic of their statecraft can be pivotal. They do not just implement policy. They initiate it and then bend it.

Two examples of countries where bureaucracy has often been regarded as running rampant—China and Soviet Russia—underline this simple contention. China, one of the world's longest surviving bureaucracies, provides an example of how what Weber called a "patrimonial bureaucracy" can survive innumerable twists and turns of fortune, adapting over and over again to new circumstances, not just through a kind of pettifogging stasis but also through constant invention (McGregor 2010). Chinese bureaucracy has often been painted as if it were an unchanging monolith for nigh on 1,300 years. But nothing could be further from the truth. Although certain elements of its makeup stayed the same, just as many changed—partly so that it could stay the same. Witness the reforms promoted by the Qing dynasty in response to population growth (Clunas 2007; Will 1990), which included reforms at the heart of Chinese bureaucracy itself: the examination system.

More explicitly, the Chinese Great Leap Forward of 1958–59 was a radical change of direction. It was almost directly antithetical to the Communist Party's previous attempts at reform, which had put titanic effort into creating a communist utopia through a grandiose package of economic, social, and cultural policies that demanded a state of mass-mobilization. The leap failed, and an estimated 30 million persons—4 percent of China's population—starved to death as a result. Until the work of David Bachman (1991), the leap had been interpreted as chiefly Mao Zedong's brainchild. But the balance of opinion now is that the bureaucracy also played a formative role in its inception: "Mao made his own Great Leap Forward, but he did not make it as he pleased, he did not make it under circumstances chosen by himself, but under conditions directly found, given, and transmitted by the bureaucracy" (Bachman 1991, 7). Bachman shows how the economic agenda of the People's Republic of China was largely controlled by economic officials and how this produced a planning and heavy industry coalition that became dominant and pursued its own interests—precisely those of the Great Leap Forward. This coalition, with its routines and conventions, drove policy and the public face of Chinese communism.

The routines of economic-policy making—particularly in a planned economy, where both plans and budgets must be formulated regularly— reinforce organizational interests. Regular staff work, negotiations, tracking of ongoing processes, and allocation of resources with only limited recourse to markets all favor bureaucratic modes of operation rather than the sporadic intervention of individual leaders responding to a wide-ranging and ever varying agenda. Leaders are not powerless in the face of organizational activity, but they are much less autonomous in the realm of economic-policy making than is commonly thought (Bachman 1991, 232).

The consequences of unequal power relations within bureaucracies were not unique to China. They shape the politics of societies as bureaucracy rapidly becomes a means of constructing a *habitus*, both for the state bureaucracy and for its citizens. The former Soviet Union is a case in point—an extreme case, admittedly, but one that still has echoes in numerous societies around the world. In many ways, the Soviet state was a vast bureaucratic machine that, through numerous officials, managed the Soviet state. But it was what Kenneth Farmer (1992) has called a non-Weberian bureaucracy in that it was characterized by personal obligation to patrons (rather than rules) as the main source of obligation; clientilistic appointments to office through the *nomenklatura* system; overlapping jurisdictions between departments, often over the same tasks; and ad hoc changes in policy. Yet this behavior was always dressed up in the discourse of Marxism-Leninism: "by the mid-1950s, the production of texts in informed officialese had become the *habitus* of generations of bureaucrats. A corpus of ideologically weighted words, phrases, and customs of writing were firmly embedded as the elements of party discourse. . . . Russians called this heavy, pompous and authoritarian language 'wooden' or 'oaken' in distinction from everyday speech" (Humphrey 2008, 5).

But, as Caroline Humphrey goes on to show, this officialese was not simply a slavish working through. Ideology was continually discussed, often refined, and sometimes subjected to abrupt shifts in direction. The life experiences of the bureaucracy—especially of party cadres—could give rise to debate and to changes, even though the process could carry very high risks for the individuals concerned. The process was especially risky for high-ranking officials, who could (sometimes inadvertently) write something "wrong," or have a text rejected for no other reason than that it fell afoul of conflicts between departments. It is worth remembering that the Soviet bureaucracy was forged in revolution, and elements of its history portrayed it as a band of brothers in the vanguard of change. But at the same time, the bureaucracy was seen as a disciplined and disciplining body, there to correct error in the general population, to provide stability, and to act as a pragmatic set of managers. Navigating between these different demands provided much of the dynamic for debate, with different symbolic and practical openings and closings becoming apparent as the debates went on. Often, timing was all. One might almost say that in the Soviet case, conflict "became the way of life of the bureaucracy" (Humphrey 2008, 28). Officials had to be loyal and yet critical; they had to show initiative and yet be obedient; they had to be conscientious and yet always ready to talk up a false position, if that was what was demanded.

As these examples show, statecraft is about the production and maintenance of a habitus that extends outward as a state mentalité into the population as a whole, whether that occurs through the various institutions of surveillance and control or through a commitment to citizens' welfare. This wider aspect of bureaucracy—its afterlife, if you like—has been best arraigned for intellectual trial by Bourdieu in his generally neglected work on the state. Bourdieu agrees that, at its worst, bureaucracy can produce a situation of political quietism, typified by the way in which the general populace in many countries with socialist states leads a schizophrenic existence. They summon up an orotund "statespeak" in public life while living quite another life in private—one in which creative and unanticipated meanings, often spun from the official texts, can circulate. However, Bourdieu's primary aim, in the strand of work that stretches from his early studies of reproduction through education to his later studies of state sorting, is to conjure up a more encompassing vision that takes up elements of Weber's observation that in every structure of domination, those who are privileged by the existing order rarely want to wield power nakedly. Instead, they choose "to see their positions transformed from purely factual power relations into a cosmos of acquired rights, and to know that they are thus sanctified" (cited in Wacquant 1996, ix). For Bourdieu, the state bureaucracy becomes a machine for the translation of social division into categories that inhabit everyday life and account for the dispositions of different sections of the population, and thus secure the cosmos of acquired rights. As Loïc Wacquant (1996, xviii) puts it in describing this locked-down world:

> The violence of the state, then, is not exercised solely (or even mainly) upon the subaltern, the mad, the sick, and the criminal. It bears upon us all, in a myriad minute and invisible ways, every time we perceive and construe the social world through categories instilled in us via our education. The state is not only "out there," in the form of bureaucracies, authorities, and ceremonies. It is also "in here," ineffably engraved within us, lodged in the intimacy of our being in the shared manners in which we feel, think, and judge. Not the army, the asylum, the hospital, and the jail, but the school is the state's most potent conduit and servant.

This vision of an all-encompassing habitus in which the state bureaucracy is able to impose its dictates with the active complicity both of those who impose and of those who submit to them — individuals whose bodies are possessed by a social field that they may recognize but that they are never fully conscious of — is a compelling one, echoed, at least in part, in the writings of other authors such as Henri Lefebvre (2009) on the state and everyday life.[2] It is, however, a little too compelling, for the version of habitus that Bourdieu is using is one that takes up the negative side of Thomas Aquinas's original use of the term but ignores the creative side, the inventions forced by the jostle between state and society.

That this is the case can be demonstrated by considering precisely the point in the social field where the pressures for conformity might be thought to be strongest: the supposedly blind and unforgiving procedures of bureaucracy that do not, by any means, simply ape official morality. Quite often, as we have pointed out in the cases of China and the former Soviet Union, they make departures that can be mortally significant. But we can go further and consider the body of evidence that arises from anthropology and history, which shows that the state's bureaucracies are rarely given such a free hand. On the one hand, and in a Bourdieu-like manner,

> Even citizens who claim to oppose the state invoke it — simply by talking of "it" in that way — as the explanation of their failures and miseries, or accuse "it" of betraying the national interests of which it claims to be both expression and guardian. In the process, however, they all contribute, through these little acts of essentializing, to making it a permanent fixture in their lives. Few ever seem able to manage completely without it. Except, perhaps, in times of quite exceptional turmoil, most citizens of most countries thus participate through their very discontent, in the validation of the nation-state as the central legitimating authority in their lives. (Herzfeld 2005, 2)

But on the other hand, social actors recast and reformulate official idioms in the pursuit of their goals and these actions, often in direct contravention of the authority of the state. Therefore, they constitute what the state is and what it can be.

While it is clear that individuals are identified by documents whose contents and use they cannot determine, the state finds itself not only continually chasing actors who do not comply with its dictates but also having to cope with its dictates being subverted in ways that it has not foreseen and that may themselves be constitutive of further actions. In particular, what Bourdieu tends to close off is a politics of articulation that allows alternative voices and practices to be passed down through the generations.[3] That proposition is nowhere better illustrated than in the history of the technologies of identification that were established by early states and, in particular, the different ways one could identify the appearance of individuals. It is easy to forget just how revolutionary these were at the time, for the establishment of identity is not, and never has been, about producing an immutable account of a person. Rather, it is about conjuring up a site of transformation of a person into a new and different condition.

Valentin Groebner (2007) has traced the prehistory of modern forms of identity labeling such as passports, biometric scanning, or DNA fingerprinting (which continuously redefine the border between the citizen's interior and exterior) through consideration of the myriad ways in which states identified citizens in early modern Europe. Late medieval means of identification, such as seals, badges, and monograms, became more and more common, and more and more systematic. Names and addresses were recorded in new ways, not least because of the proliferation of contracts of various kinds, which demanded less ambiguity, and because registers and lists had become mobile as courier and postal services became more sophisticated. Appearances started to be described in more detail, too, to make it easier to apprehend felons who might have traveled from one town to another. Clothing was a particular focus of attention, as were faces and marks on the skin such as tattoos and birthmarks. In turn, documents became more and more sophisticated at reckoning description. Letters of safe conduct, personal identity papers (*passeport*, the origin of the word "passport"), certificates of exemption, bills of health, and their accompanying registers and means of checking all became more frequent as traveling became an ingrained part of life, producing a kind of second skin of identity.

What becomes apparent is that producing stable descriptions of identities that could be transported from one site to another was by no means straightforward. The requirements of identification demanded the construction of a spatial administrative order with a centralized registration system at its heart. Indeed, by the eighteenth century, the prophets of a police state, such as Johann Gottlieb Fichte, had seized on this point:

> The chief principle of a well-regulated police state is this: That each citizen shall be at all times and all places . . . recognized as this or that particular person. No one must remain unknown to the police. This can be achieved with certainty only in the following manner. Each one must carry a pass with him, signed by his immediate government official, in which his person is accurately described. . . . No person should be received at any place who cannot thus make known by his pass his last place of residence and his name. (Fichte 1796, cited in Groebner 2007, 229)

Enthusiasts such as Jeremy Bentham wanted to go further—much further. Lamenting the disorder and confusion that governed naming, Bentham proposed a new system that would assign a truly unique proper name to all individuals,[4] identifying them beyond doubt, along with their place and date of birth. Each individual would have these details tattooed on her or his wrist.[5]

But, as Groebner (2007) points out, it is too easy to construct a linear history of direct and centralized bureaucratic administration in which these kinds of rhetorical excesses become self-confirming evidence of the impulses of our own age, beginning with the French *"état civil"* of 1792, which established a state registration system subject to central administration and ending with DNA profiling and the like as but logical projections of these kinds of thoughts, worked out over the succeeding centuries.[6] But there is no inevitability to this process. In subsequent periods in history, such requirements have seemed unnecessary (e.g., the obligation to present passport-type identity papers disappeared in most states of Western and Central Europe in the last third of the nineteenth century, at least for the well-to-do), and subversion of these requirements through forgery, theft, or straightforward avoidance has been perpetual. There has been a continual hum of protest against many of the more far-fetched bureaucratic dreams of the control of identity. Add into the brew all of the glitches, systemic failures, and aporias, and it would be difficult to argue for an all-encompassing state habitus. Rather, this state space has been built up bit by bit and in often contradictory ways by different institutions trying to do different things, using policies that often have been at odds with each other. Most particularly, it has demanded a constant record of bureaucratic innovation that pivots around the task of sorting and incorporating a yearning for signs of the body, all the way from new kinds of filing systems, reference cards, and registry numbers (an invention of bygone thirteenth-century bureaucracies) to, currently, new database designs, innovations that nearly always have been based on a logic of corralling the exception as much as on any existential condition of habitus: "A collection of essays . . . has attempted to summarize the history of citizenship in the nineteenth and twentieth centuries in one sentence by claiming that 'a nation invents its citizens'. But nations themselves invent nothing; instead, they are constituted by definition in terms of exclusion, that is, by those who are not considered their lawful members until they can prove the contrary" (Groebner 2007, 251).

To summarize the chapter so far, we have demonstrated the ways in which states are living, breathing things, miscellanies of institutions whose concrete direction is never set by the fact that they are the focus of a host of bureaucratic practices. Equally, we have shown that bureaucracies rarely follow rules blindly. They are able not just to implement but also to initiate policies that are then continually adapted to the exigencies of the moment. We have also considered how these bureaucracies shape the populations they try to control in knowing and forceful ways by multiplying categories of distinction and exclusion and by claiming to be the chief holders of expertise. For that reason alone, and for many others, it follows that bureaucratic practices are themselves political fields in which it is possible to do political things, and in turn, it follows that they, too, are a political battleground.

But to conclude this section, it is worth remembering that bureaucratic practices often have had their own distinctive and often laudable ethos. Thankfully, only a few bureaucracies conform to the example of Hannah Arendt's epitome of banal evil, the various bureaucracies of Nazi Germany, willing to commit genocide for the sake of the rule of exception. Fewer and fewer bureaucracies can be likened to those of the grandiose planned economies of the twentieth century that were tied to constructing and delivering the sacred Five-Year Plan. Fewer and fewer bureaucracies are like those of some states in modern India, still modeled in part on the imperial and the planned economy systems, bureaucracies that are an uneasy amalgam of the highest ethical standards and the lowest forms of institutionalized corruption and that often seem to function like machines that take coordination and coherence to be more important than accountability. Many more bureaucracies hold to important and laudable values. We should not be too surprised by this. After all,

> officials too are expected to make independent decisions and show organizational stability and initiative, not only [with regard to] countless individual cases but also on larger issues. It is typical of litterateurs and of a country lacking any insight into its own affairs or into the achievement of its officials, even to imagine that the work of an official amounts to no more than the subaltern performance of routine duties, while the leader alone is expected to carry out the "interesting" tasks which make special intellectual demands. This is not so. The difference lies, rather, in the kind of responsibility borne by each of them, and this is largely what determines the demands made on their particular abilities. (Weber 1994, 160)

For Weber, bureaucrats had to be capable of living up to the ethical demands placed on them by their situation: there is a "moral economy of office" (Du Gay 2008). Although, as Weber argued many times, bureaucrats may cleave to different criteria of rationality, their ethical qualities still can become clear from how they enact their personhood. As Paul du Gay (2008, 134) points out, these qualities will vary with the persona adopted on the principle that "the different personae attached to different offices represent distinctive ethical comportments, irreducible to common underlying principles." But, whatever the exact case, these offices must include (1) some form of training in expertise, howsoever constructed, usually certified by an element of examination; and (2) some notion of the office as the focus of ethical commitment and duty, as a vocation in the strongest sense of the word: "a duty of fealty to the purpose of the office in return for the grant of a secure existence" (Weber 1978, 959). In other words, "The ethical attributes of the good bureaucrat — strict adherence to procedure, acceptance of sub- and super-ordination, esprit de corps, abnegation of personal moral enthusiasms, commitment to the purposes of office — are not some incompetent subtraction from a complete (self-concerned and self-realising) comportment of the person. Quite the opposite; in fact, they represent a positive moral achievement requiring the mastery of a difficult ethical milieu and practice — a form of ascesis. They are the product of definite ethical techniques and routines" (Du Gay 2008, 136). Mentioning the whole question of the appropriate ethos underlying the comportment of the servants of the state leads us to the final section of this chapter, for it seems clear that a part of the Left's engagement with the many and serried ranks of institutions that make up the modern state must involve a sea change not just in how this ethos is conceived but also in how the ethos of political organization more generally is conceived.

This task becomes all the more pressing because a sea change is going on in how bureaucratic organization is being approached in state institutions. Whereas at one time bureaucracies were understood to be based on defined hierarchies, with each level of decision making reporting upward to the next level, it is becoming clear that, in line with many forms of organization, bureaucracies are starting to be reworked as though they were much less strongly connected but (or so the thinking goes) more adaptable networks. The idea is that, through a combination of reorganization, outsourcing to the private sector, the widespread use of information and communications technology, and a recasting of the role of the worker, the public and private sectors will interact seamlessly to provide services to the "client" on a model that is much closer to that of a private-sector provider, even when that is not the case. In turn, the demands on bureaucrats are changing. They are moving from being "shallow generalists" to "serial connectors" and from "isolated competitors" to "innovative connectors," to use Lynda Gratton's (2011) management jargon.

Counter-organization

If the modern state must cope with a constantly shifting landscape by spotting and working with potential and by regularly reinventing and reanimating its institutions, as most recently in the case of networked organization, then the same principles must surely apply to avowedly political organizations vying for power and influence and trying to shift the focus of public concerns. Constant readjustment is a necessary part of successful political organization: politics is always non-equilibrium. It is always between. The "dice must [continually] be thrown again, without nostalgia" (Stengers 2011a, 139). It could even be argued, as Gilles Deleuze and Félix Guattari did, that successful political projects depend on a notion of redefinition that is built into them, involving a capacity to shift ground, to mutate, as circumstances change and as the analysis of circumstances necessarily changes, too. Such projects do not just re-order existing political senses; they generate new ones. The contemporary antiestablishment Left, cautious of its own history of authoritarian organization and suspicious of the slide of organization into oppressive bureaucratic practices, has now begun to think of populations in this more active fashion: as cauldrons of political powers; as publics, crowds, and commons possessing particular claim to being collective political subjects with their own steering capacities and tastes for life. For example, there has been a growth of interest in Dewey's account of the formation of publics, covered in a previous chapter, as political collectivities. Again, crowds are being thought of as collective actors — for example, as revolutionary tides that wax and wane.[7] It is no surprise at all that there has been a resurgence of interest in Guattari's thoughts on the politics of group subjects (Alliez and Goffey 2011).

This search for a modern collective political subject has often been interpreted as entailing a move "beyond organization," as is clearly evident in the attempt by Michael Hardt and Antonio Negri and by Paolo Virno to redefine the people as "the multitude." In contrast to the people — or, indeed, any other descriptors that require a leader and a boundary such as the city or democracy or the constitutional state—the multitude is a "prophetic people." It is understood to be open, manifold, limitless: "the motley essence of humanity, a multitudinous subject that produces what Hardt and Negri call 'the common', which is 'language, communications, genes, images, feelings, and all the other things that must come together in a society'" (Jonsson 2008, 173). It is this common—understood as under threat as each and every one of its resources is enclosed and privatized—that Hardt and Negri see as the prime political agent, the force itself of democratic transformation, held together and given momentum through the invisible hand of the multitude rather than the market and subsisting in a flat network of interconnected groups forged out of the movement of bodies.

However, echoing Jonsson, the political implications of this approach remain opaque about how things add up or how gains are maintained; opaque about how a revolutionary consciousness arises and fires desire; opaque about how the nonhuman actors of organization that always intervene in the political process feature in the politics of the multitude; opaque about how the known institutions of politics, organized to produce results of some kind, leave all manner of traces as archives, rhetorical traditions, bureaucratic systems, and instituted powers that themselves structure political space in entangled, imprecise, and unpredictable ways. While we wait for the multitude to do its work, it therefore behooves the Left to think again about the challenges of counter-organization. If there is no self-evident magic to a collective or a people or a party, and if we recognize that many different kinds of things possess the status of political actor, what kind of organization are we looking at? To expand on this question, we want to return to the theme of worlding and to an issue first raised in chapter 3—namely, ecology. In particular, we want to expand on the notion of an ecology of practices as a way to articulate what is at stake in search of forms of organization that can be both ephemeral and resilient because they treat connections as events in their own right.

"Ecology" is a good word, as Isabelle Stengers (2010a, 33) points out, because it points to a different kind of ethos that intimates "new relations that are added to a situation already produced by a multiplicity of relations"; that always mixes the construction of these new relations with values; that is always about process, the chain of consequences on top of consequences; and that is always more than the sum of its parts: "the populations whose modes of entangled coexistence it describes are not fully defined by the respective roles they play in that entanglement" (Stengers 2010a, 34). Ecology is also a useful motif because it never mistakes consensus for peace. For Stengers, consensus is about reciprocal capture—that is, beings are co-invented by their relationship for their own benefit, but they must take a risk on what will become a shared milieu, an environment. So they might disagree, but they adapt. They do not convert. Instead, the constraints and obligations put on them create something new out of their interconnectedness in an ecology (Morton 2010).

In political terms, what Stengers is trying to portray is the invention of new practices, active propositions that are able to fashion good introductions to the other by "affirm[ing] the existence, legitimacy, and interest of other practices with divergent requirements and obligations" (Stengers 2010a, 58). That requires—at least, among the humans who populate the ecology—acts of diplomacy, with this diplomacy evolving as a set of political practices, since the varied political subjects do not know what they are confronted with but must move step by step—rather like Donna Haraway's (2008) metaphor of the cat's cradle—in a relay that can both support and intervene. For example, and counter-intuitively, diplomacy may require making the strange stranger, not more familiar, to harness a peace without consensus, as Stengers would have it. In other words, what Stengers is alluding to through the motif of ecology is the possibility of strengthening a particular direction of leftist politics—not of compromise or conversion or equivalence but of adaptation.

Seen in this way, political organization can become a series of different kinds of practices for organizing the world, which are able to coexist and, at their best, bring something new into existence or use existing features for a novel purpose that add something to all of the parties. But for that to happen, so that variation can be increased to provide a stimulus to the political ideas and practices on offer, we need to try to design an ecology. What is abundantly clear is that Stengers puts great weight on promoting shared milieux, on fostering productive environments as a means of achieving this goal. So we return, in certain ways, to the psychotopical theme of chapter 3 in that this task requires us to think in a new and expansive way about what might be counted as political arts. At one level, this simply means setting up new diplomatic channels rather like the Coordination des Intermittents et Précaires in France. But at another level, it requires a thoroughgoing reclamation and renovation of the world's spaces so that new adaptations can unfold in appropriate atmospheres. In turn, the Left needs to design worlds that recognize that all political ideas and practices are like Frankenstein's monster, made up of pieces of other ideas and practices (Morton 2010). Nothing is pure, able to be demarcated as though it could be cut off from others. There is no "clean world" (Stengers 2011b, 379). But there is always the opportunity to make something that was not there before.

What this points to is a much more open politics that is attentive to the ecology of practices that underpin politics. At the same time, it would devote much more attention to the environment as an active means of being together and bringing together but that does not automatically assume commonality of purpose, a point famously made by Deleuze and Guattari when they write about the orchid and the wasp. Their connection is an event that clearly matters to both parties, but in diverging ways. "Its achievement is not to lead the wasp and the orchid to accept a common aim or definition, but having the wasp and the orchid presuppose the existence of each other in order to produce themselves" (Stengers 2011b, 379). The environment, here, becomes a set of different modes of presence that require collectivity rather than community, which can be understood neither as a "bunch of 'I's nor [as] simply a modified version of 'alongsideness'" (Morton 2010, 127). Building these kinds of collectivity requires the Left to address the political as an ecology of spatial practices, as a resonance chamber that can amplify certain ideas and stances, depending on the tactics and tools it adopts. What is interesting here is that over the past fifteen years or so, stimulated in particular by the dislocations of information technology and the mixing of media, the Left has embarked on such a retooling, without necessarily being conscious of it as an exercise in ecological formation and transformation.

For example, a coalition of artists, designers, architects, landscape designers, media studies experts, information technology experts, and members of the general public have begun to produce a much more specific understanding of how organizing differently counts politically, based on building collectives that span all manner of actors and sites and the derivation of skills that can support this work (Thrift 2010, 2011). Indeed, so great has been this outpouring of work that it might be compared to, say, the power of Russian constructivism in the years after the revolution in its combination of zeal and zest for new ideas about how the world might be set up anew. This work moves political organization into new space in three senses. First, it hails attention to produce a degree of hesitation, a time in which to reflect: stop, look, listen. It forces consideration of the consequences of alternative engagements and attachments. Perhaps they could produce a better world; perhaps not. But think about it as you hesitate. Second, as we pointed out in the prologue, this work keeps events and beings from becoming one thing only, signaling politics as a means of keeping the doors and windows of judgment open. There is no fountainhead. There is no state of political innocence. But there is the "magical" (Merrifield 2011) craft, to return to a theme of this chapter, of the creation of assemblages out of the practices that lie at hand. Finally, it tries to build the courage to try something else. Political organization focuses on the art of political practice itself and on the knowing construction of assemblages that can support new ways of going about and acting against all the forces that point in the opposite direction.

In the next chapter, we will amplify the thoughts contained in this chapter on state institutions, bureaucratic practices, and counter-organization by referring to the case of the European Union. Our point will be that there are forms of political organization that can both satisfy the bureaucratic imperative of many kinds of political organization and contain the potential for creating an ecology of practices that values diplomacy and craft as more than incidental means of achieving political goals. We argue that the European Union might well be considered a fractured, problematic, and no doubt imperfect but still interesting attempt to create just such an ecology that can speak back in its own right, as well as represent the interests of many different collectivities.

6

eurocracy and its
PUBLICS

The gradual and largely pragmatic evolution of the institutional architecture of the European Union (EU) has produced a model of governing through diplomacy that—despite the bilious outpourings of Eurosceptics—ought to interest the Left, for it is one that has relied on the continual invention of new publics and considerable iteration between many decision-making centers and organized interests. The EU's history of progressive integration based on gradual institutional accommodation and innovation has produced a new kind of post-national political machine, with a network structure that is the sum of multiple sources of influence, filtered through a bureaucratic center bound by rules of negotiated settlement and majority consensus (Majone 2005; Rosamond 2000). Lacking the traditional tools of unitary state power and nationalist legacy, the EU has had to work hard at inventing new and more conciliatory tools of governance. Constitutional commissions, the Council of Ministers, the Committee of the Regions, intergovernmental meetings, EU directorates, the European Parliament, the European courts, EU-supported expert networks, EU institutions, lobbying groups, stakeholder networks, policy and consultative documents and forums, public referendums and campaigns, and a politics of cultural enrolment make up the fabric of EU governance. These bodies jostle for position and influence, sometimes share a division of labor, and always rub against other national, local, and transnational bodies.

The result is a veritable hybrid—part political and part bureaucratic machinery that has to work through plural political and ideological interests and through competing national and interstate or subnational priorities. It is a political invention that has attracted considerable comment and controversy, to put it mildly. Experts remain divided on whether its institutional form and practices prefigure an efficient and relatively democratic way to manage a complex, dispersed, and multijurisdictional polity that has none of the powers of the nation or the state (e.g., Majone 2005; Moravcsik 2002; Rifkin 2004), or whether they have evolved as a weak or opaque and unaccountable apparatus to further the interests of the most powerful EU nations and corporations (Gillingham 2006; Milward 2005). Although political commentary has on occasion been appreciative of the EU's declarations on peace, unity, and solidarity and of the union's provisions for justice and social cohesion, this has been overshadowed by a combination of national(ist) anxiety over an encroaching world of foreigners; a wasteful, interfering bureaucracy; and criticism of the absence of democratic accountability and public participation in the EU's decision-making processes. Discussion on political reform thus has tended to oscillate between calls to dismantle or contain the institutions of the EU and to democratize them by, for example, increasing public scrutiny and input or by transferring strategic and executive powers to its elected bodies.

In this chapter, we want to steer clear of these controversies, not because of any reservations on our part regarding their validity, but because we see them as controversies that tend to ignore the transformations in the political landscape wrought through institutional practice. Following our arguments on statecraft and the ecology of political practice in the preceding chapter, our claim is that a diplomatic mode of negotiation has emerged in some parts of the European bureaucracy to answer a need to negotiate a thorny and complicated institutional environment. This has required carving out new political space and new political practices based on reframing the language and goals of Europe (e.g., "cohesion," "subsidiarity," "acquis communitaire"), legitimating a coalitional and deliberative mode of decision making and generating a politics of interest around specific matters of concern. The result has been the remaking of Europe as a field of political contestation and practice, which we exemplify by following selected EU directives relating to regional cohesion, environmental sustainability, and technological innovation. Based on these openings, we suggest at the end of the chapter that the Left could pay more attention to the mechanics of institutional conduct, not only as a check on the ethics of procedure, but also, and above all, as a way to redesign political space.

Rethinking "Eurocracy"

The EU has developed a mosaic of governance with considerable power and reach in the form of common rules, institutions and conventions, and interstate agreements and protocols that are closer to daily life than is generally thought (Delanty and Rumford 2005; Guerrina 2002; Vibert 2001). For example, EU rules on economic and monetary union guide trade and competition; corporate, banking, and financial practices; and national economic policy decisions. The Common Agricultural Policy and the EU's food and environmental directives influence prices, products, food standards, farming practices, and the scale and tenure of rural holdings in Europe. European directives on technology, contract compliance, standards, employment and work practices, health and safety, waste management, and more shape corporate structure and behavior, employees' experience, and consumption patterns.

The geographies of everyday movement and connectivity in Europe have been transformed as a result of substantial investment by the EU in transport, communication, and infrastructure. The daily lives and life chances of millions of employees, low-income or vulnerable groups, and disadvantaged communities have been affected by various EU regional and social policies. The EU's measures on broadcasting, language learning and translation, student exchange, research collaboration, and urban regeneration have gradually altered the European cultural landscape. The work of the European courts and various legal charters resonate silently in the background, as does the regulatory force of EU directives on carbon emissions, air pollution, water quality, fishing, and other environmental issues. And there is much more.

By and large, public debate on the EU's institutions has been dominated by questions of bureaucratic power, normative intent (e.g., neoliberal or social democratic), and political accountability, overshadowing studied interest in the kind of organizational field that has arisen—for example, the changing relationship between the European professional bureaucracy, the EU's elected bodies, national governments and publics, European political elites and lobbies, and intergovernmental councils. This is a body of work that examines the EU as a new type of formally constituted political entity—neither state nor nation—experimenting with multiple and overlapping institutional forms and hybrid forms of deliberation and decision making to construct, regulate, and legitimate a very large and variegated federation of states and societies. In interrogating the intersectional dynamics of governance in Europe, it offers important insights to a Left committed to democratic institutional practice and to active public participation but faced with the not insignificant problem of achieving this in a diverse, dispersed, and often uninterested political community. It puts on the table the possibility of narrowing the gap between the politics of representation and the politics of participation by building publics and counterweights into the decision-making process and by extolling the possibility of enriching the political process by folding in what only look like antinomies such as certainty and compromise, expert and lay interests, direction and deliberation, weight and counterweight.[1]

To give just one example: Gianfranco Majone (1996) has argued that the much maligned European Commission, with its experienced experts and negotiators who are expected to skillfully negotiate EU directives through a minefield of interests, shields the policy process from crass political manipulation. This is partly a matter of the civil service providing a buffer against a political class—in the shape of the European Parliament, Council of Ministers, and member states that are obviously likely to fall prey to short-term electoral and popular pressures (Zakaria 1997). It is also a function of bureaucratic practice. The commission's directorates, led by appointed politicians, depend on teams of experts from different professional and national backgrounds bound to an elaborate process of policy formulation and consultation that tends to favor long-term, nonpartisan decisions. This is not to blunt frequently heard accusations that the commission is not an independent professional body but a corporatist power bloc in its own right, tainted by the wastage and inefficiency common to most large bureaucracies and prone to ideological and political influence. However, from Majone's description of the EU as a regulatory state (rather than super-state) can be rescued the idea that owing to the built-in involvement and scrutiny of many stakeholders at different tiers in the policy process, the rule of majority decision making, accountability, and professional responsibility results in a studied and strategic approach to future EU policy.

The plural institutional arrangements of the EU and the involvement of many actors in the decision-making process have led Bob Jessop (2004) to describe the union as a structure of "meta-governance." The term signals the mix of market, network, and hierarchical coordination involving binding rules, self-organization, social dialogue, public–private partnerships, and participation by nongovernmental organizations (NGOs) as modes of policy formulation and delivery. It captures the distribution of responsibilities between the European judiciary and its legal apparatus, political centers such as the Parliament and the Council of Ministers, and the professional bureaucracy led by the European Commission. It also highlights how EU policy structures sit alongside, overlap with, and at times incorporate structures at urban, regional, and national levels. Controversially, Jeremy Rifkin (2004) has argued that the EU's governance arrangements have to be seen as an exercise in democratic invention. He describes the EU as the world's first postmodern, "networked" polity, which has managed to invent a structure of power and authority that is decentered, plural, and inclusive.

Rifkin makes two important claims relevant to our interest in the fixtures of diplomacy. The first is that the EU possesses a structure of government without a center. Its historical weakness over the member states and the fine balance that has existed between its political, policy, and constitutional bodies have yielded a largely pragmatic approach to problems within a frame of "orchestral politics" (Rifkin 2004, 215). The EU acts more like a manager of complexity than like a force of destiny (as often assumed by its visionaries and critics), relying on painstaking diplomacy to gather divided and disparate interests around common goals and agreements. Second, therefore, for Rifkin the EU's political ethos has become one of seeking unity in diversity. Composed of many national cultures, strong regional identities, intense cross-border mobility and mixture, and only modest popular loyalty to Europe, the union is unable to appeal to a common imagined community in any strong sense. It finds unity through negotiations of consensus around common problems and shared futures but also, according to Rifkin, through a shared ethic of care for the vulnerable, the world at risk, and the commons based on old humanist, social-democratic, and Enlightenment traditions. This ethic, for Rifkin, explains the EU's success in pushing through progressive social, regional, environmental, and international development policies.

Rifkin's claims are overblown and at times forgetful of Europe's darker aspects.[2] Our inclination is to situate the EU's progressive tendencies in the diplomacies of meta-governance rather than in Europe's cultural traditions (see also Judt 2007; Slaughter 2004). The bureaucracy—less so in the arena of economic integration, which has remained under the shadow of neoliberal dogma, and more so in the policy fields mentioned earlier, which are perhaps more open to an ethic of solidarity—has had to invent metaphors, common spaces and publics, along with distinctive habits of negotiation, to find unity in diversity. One illustration is the European Water Framework Directive (WFD), an important policy achievement that began to transform thinking about water as a valuable *European* public good.

Making Euro-Water

The WFD, passed in June 2000, was an overarching piece of legislation designed to harmonize national policies on water and to improve the quality, sustainability, and security of water in all of Europe's aquatic environments.[3] The directive, which took two years to frame, is a good example of how a seemingly long, tortuous, and overly complicated decision-making process not only delivered a progressive environmental initiative in a union riddled with conflicts among nations and stakeholders in the area of water management but also, in the process, invented a new public around the politics of water sustainability. The travels of the directive from formulation to deliberation and decision tell a story of intense conflict between the Council of Ministers and the European Parliament; assiduous arbitration by the commission's Environment Directorate; lobbying of these three bodies by a plethora of stakeholders; and reconciliation of divergent national policy priorities on different links in the supply chain (e.g., on permissible pollutants, water pricing, water wastage). The complexity of the domains, interests, and actants that required alignment (from fertilizer producers and farmers to water companies, environmental agencies, and consumer groups), did not augur well for the success of the directive. Yet it did succeed, in large part because of the prevailing rules and procedures of negotiation, which included devices such as time capping the period for deliberation, building community and trust, and depending on iterative conciliation.

The EU's commitment to cooperative decision making and stakeholders' participation played a vital role in ensuring the success of one of the most progressive water-protection initiatives in the world, as we illustrate later. In 1995, in an attempt to rationalize and integrate water policies in the EU, as well as to raise public awareness of water as a valuable resource, the Environment Committee of the European Parliament and the Council of Environment Ministers asked the European Commission to formulate a new water directive. The brief was to develop a directive that would reconcile conflicts over the quality and quantity of water, address conservation and economic needs, create policies relating to surface and ground water, and resolve anomalies between EU rules on emissions and ecological protection. As Maria Kaika and Ben Page (2003a, 316) summarize, the ambition was to "protect and enhance the quality and quantity of EU aquatic ecosystems in order to ensure an adequate, but sustainable, supply of water for economic development and growth." By May 1996, draft legislation had been produced to address the problems of overuse and pollution, the two main threats to sustainability. It recommended that all water in the EU achieve the standard of "good" status by 2010, with the help of binding EU-wide sanctions against land and water pollutants and polluters, along with tighter controls to regulate water demand.

After 1997, following demands for adjustment to the directive by the Council of Environment Ministers and the Parliament's Environment Committee, the progress of the draft water directive became decidedly turbulent as the cost implications and enormity of the changes required in policy and practice dawned on the major stakeholders. The commission came under considerable political pressure to render the directive less far-reaching but interestingly on this occasion chose to use its position as the key intermediary responsible for brokering an agreement to preserve the green credentials of the directive. It did so by formally incorporating the environmental NGOs into the amendment process, knowing that they would insist on tough legislation on pollution and water wastage, in addition to disallowing national exemptions. By contrast, when the Council of Ministers debated the draft directive in June 1998, it proposed a series of important concessions under duress from the member states whose large agricultural sectors were dependent on high use of water and fertilizer and from those whose water industries had considerable private-sector involvement. The concessions included lowering the original aspirations for conservation, giving countries thirty-four years instead of twelve years for implementation, abandoning the principle of full-cost pricing, and, most controversially, dropping the original proposal that the reforms be legally binding.

An intense battle between the European Parliament and Council of Ministers ensued over the next two years, with the commission finding itself in the middle (but largely in agreement with the Parliament). In late 1998, the Parliament approved a number of counter-amendments to shorten the timescale for implementation, make the directive legally binding, prevent the release of hazardous substances into the marine environment, and reintroduce full-cost pricing. The historically powerless Parliament had decided to test the Council of Ministers in anticipation of May 1999, after which EU legislative power for the first time would be shared equally between the two bodies under the Amsterdam Treaty instead of residing exclusively with the Council of Ministers. In quick response, the Council of Ministers rejected all of the Parliament's substantial amendments in March 1999. A long stalemate followed as both sides dug in their heels, each side strengthened by its respective lobbies (e.g., the Parliament by environmental NGOs and the Council of Ministers by the water industry and agriculture).

The directive would have floundered had water sustainability not been made a matter of European public concern and had it not been for the rules and procedures of deliberation in the EU. While the Parliament and Council of Ministers continued to wrangle, media interest in the declarations of diverse stakeholders on the directive grew; this, in turn, began to generate public awareness. Through the efforts of the press and activist agitation around the directive, water came to be seen as a threatened public good. The directive was beginning to shape a new European public sphere around the idea that people and ways of life everywhere in Europe were at risk from the misuse of a single and common water space. Under pressure from a new rule approved by the Amsterdam Treaty requiring conciliation of a policy proposal within six weeks (or its automatic abandonment thereafter), the Conciliation Committee arbitrated between the Council of Ministers and the European Parliament and secured an agreement in the early hours of June 29, 2000. Indispensable to the process was the craft of diplomacy, drawing on clever wording; arbitration by the co-chairs of the Conciliation Committee; an ethos of public urgency and responsibility; and trust in the expertise, insight, and integrity of commission officials involved in formulating the directive.

The WFD finally came into force in December 2000. Despite its tortuous journey and its many compromises, it is a landmark initiative, well ahead of other cross-national agreements on environmental protection. According to Kaika and Page (2003a), it integrated national and sectorial water-management strategies; introduced river management practices based on hydrological rather than political boundaries; brought in stricter pollution controls, along with stepped-up environmental planning at the EU scale; provided clarity on what counts as "good water status" for both surface and ground water; incorporated externalities into water pricing to encourage better demand management; and increased public participation in policymaking. On this occasion, against all of the odds in a highly diverse, fragmented, and contested arena, the deliberative process secured an outcome that has to be judged as path-breaking not only for its content, but also for its ability to get member states to give up certain sovereign water rights; to get farmers, water companies, and the chemical industry to agree to stricter emission controls; to get governments to both implement and monitor new regulations they were reluctant to accept; and to get a Euro-skeptical public to agree to higher water prices.

Two aspects of this example are pertinent to our interest in the procedural dimensions of a politics of world making. The first is the potential of an expert bureaucracy to invent a new commons. The Environment Directorate possessed—or was able to gather together—the vision and expertise to fashion a new European cause and to invest it with scientific, moral, and political energy. Accordingly, water was made into an object of concern, an emblem of Europe's identity and future, a problem in need of concerted action at the EU level, and a cause that required new coalitions. The experts revealed a world of hidden connections linking different domains of water: flows across national boundaries; farmers, fertilizers, aquatic life, corporations, and consumers; stakeholders and interests hitherto held apart or at odds with each other; and the supply and demand of water for human and ecological sustainability. They also had the means and wherewithal to structure an elaborate machinery of documents, certifications, consultations, deliberations, alliances, and controversies to remake water as a European public good at risk. But as experts who were respected and trusted by diverse stakeholders (from the Parliament and the Council of Ministers to other interested parties, the media, and pressure groups), they were able to build a fragile consensus around this remaking. Diplomacy proved to be a crucial asset in preventing dissent and disagreement from quashing the directive.

Second, the example highlights the value of public orchestration of a certain kind. The prospects of a conservationist water directive were raised when "Euro-water" changed from being a matter of latent concern into a public controversy and then an object of desire.[4] Early media interest in the wrangling within the EU and the national implications of what was being proposed gave way to orchestrated debate on the meaning and value of water. This was the product of the commission's and various environmental lobbies' making available a clear argument of a commons at risk over water and proposing a European public with the right to demand ample and clean water far into the future. Thus, the case grew for a radical break with established practice — cast as prey to vested interest, particularistic concern, and economic expediency — which put pressure on the negotiating parties to find a solution that would satisfy an emerging imagined public expecting environmental responsibility from its leaders.

One European Vegetation

The ability to reinvent the European commons and weave its cause into the institutional order has been a distinctive aspect of the politics of construction in Europe. If a democratic impulse is at work, it appears in the rules and procedures of negotiating a contested organizational field, falling short of the democracy of active public engagement in the affairs of Europe but still able to collect diverse interests around a new commons. The next vignette focuses on classificatory practices — long a source of Foucauldian anxiety over technologies of division and control — to show the possibility of progressive openings when new inventories are subjected to agonistic scrutiny before they are finalized. It covers an ambitious EU initiative in the 1990s to introduce a single classification system for vegetation to help preserve biodiversity across Europe under a new Habits and Species Directive.

The CORINE Biotopes initiative aimed to give habitats and species previously listed only in national inventories (under different headings and with varying degrees of coverage) a common European nomenclature and identity. The perception was that this would help to harmonize and integrate future conservation to protect threatened habitats and species. What seemingly started out as a technical problem soon threw up all of the delicacies of extricating local classificatory practices out of rooted conventions and strongly held beliefs. Claire Waterton (2002, 181) notes that the commission started out with "a kind of imperialistic, up-to-date fantasy of a world unified by information," thinking that the new classification system could be rolled out across the member states once technical and financial anomalies were ironed out. It failed to anticipate that the new system would be seen as a threat to cherished national systems and that it would provoke local anger over the loss of authority to categorize habitats and species held to be indigenous or unique in some shape or form. It did not appreciate that the specificity of local variations, contexts, and conditions might generate significant classificatory anomalies and ambiguities — for example, concerns among conservationists that certain local varieties could not be shoehorned into CORINE's narrow and unambiguous categories.

The commission, however, soon realized that that the problem it faced was not technical but political, requiring care in the conduct of devising and implementing the classification system if local field officers and conservationists central to the classification process were to be kept on board. While governments and national stakeholders responded with varying degrees of interest and enthusiasm, the commission knew that environmentalists would be keen to participate in the initiative in the hope of getting local varieties at risk onto the European conservation register (thereby qualifying for financial, technical, and legal support to secure their protection). However, as the swell of local anxiety over the danger of imprecise or erroneous classification grew, officials turned to devising a system that would allow for local interpretation and adjustment without threatening the integrity of a single and unambiguous system of classification with Europe-wide applicability.

The European Commission came to accept, for example, that British fieldworkers who drew on the authority of the British National Vegetation Classification to bring "uniquely British questions, debates, priorities and debates to bear on the European classes" (Waterton 2002, 192) ought to be allowed to draw on their knowledge and experience to ensure proper categorization, even if this meant not adhering to stipulated class criteria. On this occasion, keen to not compromise the protection of Europe's biodiversity, the commission saw merit in allowing the hidden politics of classification to come to the fore. It did not shy away from the inevitability that "the treatment of a single category in a classification became a debate about foreign and undesirable species; a debate about British land-ownership; a debate about European integration; and a debate about the responsibility of British conservationists to a European-scale conservation" (Waterton 2002, 196).

A "simple" reclassification exercise was allowed to be ventilated by an "atmosphere of democracy" (Latour and Weibel 2005) to yield a locally sensitive system capable of underwriting a new European commons. Its success has to be traced to a moment of deliberative opening in a network bureaucracy with considerable reach that resulted in an "innocuous" invention — a machinic step — that could prove to be the bedrock of efforts to conserve the biodiversity of Europe's natural habitat.

Mapping Community

Our final example of bureaucratic invention of the commons relates to the remapping of Europe. In recent decades, many maps have been produced by the EU to classify the regions of the member states into new categories of similarity and affiliation, colorfully named the Blue Banana, Atlantic Arc, Baltic Regions, Iberian Peninsula, Motor Regions, and so on. Other schemas have facilitated the enactment of Europe as a unitary social space to encourage the mobility of workers, citizens, and tourists across the member states and to break down an idea of Europe as exclusively the space of national territorial communities. Similarly, much effort has gone into defining the boundary between Europe and its others based on surveys of public attitudes toward immigrants from outside the EU; cartographies that mark out the eastern Urals, Turkey, and the southern shores of the Mediterranean as beyond Europe; and continual efforts to define Europe's cultural values and traditions.

These mappings outline a Europe beyond its traditional imagined communities, tracing relational topologies — virtual, transnational, inter-regional, diasporic — that disturb the map of Europe as an agglomeration of territorial formations and affinities. They are the creations of a bureaucracy that is actively involved in redrawing the boundaries of communication and community in a new old land, offering up alternative cartographies, classifications, and technologies of togetherness and difference. To date, these inventions have fallen short of dismantling the strongly felt legacies of place, state, and nation in Europe, but they should also be judged as frames that subtly work on the precognitive as new spatial orderings. The EU's many information and communication technology–based policies to reduce social and spatial distance in Europe provide a pertinent illustration.

Sarah Green, Penny Harvey, and Hannah Knox (2005, 807) have argued that the EU's information society program, for example, which has spent billions of euros to upgrade the connectivity of disadvantaged regions, should be seen as "an exercise in spatial imagination and place making" based on redefining "spatial location," "senses of place," and "spatial relations in practice." The program, which gave the regions access to information technology resources in more than thirty areas of activity, including e-government, e-skills, e-safety, e-learning, and research and development, offered the regions the promise of a place in an "open-ended and flexible" network space freed from the constraints of a bounded and predefined community. Drawing on an ethnography of Infocities, an initiative in Manchester that was part of the EU's Telecities program, Green and her colleagues (2005, 807) argue that the information society venture gave the regions with "both a 'moral community' sense of connection and a 'flexible network' sense of connection."

Infocities linked seven European City Councils, each responsible for a particular aspect of urban public life (e.g., culture, education, public services, electronic commerce) and charged with making information available and commensurate across a common broadband space. Manchester had the task of making cultural information on the seven cities available in a common virtual space. Pragmatically, this allowed the cities to compare, share, and learn from each other's cultural legacies and provided a portal for all of the cities to the site's visitors. Symbolically, however, the initiative—and, more generally, the Telecities program—can be seen as an attempt to construct a single European cityscape with shared assets distributed in different locations, in contrast to the extant idea of Europe as a space of separate urban entities.

The EU vision was that the "generation of connections between artifacts across Europe would highlight a European cultural heritage" (Green et al. 2005, 811); its implementation, however, was by no means guaranteed or straightforward. Like CORINE Biotypes, Infocities came laden with interpretive difficulties. Local teams, pressed to catalogue their cultural heritage under standardized categories, worried about the loss of local granularity and meaning and questioned the motives of those who were promoting information and communications technology in this way. They were not naïve about the implications of joining a software-driven imagined community shaped by distant interests. But the terms of engagement allowed sufficient space for the local actors to participate as knowing partners. They managed—without punitive outcomes—to work around the limitations of the "technical reference model"; they saw through the hype of the European network society; and in the course of participating enthusiastically in the new virtual European cityscape, they sought to increase local returns. For example, alongside developing the portal linking the cultural heritage of the seven European cities, Manchester's City Council opened up the Infocities broadband to local community groups to help poor residents find socially useful services on the Internet.

Infocities could have ended up as a top-down bureaucratic imposition. Instead, like many of the EU's cohesion or environmental policies that strive for an inclusive and sustainable Europe, it succeeded in building local interest into the policy process not only at the implementation stage but also at the design stage. While this may reflect the normative ethos of particular directorates within the European Commission, we contend that it is also a function of the commission's organizational status as a maker of Europe that depends on knitting together diverse interests and stakeholders under particular visions of possibility. The commission cannot act on its own; it has to follow distinctive bureaucratic procedures, and it frequently fashions distinctive imaginaries of the future to build coalitions of interest around its cause. Into the gap opened insert themselves diverse actors, new procedural arrangements and compromises, and unanticipated geographies of communication and affiliation. Infocities, for example, spawned a new "desktop society" (Kelty 2005) composed of altered local ties and membership to a new European cityscape.

Conclusion: Publics, States, and Bureaucracies

Leftist commentary on the EU makes a point of distinguishing between techno-politics and democratic politics. This is most vividly captured in Andrew Barry's (2001) critical study of the politics of EU directives on technical standards and on air and water quality. Barry argues that these were top-down directives that deprived Europe of the possibility of a deliberative politics of science and technology and suppressed public debate by making the issues they tackled appear simply to be matters of pragmatic regulation. Instead of launching new matters of concern and debate into the public and political domain, so that "new sites and new sights" of difference, protest, and possibility could arise, the European public was offered a "technicization of problems" at the expense of their "*mise en politique*" (Callon 2004, 131, 133). No doubt, many an EU initiative has been pushed through on technical or pragmatic grounds instead of helping to form a vibrant European public sphere. On the other hand, the examples in this chapter uncover a process that can unlock the kind of policy politics proposed by Barry and Michael Callon. The jostling among EU institutions and with national governments, the involvement of external bodies and lobbies, the rules of policymaking, and the fervor aroused by EU visions of the future have also managed to produce a politics of scrutiny, disputation, and invention around EU proposals.

The vexed question is whether such a politics can be counted as democratic or conducive to radical possibility. An obvious criticism is that the dynamics of negotiation are stacked up in favor of expressed rather than latent interests, lobbies with the most power and influence, and parameters set by initial recommendations. The result is a jostling around only the mainstream middle (for an illustration of how EU financial directives have worked in this way, see, e.g., Bieling 2006) and, furthermore, a jostling without much in the way of public involvement. It is well known that EU proposals and policies—despite the occasional public flurries aroused by media coverage of them as the impositions of an interfering bureaucracy—have not fired up a politics of public involvement or the formation of a European counter-public. The critical Left tends to see Europe as a "democracy without a demos" (Mair 2006, 25). For Perry Anderson (2009, 17), the EU, in lacking a constitution, an effective Parliament, popular credibility and involvement, and parties fashioned at European scale, has suppressed "politics of any kind" and is slave to a "cartel of self-protective elites" negotiating only with itself to reach agreements steamrolled over national legislatures and the public. The EU, for Anderson (2009, 17), has sacrificed the "the open agenda of parliaments into the closed world of chancelleries."

These are only partially valid observations. In particular, they caricature the politics of conduct in the EU by neglecting the actual practices of decision making. There is sufficient ambiguity, dissonance, and centrifugal force in and around the institutional habitus of the EU to allow the sorts of inventions, inclusions, and progressive outcomes we have considered in this chapter. For example, a Europe of instituted and extended diplomacy might have pushed back at the onslaught of the more powerful member states and their command centers in the EU on states entrapped by the current financial crisis—states that hold only partial responsibility for the crisis but that are treated like irresponsible children by the bailout institutions. Similarly, it might have pushed back at the tendency of the "closed world of chancelleries" to pervert just cause in Europe's own and neighboring conflicts by either failing to act or falling in behind more powerful geopolitical interests.

A politics of institutional form and conduct should also be of interest to the Left because, as we have argued throughout this book, the modern political field is a hybrid field composed of multiple sites, interests, actors, and modes of expression that daily weaves means into ends, ideals into practices, passions into objects, and affects into the "prepolitical." The resolutions of democracy in this field are not confined to the balance between representation and participation; the relationship between legislatures, publics, and bureaucracies; or the other parts of the base of formal politics. They are also dependent on working through—and with—this hybrid field to promote outcomes that improve the prospects of the many, including acting on behalf of others.

Thus, in the long and far from assured wait for an active European public sphere to emerge to ventilate EU politics, the Left might wish to consider the interstitial jostling of the EU as a democratic opening: the peculiar blend of checks and balances between Brussels, Strasbourg, and member states; the friction between experts, idealists, and interests; the ambition for a new kind of transnational polity that must be approached delicately; the involvement of many stakeholders. Indeed, this jostling might be seen as a way to build meaningful European publics around specific matters of common concern—publics that might eventually stack up to form a living European public sphere. With this kind of civic filling in, the radius of public support might expand for European leftist projects such as a Social Europe that values social and spatial equality, workplace democracy, social enterprise, public goods (health, education, insurance), state insurance, and protection of the commons.

More generally, and looking beyond European "diplomacy," this chapter has been concerned with some of the practices of statecraft. Our argument has been that a consideration of the crafts of state—a topic the Left has either seen as Machiavellian or taken up unthinkingly when in power—allows new connections to be made between bureaucracy and democracy. Indeed, making this unholy connection also allows the discussion of democracy to move beyond the commonplaces of current leftist dispute around democracy, in which some defend the franchise, some defend representative politics, and some defend revolutionary or anti-corporatist stances. As we noted earlier, the Left has always had an ambiguous relationship with the arms of the state. On the one hand, it has often depicted the state as an oppressive force. On the other hand, the Left in power has often expanded its remit and, in a few cases, attempted to make civil society into simply its mirror image. What seems certain is that the Left, confronted with the practices of the state, needs to become cannier—craftier, if you like—if it is to produce the commonplaces that are now so important.

So how should we frame politics when it so often seems to be threatened on all sides? Certainly, the political sphere in the West often seems squeezed—by the self-interested and partisan wishes of corporate interests, by the machinic nature of state bureaucracy, and by the instrumentalization of passions. The virus of totalitarian democracy may not have infected all Western politics yet, but the signs are there. Think only of the general increase in paranoid thinking brought about, especially, by carefully modulated media campaigns mounted by various parties: over migrants and immigrants, over crime and punishment, over almost any threat from overseas. Paranoia works in part because it *feels* good. The paranoid frame of mind strikes us as one of the greatest dangers to rational political thought, yet it is currently rampant across much of the political spectrum, closing down imaginative resistance. The fact that history is not a product of conspiracy and that political events are often highly contingent is something that paranoia simply casts aside.

What seems very clear is that a simple defense of the virtues of democracy will no longer do. The "democracy is always good" defense is simply inadequate to the task we now face. After all, democracy is an imperfect beast, at the best of times. In a pessimistic frame of mind, one might argue that it too often produces results that are not optimal. Equally, the apparatus of democracy often disallows citizens the opportunity to register what they think, except through protest. For example, the Iraq War produced mass disaffection, but the electoral cycle was out of sync with allowing most electorates to register their opinion at the ballot box. Again, one cannot claim that democratic elections routinely enact a Pauline moment of clarity, in which the majority awakens to the task of slaying a hegemonic dragon. Finally, as we have seen recently, democracy can simply be used as a front for a haughty kind of imperialism. In other words, a case could be made that the "crisis of democracy" is not "something that happens when people stop believing in their own power but, on the contrary, when they stop trusting the elites, when they perceive that the throne is empty, that the decision is now theirs. 'Free elections' involve a minimal show of politeness when those in power pretend that they do not really hold the power, and ask us to decide freely if we want to grant it to them" (Žižek 2009, 6).

But the alternatives are usually no better. The revolutionary Left's case against elections (e.g., Badiou 2009) often sounds like the worst kind of "we know better" elitism, and historically, when instituted, it has usually resulted in more or less—usually less—benign forms of dictatorship. Equally, this case almost always ignores the rise of monitory democracy whose institutions' purpose is "the public chastening of power, a way of life that creates spaces for dissenting minorities and levels competition for power among citizens who are equals" (Keane 2009, 848). In other words, the practices of democracy have not stood still and now extend far beyond elections.

The promise of democracy relies on its potential. We mean this as more than a kind of Rortian pragmatism, a potential that is a glimpse of other possibilities, as John Keane (2009, 853) claims: "when democracy takes hold of people's lives, it gives them a glimpse of the contingency of things. They are injected with the feeling that the world can be other than it is—that situations can be countered, outcomes altered, people's lives changed through individual and collective action." With such potential, the push for a bureaucracy that works for democratic ends can arise by forcing institutions to change. A first step would strengthen the institutions of monitory democracy, institutions that act both as checks on state power and exemplars of how to go on. The proliferation of these institutions is one of the most important developments of the past few decades, and although individually they may vary in their degree of democratic openness, together they can be seen as providing a means of scrutinizing the exercise of power that hitherto has been lacking.

A second step would rework what we mean by democracy in an age in which it often seems that civil and political rights are premised on immunity to the contagion of the possibility of community, in turn leading to a situation in which what is common ends up being put at risk as immunity turns on itself (Esposito 2008). At the very least, we need to assert that there is no democracy without representation. But that is a problem. For what, exactly, does representation consist of? Representation is a moveable feast: it must mean more than just periodic elections. To make more (literally) of this term, we want to return to the work of Bruno Latour. For Latour, representation can never be a simple act of translating fixed views and interests into policy. Rather, it allows politics to be transformed and expanded by facilitating the formation of identities and interests (Urbinati 2006). In other words, a representative is a mediator, not an intermediary. Politics becomes an experimental practice of modification, rather like the conduct of science in the laboratory, in which "no being, not even humans, speak on their own, but always through something or someone else" (Latour 2004, 68), thus chiming with the Tardean viewpoint. It follows that "the representativity of a claim is to be judged not by the accuracy of its resemblance to some measure of reality that would have been fixed in advance (the 'preferences' of voters or the 'thing-in-itself') but, rather, on whether or not the system of representation has conferred agency on the represented" (Disch 2008, 92).

A hard test of representation follows from this: are the represented "allowed to make a difference in our thinking about them?" (Latour 1999, 117). In other words, representation can exist only when the process of representation confers agency on the represented. That means a big change in thinking. It means that politicians will repeatedly have to take the risk of attempting to form an "us" that will inevitably prompt refusals in the face of the fact that politics seems to "let us down [because] we keep comparing it to our ideal narratives, to politics on TV or in the movies, which is tidier and better fits [simple event] structures" (Lakoff 2008, 27). Politicians must therefore pursue a work of fiction — tell stories that alter the way citizens define their situations and change their loyalties — even as that work demands that they be able to articulate firm identifications (Rosanvallon 2006, 24). Of course, politicians already do this — and, perhaps, all too well with the help of an army of political consultants. But what about producing immunity to such rhetoric by producing an apparatus "whose protocols would render voters robust enough to simply defy their interlocutors in the way that nonhumans do" (Disch 2008, 95)? The challenge, then, is not, in the manner of deliberative democracy, to get citizens to make their claims more precise and to communicate them without distortion to their representatives through devices such as citizens' juries and deliberative polling. Rather, the challenge is to produce means by which we can go beyond a politics of opinion, with its apparatus of elections, letter-writing campaigns, marches, and so on, to something even more productive.

A third step would redefine what is meant by political activism, a step already hinted at in the previous chapter. Perhaps a new sentiment of democracy might change how we figure the democratic citizen. There is a view of the political activist that is nicely summarized by Michael Walzer (1998, 313): "self-confident and free of worry, capable of vigorous, wilful activity." This is very much the activist as hero, even as soldier, almost certainly as male. And it is an understanding that is off-putting to a great many people who do not feel that they can possibly live up to it (Eliasoph 1998). But looking around the world and through history shows that there are other ways to proceed — indeed, there is a vast archive of alternative models of activism to delve into, each with its own compound of sentiments galvanizing action. Thus, activism involves a whole range of affective dispositions that can be worked on. So, for example, how might it be possible to understand forms of bravery and courage other than that of the self-confident hero who is clear about what needs to be done and even give those forms a boost? Cultures vary widely in their understanding of bravery and courage, from the martial notions of bravery and courage that can be found in some hunter-gatherer tribes to the much more stoic and encompassing notions of bravery and courage that can be found in avowedly nonviolent cultures such as the Quakers (Thrift 2010). The same variation can be found in a whole series of other affective dispositions relevant to the makeup of a citizen in the political sphere.

There are other ways to proceed than with the martial model of the activist, as modern feminism, for example, has shown only too well. The Left might usefully turn to those disciplines that have made understanding affective disposition and how to use it in new ways their life's work, disciplines that occupy the uncertain divide between the social and the biological as they try to produce new activist instincts. For example, there is the vast archive of valuable performance as a means of both understanding states of mood and creating new affective mixes that would better allow us to think how we think and feel the political. A commonly cited source is the use of exercises that combine the ascetic with the aesthetic, a frequent motif since at least the sixteenth century, with roots going back much further than that. Or take the example of acting skills. "The method" is one moment in a battery of acting techniques. Based on the key concept of "emotional memory," it is intent on producing actors who are able to summon up the emotional patchwork of a character and so experience real emotion on stage (Krasner 2000). This transformation comes about through a range of techniques, such as making a performance physical through, for example, exercises that imitate animals, to get at pure behavior, and to "real doing" rather than indicating or pretending. Such a method can be used to reconstruct the emotional makeup of individuals, so producing new templates for action.[5]

One final step, which brings us back to where we began, would address the topic itself of bureaucracy. As we have already pointed out above in references to the work of Weber and du Gay, it is quite in order to think about bureaucratic ethos that focuses on more than efficiency. Indeed, it is probably more necessary than ever before, both as the audit society seems to press so hard and as so much evidence mounts that shows what happens when bureaucrats only do what they are told or what happens when standards slip to the point that corruption becomes institutionalized. Producing a viable ethic for bureaucracy may not seem like a primary political task for the Left, but it is worthwhile reflecting on just what a difference could be made by transforming the status of bureaucrats so that they were assumed to be important and principled actors in their own right (Du Gay 2005). Indeed, it could be argued that bureaucracy has become a condition of freedom as much as it has become a constraint. The Left can learn from the kinds of diplomacy that a small executive in the EU has had to invent to sustain a program of progressive policies, for there are options for participating in existing bureaucracies and building counter-organizations that can help to fix the gains of a fair and just society.

7

affective
POLITICS

It is generally assumed by students of politics that political judgments are—or should be—made in a rational or deliberative manner. Emotions and emotional capture are judged to be at worst a distraction or distortion and at best a means of getting publics behind a cause fashioned on the anvil of reason. Good political decisions should be the result of considered arguments and deliberations that can iron out irrational desires, so the argument goes. Emotions get in the way (or should enter the fray once the argument has been formulated). The history of Western political thought is littered with such signposting.

This chapter takes the opposite stance. It takes politics to be shot through with emotion from start to finish. Political ideas are frequently born out of passionately held beliefs; many political impulses are contagious precisely because they work on feelings. Thinking itself—we now know from neuroscience—involves considerable sensory and emotional pre-mediation, and political judgments follow the contours of emotion. This is precisely why many deliberative democracies, and the United States in particular, have developed sophisticated technologies to both track and work on public emotions and to build political content and direction, often guaranteeing success to the political forces that are most able to chip away at the hyphenated joint between thought and feeling.

The first half of this chapter, building on the evidence of how the Left made its first significant gains one hundred years ago, focuses on the workings of this affective machinery—its role in constructing publics and commonplaces, in reformulating the spaces of the political and the means of making progress, and in making certain public emotions and their sites count for more. Much of the account is critical of what exists, readily acknowledging the manipulations and stupefactions involved and the frequent stoking of negative emotions to appeal to the lowest common instincts. But the purpose of the criticism, given our premise that people have to care if they are to act or be acted on, is not to steer the Left away from the machinations of affective politics. Instead, it is to press for the Left to take a greater grip on the machinery of affective politics. What is needed is active cultivation of alternative feelings so that new affective connections can be forged and a general desire for other ways of being in the world can emerge, and can be built into new political causes. We need to break the spell of capitalism by casting new affective runes (Pignarre and Stengers 2011).

The thesis of this chapter, following our opening commentary in chapter 2 on the pre-personal and psychotopical, is that affect precedes decision, rather than the other way round, and that in modern democracies, mastery of the means of affective capture is essential for making political gain. That means that the Left has to reclaim or reinvent an affective politics that has been wrested away from it by the Right by using and developing the psycho-technologies that engineer collective feelings, but in a non-cynical way. The second half of the chapter outlines the shared structures of feeling that the Left needs to work on to sustain the desire and impetus for an open, just, and collectively rewarding world. The structures of feeling named—intended as examples rather than as a checklist—include feeling committed to labor, to fairness, to impurity, to living as a craft, and to steadfastness. In closing the book, we show how the mobilization of affect along these lines, along with the mastery of other political arts such as organization and inventiveness, can change the political landscape by making public latent or common concerns in novel ways.

The Public and the Construction of Commonplaces

We live in a time of very large publics. For politicians, negotiating with these mass publics has become a good part of what they do. Even a supposedly local event can be turned into something larger and, well, public, given the tools of the modern politician's trade: newspapers, radio, television, the Internet, blogs, social networking sites, and Twitter. This section turns to how publics in deliberative democracies are being tuned to resonate at the same frequency instrumentally to achieve particular results.

This analysis is not meant to be a nostalgic one. Many commentators have located a golden age in which politics was conducted untrammeled by the restraints of place or position, in which a process of rational cognition or organization was engaged in by a polity in which all had equal voices: the Athenian polis, the newly independent United States, Scandinavia in the 1950s and 1960s, and so on. We can reject these moments of nostalgia while at the same time being more than concerned about the way in which a new level of political organization—a powerful coalition of the media, political parties, donors, and political advertising and public relations consultants—is increasingly able to obtain determinate electoral results through the manipulation of affect. Although the practices of this coalition may have reached their "height" in the United States, they have now spread to most parts of the world.

To understand why this coalition is so threatening, we need to start with some fairly simple propositions about thinking in general, which, in turn, have deep political resonances (Lakoff 2008; Westen 2007). They can be seen as concerned with what Max Weber called "states of mood," existing somewhere between what he called the social and the biological realms. Weber was skeptical of biological orientations to the social sciences, but he also understood the importance of what he termed mechanical and instinctive factors in certain kinds of intentional action—in many types of "traditional action" as habit; in many aspects of charisma; and, crucially, in a number of forms of psychic "contagion" (Turner 2000)—thereby foreshadowing what we now routinely call the biopolitical realm.

Since Weber's time, the role of mechanical and instinctive factors in the formation of intention and action has become much clearer in three ways. First, and most particularly, we have come to understand that there is no such thing as thought that exists free from emotion. Emotion is a key part of how we think and make decisions. Second, human thought is rarely aware in the sense of having crystalline clarity about a situation, since very few individual actors have anything like a substantial amount of information available with which to make choices; nor do they have pristine cognitive thought processes, in that most thought is semiconscious at best, picked up from the cues provided by other people and a few scraps of information; nor is it individual, in the sense that nearly all thinking is corporately held and mediated in various ways. Third, human thinking is assisted by various prostheses that aid its formation and expression and stabilization, from practices of reading and writing through all manner of mass media. We might see thinking, then, as something akin to an assemblage in which different actors, including things that are variously empowered to act as cognitive proxies, constitute something not dissimilar to a laboratory that empowers some things to represent others, or to a continually reconstituted parliament in which representatives come and go according to the issues to hand.

All of this means that public thinking is therefore nearly always indistinct and imitative, borne this way and that by waves of emotion that register semiconsciously. The best model for this state of affairs is still provided by Gabriel Tarde's irreducibly processual, relational, and contingent sociology. Tarde proposed a model of society as being propagated and carried along by processes of affective *imitation*. For Tarde, society was not an organic unit, distinct from its constituent parts. Rather, it was a circulating flow of imitations, constantly moving through individuals in semiconscious ways, producing infinitesimal variations as they went along. While Tarde's work on psycho-social contagion can be accused of shrouding objects and agencies in a certain metaphysical excess (Tarde 2012), his basic propositions about imitation, affinity, and invention are still cogent and can still be applied.

Tarde's work more than a century ago relied on the premise that we only rarely control our own neural systems. It has proved prescient in all sorts of ways, prefiguring work in a variety of disciplines since. Take the case of imitation. Various studies have confirmed that imitation is rapid, automatic, and semiconscious and involves emotional contagion (including such phenomena as moral responsiveness); it is part and parcel of a widespread human capacity for "mindreading." What seems clear is that human beings have a default capacity to imitate, automatically and unconsciously, in ways that their deliberate pursuit of goals can override but not explain. In other words, most of the time humans do not even know they are imitating: their reactions are involuntary and precognitive. Yet at the same time, this is not just motivational inertness. It involves, for example, mechanisms of inhibition (or, if you like, immunity), many of which are cultural.

Thus we arrive at the subject of *automatism*. Generally, affect is a semiconscious phenomenon, consisting of a series of automatisms, many of them developed in childhood, that dictate bodily movement. They arise from suggestion and are not easily available for reflection. These automatisms may often feel like willful action, but they are not, and they have powerful political consequences, not least because they form a kind of psychic immune system that means that certain issues can be avoided or perversely interpreted as a matter of course. Equally, suppositions of causality may become firmly entrenched. For example, it is relatively easy to promote in populations feelings of responsibility for events over which they could not possibly have had any purchase and, as a corollary, feelings of denial of their influence over events for which they quite clearly did have some responsibility. In other words, there are highways of imitation-suggestion that are continually being traversed. As Daniel Wegner (2002, 314) puts it, we live in a "suggested society" in which "the causal influences people have on themselves and each other, as they are understood, capture only a small part of the actual causal flux of social relations." In other words, societies are thought of, quite literally, as *entranced*, as only half-awake. This somnambulist diagnosis—Tarde's diagnosis—suggests a certain lack of free will: people have little or no agency over their bodies or environments but are under the control of affective forces. That is, they are powered by automatisms: the body is the medium for the transmission of force but usually without any conscious volition. Unconscious—or, rather, semiconscious—"thoughts" cause the bulk of actions, including those associated with the political sphere.

With this background in mind, we can move on to a consideration of modern political feeling and back to Weber's states of mood. Note the word "mood." It is the right word. After all, social life seethes with passions, moody force fields moving back and forth through bodies and things, kept alive by cascades of imitation and suggestion. Warfare—often called politics by other means—is a good example. It is one of the most passionate of human pursuits, releasing the full range of affects to greater or lesser degree according to circumstance. (Indeed, some of the best empirical research on the passions has been carried out with soldiers on battlefields, capturing the way in which bodies and spaces are affectively intertwined). The current international political situation shows the power of passions all too well. The different passions that sweep the current political scene are a part of how we reason politically, not just an adjunct. Think only of the famous Russian newspaper cover that simply shows an outstretched hand flipping the finger to the rest of the world. To ignore the affective, passionate element of reason is to delete much of what reason consists of.

That proposition is made more urgent by the times we find ourselves in, for what we can see is democracy being eroded by forces whose primary concern is to knowingly align feelings in pursuit of their political goals. This turn to "totalitarian democracy" has been commented on by many thinkers, including Sheldon Wolin and Slavoj Žižek. Totalitarian democracy arises out of the increasing concern with "manufacturing consent," a term first coined by the American journalist and liberal Walter Lippmann and subsequently made famous by Noam Chomsky. Lippmann did not intend the term to have the pejorative meaning it has subsequently acquired. Concerned that democracy could be compromised by herd instincts, Lippman (1921, 310) argued that what was needed was a "specialized class whose personal interests reach beyond the locality," a Platonic elite able to short-circuit what he perceived to be the chief defect of democracy—namely, its inability to produce well-rounded, "omnicompetent" citizens able to see all sides of an argument. In its stead, argued Lippmann, citizens were left at sea in a mass of local opinion, ill-served by a press that was too quick to come to judgment and hampered by its own limitations.[1]

Whatever the exact pros and cons of Lippmann's views, they seem quite prescient in our mediated age in that they foretell that democracy's potential would become threatened as political deliberation was reduced to simulations by a combination of the media and the naked pursuit and exercise of power to protect corporate interests. The media become a source of events that either distort or distract while, behind the façade, the state becomes ever more authoritarian, able to justify this stance by spinning selected events as threats so that what were extraordinary measures become ordinary. In particular, totalitarian democracy plays exactly to the limitations of the individual citizen that Lippmann saw as limits to democracy's functioning, working hard to sustain them as a means of exerting power. Žižek (2009, 7) issues a general warning about what can happen under these conditions when he compares Silvio Berlusconi's hegemony in Italy to *Kung Fu Panda*, a hit cartoon in 2008:

> The fat panda dreams of becoming a kung fu warrior. He is chosen by blind chance (beneath which lurks the hand of destiny, of course) to be the hero to save his city, and succeeds. But the film's pseudo-Oriental spiritualism is constantly undermined by a cynical humour. The surprise is that this continuous making-fun-of-itself makes it no less spiritual: the film ultimately takes the butt of its endless jokes seriously. A well-known anecdote about Niels Bohr illustrates the same idea. Surprised at seeing a horseshoe above the door of Bohr's country house, a visiting scientist said he didn't believe that horseshoes kept evil spirits out of the house, to which Bohr answered: "Neither do I; I have it there because I was told it works just as well if one doesn't believe in it!" This is how ideology functions today: nobody takes democracy or justice seriously, we are all aware that they are corrupt, but we practise them anyway because we assume they work even if we don't believe in them. Berlusconi is our own Kung Fu Panda. As the Marx Brothers might have put it "this man may look like a corrupt idiot and act like a corrupt idiot, but don't let that deceive you—he is a corrupt idiot."

Politics has always consisted of tapping into currents of feeling, but now states and other political actors such as parties, corporations, and various civil society groups have become increasingly skilled practitioners of the art. We want to argue that a good part of contemporary statecraft consists of modulating these passions, not least because states have become better at "explicitating" a world in which these passions cannot necessarily be controlled but can be metered and modulated. We are not, of course, claiming that addressing the importance of mood in political life is something new. The passions have been a focus of political activity since politics was invented. For example, when Aristotle declared that we are all political animals, he underlined the importance of passions for good moral judgment and drew attention in *Rhetoric* to passion as a key component of political oratory. Equally, politicians routinely ask the "How do they feel?" question before they talk to expectant audiences, recognizing just how important that question is. And they are, of course, continually being accused of preying on people's hopes and fears, the two emotions to which they are most likely to appeal.

All that said, few canonical political philosophers and even fewer contemporary political theorists have tackled the role of mood in politics, even as they have spent a good deal of time challenging the supposed certainties of liberal political theory. But that is not to say that there is nowhere to turn. Think only of Paul Lazarsfeld's seminal study of political communication and voters' decision making during the U.S. presidential election of 1940 (Lazardfeld, Berenson and Gaudet, 1944); Richard Hofstadter's (2008) classic essay "The Paranoid Style in American Politics," expounding on the power of "angry minds"; George Marcus's work on affective intelligence and political judgment (Marcus, Neuman and MacKuen, 2000); Lauren Berlant's remarkable series of works on affective democracy and compassion (e.g., Berlant 2008, 2011); and a growing body of feminist literature on politics. But it is fair to say that much of this interest has not been systematic and has been bedeviled by the view that politics ought to be about conscious, rational discourse, with the result that affect is regarded as an add-on, at best, and a dangerous distraction, at worst.

But there is one tradition of thinking about politics that has never ignored the passions—namely, rhetoric. Indeed, the arts of rhetoric have been a staple of political life precisely because they are concerned with raising and directing passions. Originating in Greece among a school of pre-Socratic philosophers known as the Sophists circa 600 BC and subsequently codified in numerous primers, rhetoric was later taught in the Roman Empire—think only of the example of Cicero—and during the Middle Ages, it was one of the three original liberal arts, or *trivium* (along with logic and grammar). In the history of Europe, rhetoric concerned itself with persuasion in public and political settings such as assemblies and courts. Although rhetoric is often said to flourish in deliberative societies with rights of free speech, free assembly, and political enfranchisement granted to at least some portion of the population, as celebratory (or epideictic) rhetoric, it is just as important an element of authoritarian regimes that are not open to debate on any equal footing. Indeed, it might be argued that some of these regimes are the most practiced modern exponents of the art.

Rhetorical arguments do not make use of demonstrable or tested truths. Rather, they resort to fallible opinions, popular perceptions, transient beliefs, chosen evidence or evidence at hand (such as statistics), which are all properly called *commonplaces* because they help to establish a commonality of intellectual and emotional understanding between the orator and his or her audience. Although contemporary studies of rhetoric draw on a more diverse range of practices and meanings than was the case in ancient times, and tend to take a much wider view of what can be included under the term, the general thrust remains clear: to persuade. In particular, the role of commonplaces as, quite literally, common places, in which spatial organization is an integral part of the art of persuasion, has become more and more explicit. In the Greek polis, it is at least possible to argue — as, indeed, Peter Sloterdijk has with gusto — that the most important innovation of ancient Greek politics was the production of a space that could dampen emotions sufficiently to produce a time structure of waiting one's turn to speak. Subsequently, the role of space and spatial arrangement as a key element in swaying constituencies by both producing protocols for and underlining the use of affective cues and appeals has become ever clearer. Think only of a book like Thomas Wilson's *The Art of Rhetoric* (1553) and the careful attention it pays to staging as an affective key. Or think of the minute attention to the detail of staging space at the U.S. party conventions.

The point is that rhetoric, in explicit or implicit form, as the pursuit through a variety of devices of the establishment of a communion of feeling — however brief that may be — is a key to making contact with publics. At the very least, it is "the truth well told," to use the phrase from H. E. McCann's philosophy of advertising. And telling truth well requires research — howsoever defined — into how people feel. One of the key weathervane questions in any modern political campaign is the affective proximity between a politician and the electorate. Modern politicians have to be seen to extend care — they have to be seen to relate and not just communicate — and this requires emotional contact. "The battle is ever more for hearts, not minds" (Harding 2008, 7). In turn, that requires being able to draw on a series of technologies — we use the word "technology" purposefully — of feeling that will achieve this end. We make no excuse for concentrating on these technologies of mood that are being put to use in creating collective political subjects, but too often in grim mockery of what is really needed.

Technologies of Mood

The study of the automatisms that are the grist to the mill of modern politics has had a long history, going back to at least the eighteenth century. But what is different now is that these automatisms are increasingly available to be worked on and cultivated through a kind of performance management, both because they are more easily measured and because the cultural vocabulary of emotion has changed. For much of the time, Western democratic cultures tend to be disengaged or reluctant to engage — actively passive as Nina Eliasoph (1998) puts it — but they can be "switched on" by particular issues with high affective resonance. Thus, a growth in disengagement and detachment is paralleled by moments of high engagement and attachment. Such tendencies have been only strengthened by the growth of the mass media that makes it much easier to work on the semiconscious realm, especially through the ability to arrest time and examine and work with it. Delay in time allows detail that has lain dormant, so to speak, to be noticed and molded. During periods of deferral, action can be pre-treated in various ways, allowing new automatisms to become embedded in that action — hence, the rise of the range of techniques that Sloterdijk calls "psychotechnics."

At the same time, the advent of mass media has almost certainly been speeding up the reception of events so that giving any considered political voice the luxury of time to consider and reflect becomes increasingly difficult. Indeed, notwithstanding a general increase in news outlets (Bennett and Entman 2001), this considered political voice tends to be restricted to certain widely circulated clichés of presentation that foreground affect as a means of gaining a speedy impact, an effect that is only exacerbated by the heightened levels of competition to find presentations with grip. For example, mass media images of risk nearly always focus on suffering: "more often than not, 'risk' is communicated for public attention in graphic portrayals of bodies in pain and harrowing images of people in mourning and distress" (Wilkinson 2005, vii). In particular, an affective platform such as melodrama, which involves the generation of high levels of involved anxiety, has become through the media an accepted affective automatism (Delli Carpini et al. 2002; Thrift 2010). Furthermore, the proliferation of the mass media tends to both multiply and keep this kind of affective platform in the public mind in a way that promotes an anxious melancholy and can sometimes even produce states of cultural obsession or compulsion. "Emotional constitutions" can be written and backed up, set for stock affective responses that dictate political response, as in the case of Republicanism in the United States over the past twenty-five years (Westen 2007).

In other words, what we are trying to point to is the rise of more and more psycho-technologies for influencing mood, premised on making appeals to the heart, to passions, to the emotional imagination, through a realm of affective push that is present along with the psychic and the emotional rather than the intellect and reasoning. To put it another way, we want to recall Tarde's work by paralleling imitation with invention. A quarter of a century ago, Serge Moscovici (1985) was writing about another, less mediated time, but his work seems particularly relevant to the new mediated age of the imitative crowd we now inhabit, an age that might well be caricatured as the age of mass mesmerism (Barrows 1981). Moscovici argued that affective appeals try to create an "illusion of love" via a range of techniques — affective, corporeal, and psychological — aimed at maximizing processes of suggestion and imitation, including the use of symbols, images, flags, music, affirmations, phrases, speeches, and slogans, all jammed into the half-second delay between action and cognition. These signs are delivered through the hypnotizing use of repetition rather than didactic command and instruction. Thus, the population is touched in ways that are semiconscious and may well instill the feeling that they are the originator of that thought, belief, or action rather than simply and mechanically reproducing the beliefs of a charismatic mediatized order. Waves of affect are transmitted and received, transmitted and received, transmitted and received. The goal, in other words, is to extend and then reinforce "mental touch" for instrumental reasons.

That politics since the rise of the mass media is susceptible to, and based on, many of the same subconscious processes of imitation as other affective fields (e.g., those pertaining to corporations and consumerism) is clear from many examples. Take just the realm of political advertising. Think of the classically hopeful "Morning in America" ad campaign for Ronald Reagan in 1984 or the scary "Daisy" ad of 1964,[2] which portrayed Lyndon Johnson's opponent as the harbinger of a nuclear holocaust. Each of these campaigns, repeated many times since in different variants, testifies to the influence of mood on politics and the importance of imitation as a constituent element of affective contagion. And this is no surprise. As Samuel Popkin (1991) pointed out in the classic *The Rea-*

soning Voter, a good part of politics in a mediated environment is based on intangibles that briefly fix attention—what he calls "low-information signalling"—chiefly affective shortcuts that convey just enough of the character of candidates to voters and that are open to all kinds of manipulation, particularly via the use of nonverbal cues such as music and imagery. Such fleeting impressions—momentary neural bindings, if you like (Lakoff 2008)—in which, as Ted Brader (2006, 26) puts it, "Our brains often identify cues and respond to them without our awareness" through various frames, metaphors, and general bodily dispositions, that often count for more than cogent policies and can often pass as voters' political reasoning. In turn, this change puts much more emphasis on the individual politician whose personality acts as a kind of affective bellwether. Indeed, recent work in political psychology suggests that voters can often make inferences of competence based solely on the facial appearance of candidates, and they do so remarkably rapidly—within milliseconds sometimes.

In particular, a gathering of political technologies have been gaining momentum since the use of the radio as a political tool in the 1930s. Many of these technologies take their cue from corporate practices of generating engagement. Although such technologies supposedly make the conduct of electoral and other forms of politics more effective, too often they confuse the consumption of democracy with the practice of democracy; too often, they emphasize personality, perception, and organization over genuine debate. It is a familiar criticism that modern politics tends to emphasize style over substance, but it is also true. Remember "James Callaghan's retort to the marketing industry's encroachment on politics: 'I don't intend to end this campaign packaged like cornflakes. I shall continue to be myself.'" He did. And he lost" (Harding 2008, 216). Remember Gordon Brown's fateful appeal during the televised debates of the British elections in 2010 to be valued for his policies. He pleaded, and he also lost.

Technological Change in the Political Sphere

| 1930s | National polls (Gallup, Harris, Quayle); use of radio |
| 1940s | Audience research, precursor to focus group developed by the U.S. military |

1950s	Segmentation studies and motivation research done by psychologists such as Ernest Dichter
1969	First intensive polling firm
1970	First filmed political bio-pic
mid-1970s	Telephone polling and focus groups and direct mail fundraising; first attempt at behavioral demographics
1976	The permanent campaign
1992	Dial groups
1980s	Daily tracking polls
1990s	One-on-one sessions in shopping-mall offices
2003	Use of Internet campaign to organize monthly meet-ups (create own crowds) in Howard Dean's decentralized campaign using websites; use of email and blogs instead of focus groups to gauge opinion.
2008	Use of social media in Barack Obama's campaign; large-scale data mining

Four processes seem particularly important to note in relation to the Left's ability to regain political influence. The first, and most obvious, is that politics has been mass-mediatized. It is something of a cliché to note the influence of the media on politics, but this has now become pervasive, based especially in the interaction between techniques such as opinion polling and media presentation, the result of an increasing familiarity with television technique, increasing professionalization of the presentation of politics (as symbolized by growing numbers of consultants and the fame of formative guru-cum-inventors such as Ned Kennan, David Sawyer, Scott Miller, Mark McKinnon, Mandy Grunwald, Lee Atwater, Dick Morris, and Karl Rove), the burgeoning of available media outlets and the subsequent expansion of political programming, and increased media access. When a spin doctor for New Labour in Britain declares, "What they can't seem to grasp is that communications is not an afterthought to our policy—it is central to the whole mission of New Labour," it is time to concede that this is no longer a partisan point. It is typical of the modern mediated Western democracy.

Second, political actors are increasingly treated as commodities to be sold, partly, perhaps, because so many citizens lack the attention span or inclination to follow political issues and tend to invest their trust in the low-information signals emanating from iconic figures instead. Such marketing involves more and more use of the small signs of affective technique structured as various kinds of performance of style. A politician's ability to perform in public becomes a crucial asset, but it is very often a performance in which unexpected emotions are bleached from the process because of the dangers of "expressive failure." Spontaneity has to be carefully structured. So, for example, the practices of celebrity are becoming more and more common in the political arena. Think only of the way in which Ronald Reagan's face has become an abiding source of contemplation for political commentators because of the affective power of its ability to convey comfort and avuncular authenticity and warmth and even serenity, or the careful prepping of Bill Clinton's body language in key television appearances.

Third, if political actors are commodities, then it should be no surprise that political campaigns are increasingly treated as forms of marketing. This tendency toward retail politics is only strengthened in first-past-the-post systems, where the outcome of any election is disproportionately influenced by a few swing voters whom it is important to locate and communicate with, against a background of increasing speed that we noted earlier. Thus, polling techniques that can gauge intensity of feelings and the general quality of mood have become a key to many political campaigns. Parties and other pressure groups have adopted a series of these practices: all manner of polls, focus groups, voter databases, geographic information systems, customer relations management software, targeted mail and e-mail, and so on, especially to target particularly passionate constituencies. In the United States, these techniques have become far advanced since the 1970s. In each case, the goal is to identify a susceptible constituency as accurately as possible through continuous polling and to boost affective gain by making voters feel differently—for example, by finding wedge issues. But more than this, it is also to identify individuals and their interests and concerns as exactly as possible, thereby turning them into "intimate strangers."

Fourth, the political process, in an odd simulation of the original ambitions of democracy, becomes a continuous one based on a model of permanent tracking that can be used outside elections, as well as in them, according to the play of events. In the "permanent campaign," a term first used by Pat Caddell in 1976, media time and election time begin to merge and techniques for campaigning and governing gradually coalesce. The aim, it might be hypothesized, is to produce a semiconscious inflow of political imitation-suggestion that is unstoppable and that can be played into to produce affective firestorms that, in turn, can be modulated by the new technical means now available. A whole array of corporate, Internet-related techniques, from websites to blogs to social media, have been used to tap into and work with voters' concerns. The idea is to maintain constant contact with voters and mobilize their concerns for political ends. At the same time, it is worth remembering that these are also the arts of *not* swaying constituencies. Sometimes what is needed is to "reduce the juice" by inducing apathy in its many forms. But apathy, as Eliasoph (1998) wonderfully shows, can involve a whole series of denials, omissions, suppressions, and evasions that add up to much more than a simple absence of thought and action.

The technologies we have outlined undoubtedly were born in the United States, but they are now diffusing to all democracies at higher or lower speeds, following an increasingly insistent media-marketing logic pushed by a motley crew of consultants. As James Harding (2008, 218) puts it, "Their craft worked. It did not guarantee success but it improved the odds." Nearly every election in a democracy or a becoming-democracy now depends on consultants being pulled off the shelf to assist. The case of Italy's totalitarian democracy under Berlusconi is perhaps the most extreme. There, Berlusconi was able to turn a potent mixture of marketing and celebrity into a politics by drawing on the work of Frank Luntz, a Republican political consultant for Newt Gingrich's "Contract with America" campaign of 1994. Berlusconi's "Contract with the Italian People" followed an almost identical model. The case of Russia is similarly instructive: from the time of Boris Yeltsin, pollsters and consultants have been involved in elections. The case of the United Kingdom also bears some consideration: since 1992, something like a permanent campaign has been in operation, the result of its adoption from U.S. sources by New Labour. While the permanent campaign in Britain does not run at quite the intensity of its North American counterpart, the result of a slightly longer electoral cycle, nearly all of the techniques found in the U.S. permanent campaign have gradually made their way across the Atlantic, fuelled by the hiring of U.S.-based consultants at various times. As if to underline the point, in 2007, the "Conservative Party hired a spin doctor and agreed to pay him two and a half times the salary of David Cameron, the party leader" (Harding 2008, 216).

As important, the greater sophistication of databases—in particular, the scope and thickness of the data that are available; the fact that so much data can be gathered interactively with citizens through sources such as texting, blogs, and social networking sites, as social relations increasingly become communicational relations; and the addition to the data of all kinds of spatial referents that make it possible to continuously map out connection, interaction, and affinity—has opened the door to tracing out waves of feeling and operating on them.[3] Political consultants now routinely trace out emotional landscapes, mapping various communities of feeling (Woodward 2009).

Now, the institutions of the state are doing the same. Not only are state campaigns more and more likely to appeal to emotions as a matter of course, but, equally, citizens are increasingly perceived as emotional entities. Recent attempts to meter the "happiness" of citizens are not just about new ways to calculate gross domestic product but also about beginning to collect data on emotional response in the same way that all kinds of other data on citizens are collected. A similar observation can be made about new forms of citizen consultation by states, such as citizen juries. States also are beginning to take notice of the kinds of feelings that are often engendered by state bureaucracies, including anger, frustration, and even depression (Woodward 2009). In time, this measurement of emotional states is likely to produce an emotionally literate state as states begin to map fates.

It is crucial to understand how mapping is now a vital part of political psychotechnics. Maps, of course, have a long and involved history as handmaidens of the state.[4] They have become a standard part of how a state thinks about itself. Indeed, in their current form, they seem to have reached well beyond the previous high point of map use at the end of the nineteenth century, when new technical inventions made maps a vital part of journalism, saturating the popular and bureaucratic consciousness. Maps nowadays not only have their traditional uses in finding one's way and identifying spaces; they have also become itineraries that themselves are categories. This new generation of maps increasingly resembles a kind of bureaucratic "satellite navigation" system, automatically searching out what and where for each and every event. They have become a way to file the world. In this sense, they refer back to Sloterdijk's spheres in that they make it possible to produce worlds *and* they make it possible to provide route maps through them *and* they provide notice of the real or virtual migrations of different kinds of communities in a manner akin to the itinerary histories of the Aztecs and native North Americans (Thrift 2011).

We are still trying to come to terms with the kinds of imaginative forays and extensions that such mapping makes possible, for new types of maps do not tell us just how to reach a destination. They also tell us how to be—that is, they "reflect shifts in our perception of who we are and where we are going . . . shifts in our imagination of the world, our reasons for travel, and what destinations are possible" (Akerman 2007, 63). But what is interesting is the number of leftist artistic and other experiments that are currently taking place with the explicit intent of reworking what we think of as the map. These experiments can now be seen to have real political import. As maps become the new files, interrogating and extending their possibilities becomes a genuinely political move.

Alternative maps of being and affiliation (e.g., relational worlds, imagined utopias, diasporas, ethical identification) disclose new possibilities of organization, new emotional communities. This, in some shape or form, the Left has always known in trying to break free from the maps of legacies presented as natural, inviolable. Now, however, sophisticated databases and software manipulation allow these maps to be populated, mined animated, visualized in their details, available to the Left to fashion and hold together new affective communities; to simulate dangers, risks, and possibilities; to track emotional responses against simulated futures. Similarly, the proliferation of political technologies of mood offers the Left new possibilities. If mediatization is built into the political process, the Left has to recognize that without it, there is no public or commonplace. It has to work the grain the best it can (knowing that powerful vested interests with extraordinary resources patrol the media), along with exploiting new media outlets and technologies. It also must attend to the politics and techniques of charisma, structured spontaneity, permanent tracking, emotional reach, staying close to the electorate. There is nothing guaranteed in this, and the danger of mood manipulation to preserve the status quo or serve vested interests must be avoided. Still, the opportunity to work a whole new range of media-scapes (from blogs, Twitter, and webcams to videogames and community broadcasting), with the help of databases and software intelligence that get close to the ground of mass experience, should not be avoided by the Left as it looks to power up new sentiments for new causes.

Leftist Structures of Feeling

Following from the preceding discussion, the Left needs to become associated once again with particular structures of feeling—to resurrect a term from Raymond Williams—to regain its relevance and influence. It has to involve itself in the genesis of desire for just, equal, and responsible ways of being. Without desire, the momentum for change will falter, and importantly, it is from new desires that leftist political causes will arise, melding existing and latent concerns into a future-making project. Put differently, we do not believe—as many leftist pundits do—that the Left will succeed when it can name a new project and then give it affective push. Too much has gone wrong when blueprints have been rolled out in this way (Jacoby 2005). We believe the opposite to be true on the basis of our reflections in this book: it is feelings (more accurately, their entanglement with inventions of thought and organization) that convert concerns and controversies into sustained and supported political causes, into care for a different world (Goldfarb 2006; Winter 2005). Structures of feeling—inexact but powerful constellations of affective account and evaluation running through the mill of everyday practice—are therefore shorthand for orientation to the world, in itself a powerful political site in which the world takes on shape as a form of emotional constitution (Ahmed 2010).

In what follows, we outline some of the key structures of feeling that we believe the Left must claim—or reclaim where they have become stuck in certain emotional alignments. Our aim is to summarize their normative orientation and indicate some of the substantive areas of concern and ways to respond to them. These structures of feeling are affective fields structured by practices instituted through specific forms of political action and organization. It follows that an affective field does not involve people alone. Its energy extends into particular forms of space, other living beings, assemblies of objects, and, of course, bureaucracies of various sorts—precisely those social formations that are seen as being most immune to feeling. This is how care for the world will be carried forward and held in place, regardless of the idiosyncrasies of human behavior.

A first structure of feeling has to be *labor*, understood as a validating activity that holds the world in place. Historically, the Left has always pressed for labor as a source of meaning. But what is equally certain is that the meaning of labor is going through theoretical and practical change. Thus, many theorists are trying to broaden what is regarded as labor (e.g., to take in the contributions of excluded groups and different forms of unpaid work) and to link labor more closely to expenditures of creative energy; they are concerned about bringing in the efforts of other, nonhuman actors, without which any desired outcome would be impossible. On the practical side, capitalist firms are trying to prospect across the range of talents that workers might have; to redefine work so it takes in activities that were formerly regarded as not within the organization; to free up the loads on some workers while increasing those on others; and to experiment with different ways in which individuals come in and out of the system as workers trained, retrained, and dropped. The result is that labor can no longer be easily associated with just the world of work; has genuinely come to be understood in the Marxian sense as the combination of manual and mental effort; is the subject of a striking new series of environments that are meant to cement these insights; and is viewed by individuals as an activity that needs their continual effort but is also part of many other forms of daily activity.

One consequence is that a left politics of labor that is reduced to a politics of work or particular categories of workers is likely to miss many of the most significant issues about what labor is becoming. For example, one might argue that one of capitalism's main ploys currently is to draw on activities carried out by workers in their free time—that is, to draw into the sphere of labor activities that conventionally were not regarded that way. But at the same time, such redistribution might present an opportunity for the Left, since it raises a whole series of political issues such as the nature of open innovation, intellectual property, and what work is for. Another consequence of capitalism's ploys is that elements of labor that were always present but not valued are now being valued, for example, for their ability to intermesh with others, to strike the right tone, to give off the right signals, and so on. These have become major attributes of certain forms of valued labor. A third consequence is that the changing nature of technology makes it both more and less central to labor. Technology frees the body from manual toil (in some parts of the world), but it also produces new forms of precariousness, wage slavery, and degrading of skills. Again, there is a political opening for the Left in fighting for jobs that do not produce a new state of precariousness or deskill the labor of workers, not only on grounds of welfare but also, it has to be said, on grounds of efficiency (e.g., the absolute necessity of repair and maintenance work in the most software-sorted systems). This fight for jobs, however, has to accept that labor has now become so interwoven with technology of one sort or another that any anti-technological stance is simply unrealistic and may force more thought about controversial political arenas such as genetically modified organisms, genetic implants, and medicated labor (as workers become increasingly reliant on pills).

As the meaning of labor changes shape, the expectations and organizations that arise from it also change. The Left has made some progress in trying to take these changes into account. For example, there is much talk of the prevalence of affective labor, immaterial labor, and so on, all signaling a need to understand how what were regarded as non-work characteristics have become central to work. This momentum needs to be maintained and periodically renewed. In particular, that must involve a thorough reconsideration of the available institutions of transformation. Why, for example, does unionism no longer have the same emotional pull? What can the Left do to offer hope against various tyrannies of labor, through new institutions of organized labor with an enhanced affective reach, and through new causes that clearly resonate?

Clearly, the Left needs clarity over the kinds of labor that need to be defended. The old commitment to the romance of manual labor may be long past, but there are real issues over what is to replace its most debilitating forms — not least as more and more areas of work, including domestic labor, emotional labor, and even craft understood as an updated stance that sees work as a satisfying vocation, have been valorized. However, a romance of labor as fulfillment could help to select for particular kinds of work. If a politics of unswerving commitment to the wholeness of labor were given real impetus, along with a generalized understanding of work as both rewarding and socially defining, the moral case for the precarious, unprotected, and exploitative forms of work that seem to be proliferating might be significantly weakened. The case for such forms of work would need to be made against the tide of general opinion, against their acceptance as normal in a neoliberal ethos of social being.

The issue at stake thus becomes: what counts as fulfilling work? Human bodies are designed to interact with the world in forceful ways that can be regarded as work. People get considerable satisfaction from the exercise of work. For too long, the Left, contra Marx, has tended to equate work with toil; however, the fulfillment that sheer hard work brings should not be underestimated. The problem is more the degree of direction that each worker has over his or her work and the social recognition that this work contributes to the common good. Work very often produces good feelings, ranging from "a good day's work done" to the pleasure gained from finishing a task well. Instead of obsessing about those skills, professions, and activities that need to be preserved over others that are somehow regarded as of a lesser nature, it might be better for the Left to think about how work of all kinds can become a source of everyday satisfaction. Isn't this, after all, what unites Marx with John Ruskin and William Morris?

A second structure of feeling is *fairness*, opportunistically resurrected by the newly formed Conservative–Liberal coalition government in Britain but worthy of more leftist consideration, since a substantial part of Left's political action has been bound up with it. Throughout the history of the Left, fairness has been one of the key gut reactions that has driven the movement. At times, this feeling has manifested itself in the form of demands for justice; at other times, in the form of demands for equality; and at yet other times, in the form of demands for fair play. What seems certain is that an unequal distribution of rewards causes political stirrings. Whether, as Robert Dahl (2006, 39) claims, "Human beings are naturally endowed with a sensitivity to the unequal distribution to others whom they view as comparable to themselves in relevant ways," it seems certain that "what a human being sees as fairness and injustice will often arouse strong emotions. Given the opportunity, these emotions will then express themselves in actions, which may range from an immediate verbal expression — it's not fair! — to behavior intended to bring about a fairer distribution, whether by peaceful persuasion or violence, and whether by acting individually or in concert or others."

In recent years, a whole set of new claims about sexuality, disability, immigration, citizenship, and so on have also been made around fairness. At a time of considerable leftist lament about the unfairness of the contemporary world, what is striking is the enormous expansion of movements devoted to instituting forms of fairness. As a result, the traditional care of the Left for important gains such as human rights, distributive justice, and equality of treatment and reward has to be accompanied by new forms of care, which, like these preceding ones, also need some form of institutionalization. This is not to argue simply that no more action is required in the traditional arenas, but it is worthwhile for the Left to reflect on the gains that have been made recently through the expansion of what is counted as fair and through the enshrining of some of these principles in legislation and their own institutions. There is a stark geography of fairness that in itself can be understood as a structure of feeling. It is hard not to be outraged by the grotesque disparities of income between North and South; by the difficulty many people in the South have in gaining access to the basics of life; by the structures of power that guarantee the continuation of these iniquities; and by the elaborate efforts in the North to keep the world's poor and traumatized at bay. One of the more interesting, though still hesitant, developments of recent years is the rise of global networks of nongovernmental organizations, from time to time accompanied by promises to the South by the major industrialized nations aimed at righting some of these wrongs. This is a far from adequate development, but it does highlight the scale of what has to be fixed to eliminate these persisting spatial inequalities. It also captures something important about fairness as a structure of feeling. In the absence of global institutions that make fairness their concern, much of the momentum built temporarily by social movements, international agreements, and local campaigns cannot be sustained. However, whatever the global architecture that is put into position, it will never solve the problems of injustice and inequality on its own. That requires the constancy of cross-border solidarity—the denouncing, regardless of jurisdiction, of these problems as unacceptable.

Strong public feelings of fairness force institutional attention and keep feelings of blame and aversion at bay. But as times get hard—and we are beginning to see this as the current economic crisis rolls on—the stranger, at home and abroad, is cast as a threat to community, security, tradition, nation, economy, and more. As subsequent feelings of aversion grow, sweeping in their train publics and institutions, what was once seen as fair is suddenly felt to be unacceptable; the very same victim of poverty, oppression, or deprivation regarded as possessing the right to various kinds of entitlement, is refashioned as the threatening alien to be tamed or ejected. This change is often the result of the emotional repositioning of the stranger, which is mercilessly exploited by political parties for easy electoral gain.

Similarly, as a sentiment returns that, through a mixture of fear and aggression, seeks comfort in a pure society, the Left needs to reinforce a third structure of feeling: a commitment to *heterogeneity*. All things are mixed and will remain so. Too often, political movements, including those on the Left, have tried to purify the world in ways that work against its grain and sometimes have dire political effects. Classically, this kind of attempt has been framed around issues of identity and belonging, resulting in the terrible oppression of minorities, outsiders, and dissidents. However, it is just as important to mark heterogeneity as a characteristic of other parts of human life. This includes economic life.

Modern economies are inherently mixed, containing many modes and practices of organization and delivery. In some of their parts, they may not even be characterized by monetary exchange or by organization driven purely by exchange value. To caricature the economy as singular is as erroneous as is the attempt to construct a single type of economy, laissez-faire or managed, private or public (Gibson-Graham 2006). Variety is an evolutionary force in economic life, too, and it requires a considerable degree of coordination and regulation. The Left's challenge in facing economic heterogeneity, therefore, is to ensure that it can be harnessed as a resource for the benefit of those working or otherwise implicated in the different sectors of the economy—for example, by making social enterprises more durable; by democratizing large corporations; by spreading the rewards of the knowledge economy more widely; by ensuring that micro-firms can emerge to populate markets; by regulating against monopoly and centralization; and by extending public ownership and control in the baseline industries and services, especially finance. Such regulated heterogeneity also serves to question the existing order and to illuminate new possibilities—for example, by legitimating new forms of profit and value that may be less predatory than those that went before.

A politics of heterogeneity thus requires the Left to think imaginatively about why economic variety matters and to intervene in bold ways to harness its potential. This means, above all, joining in global efforts to prevent totalitarian capitalism from holding sway. Such a step has to include fighting hard and in unison for a new set of global economic rules on trade, monopoly, minimum wages, and corporate responsibility, and resurrecting Keynesian-type demands for world-level regulation, something that entrenched neoliberal interests persistently have opposed. It also means valuing slack—or, at least, knowing the limitations of organizing for growth and efficiency at all costs. Underutilized and wasted capacity is a genuine problem in most economies, one that will soon spiral to alarming levels as a small set of economies with high labor pools, big internal markets, and low costs out-compete the remaining majority and invalidate alternative economic experimentation. Expecting these economies to act as the world's welfare basket is unrealistic and will fail to ensure better redistribution of economic capacity. The shift to an economy that values labor in all of its forms and that measures efficiency broadly to include such criteria as social empowerment and utility will require worldwide pressure to harmonize work standards and upgrade trading habits.

Economic heterogeneity is just a part of the story. Social and cultural heterogeneity can be understood as just as important. As societies become hyper-diverse, equality comes to mean something very different. The Left, through its original commitment to recognize all citizens as equal, is more in tune with this than is the Right. It is the Left that has championed the politics of difference around this building block, attending to the rights of minorities, migrants, women, cultural formations, and differences in human aspiration. Against this background and the stubborn variety that circulates the world, it simply makes no sense to insist on a politics of sameness. We are, though, not in favor of cultural pluralism unchecked. Rather, we favor the expansion of mechanisms of diplomacy that recognize difference but also attempt to negotiate it to reach ends that the parties may set but that are not ends in themselves.

This point becomes particularly salient in the case of religion, which by definition is an affective formation and is often immune to forms of leftist secular rationalism. Here, where worldviews are so likely to be entrenched, the work of diplomacy becomes even more important. There is little point to hoping that diplomacy will reconcile difference and make friends out of enemies. Rather, the intention is to find minimal forms of accommodation to build longer-lasting structures of reconciliation. This process involves recursive and studied intermediation between warring parties, not separation, because in the modern world, separation is no solution. It requires getting the parties to abide by a situation so that each one is forced out of the comfort zone of certitude. It does not mean the simple proliferation of difference in the hope that plenitude alone will automatically result in parties' accepting their place in a plural world.

Diplomacy, fairness, economic solidarity, and other aspects of a stance toward the world as a shared commons feed off another important structure of feeling: to set out to live life as an *accomplishment.* We want to distance ourselves from ideas such as happiness or contentment or other synonyms, which presume the arrival at a state of satisfaction while often neglecting the work and effort involved, the welfare of others and the world at large, and the labor and sacrifice of others. When we write about accomplishment, we are interested in the ability to reach out and change the social fabric, which, of course, may include the fulfillment of individual aspirations but cannot be reduced to that. It follows that some degree of material attainment can be included, but accomplishment cannot be limited to that yardstick, not only because the relationship between the two is not direct, but also because many kinds of fulfillment derive from the care put into social relations, world disposition, and material arrangement. We have in mind an idea of accomplishment as a general freedom to develop in a multiplicity of ways: generosity and curiosity as a mode of being. We are looking for the Left to regain something of what Marx envisaged as a utopia offering all subjects the freedom to develop varied interests and capabilities, but as a rolling process that takes place in the present and that involves care for that which surrounds us.

This move means replacing dominant Western modes of selfhood or personhood, which are contained and instrumental. Many models of personhood could be adopted—for example, one that does not make strong distinctions between the self and the other and therefore is more likely to be able to take in other claims and claimants; or one that is finely tuned to the dynamics of the commons; or one that demonstrates the humility we documented in a previous chapter. It also means developing a sense of giving to the world as being a fundamental human value, shored up by designing environments in which such activities become normal. Finally, it means getting used to not asking for or expecting too much, a modesty of claim worked into the cultural fabric of society through appropriate reforms relating, for example, to fiscal and welfare redistribution or to lowered standards of consumer satisfaction.

But we want to go further than this. In using the word "accomplishment," we want to signal a more general condition: fulfillment as it applies to the world as a whole. We might argue that, at the limit, leftist politics has been about ways in which being itself can become fulfilled. That means paying attention to beings other than human beings; it means paying attention to the condition of the spaces of life and the environment more generally, up to and including the planet itself. It could even mean considering the state of the object world and the means by which that world can speak back. If the certainty of what we mean by terms such as "a people" is taken to be at issue, then the whole question of what it is to be human is cast into the open. Humanity could include all kinds of entities in all kinds of combination, not just bounded biological human beings.

Accomplishment is also about working with others. Of course, the most obvious others are other humans, but we cannot assume this. For example, scientific work on animals consistently demonstrates that, in the ability to cognize, they are much closer to human beings than formerly thought. Again, the load of cognition faced by humanity is increasingly being taken on by machines and boosted neurological systems. And, again, the cognitive potential of the human body may itself be open to change. In turn, these kinds of changes are producing some of the most potent ethical questions currently being faced (e.g., euthanasia, right to life, animal rights, drugs for tackling attention deficit hyperactivity disorder) — questions that have clear implications for leftist politics, not only because new sites of political attention have appeared, but also because some of the basic tenets of apparently human accomplishment are being problematized by contemporary human–animal–science interfaces.

One of these implications concerns how we define and deal with the processes of rationalization now that we know that rationality is such a clouded glass. For example, as we argued earlier, voters do not make what most people would regard as strictly rational choices. Equally, we know that the political issues on which they fix — whether it is the desire to extend life, the future of badgers, or a fear of genetically modified organizations — often seem tangential to the Left but may be a matter of the greatest concern to them. So the Left's traditional interest in rationality needs to be tempered or even rethought. Another implication has to do with the politics of disclosure. More and more elements of human differentiation are revealing themselves. For example, genetic information will undoubtedly become a means of tagging individuals, and thereby a new mode of control. Should the Left press for an optimistic pan-humanism that takes these new prompts as signs of a new kind of humanity? Or should it regard them as one more elaboration of the panopticon? A third implication is the enhanced understanding of basic dispositions that has become possible in the past twenty or thirty years, which provides a new terrain for political operation. In particular, it has become much easier to detect and read the "honest" signals arising from the human body (e.g., muscular alteration, facial expression, gesture) and to play these in the large via the media. While the political mainstream is now responding to this new biological stratum more seriously, either through new technological responses or by incorporating the signals into vote-catching machinery (as hinted earlier), the Left by and large still does not know what to do with these signals other than to deny them space in the political field, trapped as it often is in a humanist conception of authenticity.

It is important to add into this brew a final factor: the fact that environments themselves are beginning to cognize through various forms of software and new kinds of detection instruments that build thinking, action, and reflexivity into the technological fabric. This process is replete with numerous forms of hidden politics that the Left is only just beginning to recognize. Much of this recognition focuses on the disabling or threatening nature of these hidden engines, but it need not be so. For example, we might begin to think of these environments themselves as sentient: the battery of scientific paraphernalia that surround the measurement of climate change might be understood as the beginnings of an institution that can care for the planet and allow it to fulfill itself. The sum of all of this is a new form of post-humanism that has either far exceeded the agency of humans or has redefined humanity in such a way as to bring in many other forms of agency. What might accomplishment cultivated as a craft mean in these circumstances?

One thing it might mean, were the Left to work actively on the implications of human proscription along these lines, would be to tackle head-on the culture of blame that has become pervasive as a result of the rise of modern individualism. In all walks of life, coming in second or not meeting the target is taken as a sign of failure, a reason to blame oneself or someone else. Institutions push in this direction, and the more they push, the more people take their personal circumstances to be of their own or someone else's volition. It is as if the hidden power of so many other forces—human and nonhuman—does not exist. The result is rejection, a sense of hopelessness, trying to get along by stepping on others rather than finding value in doing one's best, trying hard, being part of a common endeavor, working with others. To tackle this culture of blame and despair, the Left needs to be able to offer a different vision of fulfillment and hope that offers conviction and steadfast commitment.

It is *steadfastness* itself that we wish to propose here as a final key structure of feeling (as much, of course, as the content of leftist conviction), for in its beleaguered state over the past few decades, the Left has sometimes lost the courage to hold on to its sense of rightness and wrongness when the wind has blown in different directions. Thus, pragmatism has been reduced to opportunism, leading to following, and mapping to positioning while the politics of conviction has been killed off or handed over to the Right. Steadfastness has become a synonym for stubbornness and inflexibility, torn apart from any sense of the worth of knowing which lines not to cross. The Left needs to recover this sense and show the value of behaving in this way: the strength that comes from weathering the storm and breaking free of the constant pressure to conform and to do better without knowing why, from holding firm to an idea of what is right in a situation that will inevitably vary day by day without lapsing into the kind of righteousness that has so often acted as a powerful political deterrent.

The Left has a role in working through these ethical formations and can do so effectively by being very clear about certain dispositions that really do count. It is exactly a stance on such things as fairness, harm, and injustice that underlies the Left project. After all, how many people can offer a finished critique of capitalism and its depredations so as to act and feel leftist? Instead, they operate as if something is wrong in the world that needs to be put right. It is steadfastness to such feelings that can once again become a compass for individuals to make their own way in the world and connect purposefully to others in it. The engineering of such ethical certainty is unavoidable. This is what cultures have done since time immemorial in their own ways, and today, the politics of fear plays in just such a register, trying to usher people toward narrow conclusions about the world. Again, the bulk of the output from the media industry retails attitudes and stances that confirm particular feelings about the world.

The Left must work with and against these flows of feeling by producing its own institutions. We see steadfastness not so much as a personal quality as the product of collectives, steeped in particular ways of going on that were learned early in life through institutions that in their own right demonstrate such qualities. The range of possibilities for putting into place a machinery of ethical responsibility is vast. It includes education, the layout of public spaces, simple rules of everyday conduct, the structure of promises in the economy, and even such pervasive ideologies as romantic love. The current economic climate provides an open door for considering these kinds of politics of concern if only we have the wit to step through it.

If we add all of these structures of feeling together, we start to get a sense of how the Left apprehends the world differently. Specifically, the Left both assumes and works with an open political horizon, in which the game is never up, things are never fixed, and societies can be changed for the better. Of course, we all know of situations in which this has not happened, but in the end, this forward-looking stance seems to us to be crucial: at the root of leftist styles of thinking is the disclosure of worlds yet to come into existence. This ability to make imaginative leaps is accompanied by a sense of longing for these new worlds. And it is this longing that will sustain momentum, bring different voices and interests into coalition, and, above all, act as a magnet.

If the Left has a new task in front of it, it is to make much more of this process of worlding. Other agencies have already accumulated large stores of practical knowledge about how to produce worlds. The Left has tended to leave this work as a specialist domain to artists, filmmakers, and the like, but it is pivotal in producing a leftist project and demands a coalition of immersive skills through which many can make their place. In other words, we are making the case for a different kind of manifesto that operates not just at the level of cognition but in all the other registers of the sensible, working as a kind of intelligence across the slope of political skills. This is a manifesto in more than words, working with the crafts of art, explicitation, emotion, practice itself, and hesitation, plus a discursive program that has more force as a consequence.

In case all of this seems unworldly, let us point to one example: the

2008 presidential campaign of Barack Obama. What Obama undoubtedly managed to achieve was a genuine sense of hope in quite a large part of the U.S. population who were split by region, class, gender, and lifestyle. He did this not by articulating some extraordinarily detailed agenda, but by presenting a stance to the world and, through it, a sense of how the world might be different. It is this sense that fired the imagination of so many voters, not simple calculation of their own best interest. Writ large, this surely must be what the Left project has to entail? We are not naïve about this. Obama would not have won without the benefit of good political timing, widespread discontent with the status quo, access to airtime, and billions of dollars' worth of resources that funded advertising and organization. But we cannot reduce Obama's campaign to these factors, not least because the billions of dollars came in large part from small donors fired by his vision. What Obama achieved was the concatenation of invention, affect, and organization — the three political arts stressed in this book.

In its best guises, the Left has been a machine for generating new dawns. It seems to us that we need to go back to this vision, not forgetting the lessons of the past, but not allowing ourselves to be weighed down by them, either. This is needed with urgency at a time that capitalism itself has moved enthusiastically into this business. As Paolo Virno (2004) has pointed out, modern capitalism works to fashion worlds that then come into existence through numerous mechanisms, including working directly on affect, but usually for reasons connected simply with profit. This energy can be harnessed in different ways to produce better worlds. The fact of the matter is that the Left must out-compete these imaginary realities or it will find itself out-motivated. None of this means that we should bring to a halt the work of complaint about the effects of capitalism, but it recognizes that a new door has now been opened on motivation — one that the general population must be primed to go through.

epilogue

Is it enough to end a book on leftist renewal without making an explicit case for what makes the Left "left" in terms of its moral compass or objects of attention? What ensures that the case for a world-making politics based on prizing open the political as a zone of engagement will steer inexorably toward an equal and just society? These are important but difficult questions for a book that focuses on the arts of political innovation and maintenance, for no self-evident moral stance or manifesto necessarily springs out of such an endeavor. However, from the historical examples that we have celebrated, from the affective motilities that we have singled out, from the organizational innovations that we have noted and praised, and from the accompanying procedural stances that we have commended, it is possible to synthesize a certain normative stance. It is one of forcing and sustaining a distinctive politics of justice out of the many disorders of the moment.

Historically, the Left has distinguished itself by the consistent tenacity it has shown in combating oppression and exploitation. This stance has fired the socialist, feminist, communist, antiracist, and anticolonial causes. Arguably, the history of the environmental movement has also been one of redressing exploitation and oppression of the planet and its varied forms of life. Harnessed to political economy, the leftist stance against oppression and exploitation has looked to ways in which the material conditions of existence can be changed—for example, through socializing the means of production. But the targets of intervention have changed, something the Left has had to learn painfully from its periods of fixation with the so-called essentials of freedom. The success of the Left has lain in continually adding sites of exploitation and oppression to its portfolio of concerns. It is this focus that most clearly marks the Left from the Right, which has so often looked back to the past for reassurance and has rarely been bothered when the "flow of history" has brought injustice in its train. In contrast, the Left at its best has had a future orientation. It has shown a capacity for inventing invention, always looking out for emerging sites of harm so the road to a better world can be laid out on the ground. It has retained a capacity to be surprised, accepting that the world does not always turn up in the same way and that this variance can be regarded as a good thing. And it has shown an appreciation of heterogeneity, continually taking new communities into its world and seeing them as a source of inspiration rather than as a threat. Leftist hope in a just future thus accepts that the future has its own existence.

One consequence of this open stance is an acceptance that the Left must operate across a vast terrain of concerns. Given the ubiquity and obduracy of contemporary exploitation and oppression,[1] this should come as no surprise, and it is a cause of wonder to us that certain sections of the Left would want to focus on just a few of these sites — for example, those most closely associated with capitalist business, with the state, or with nature. Instead, in seeing the Left as a historical accretion of concern for the world, we do not see any widening of the field of attention as a dilution of focus and effort, just more involvement. With 7 billion people in the world, there are plenty of sites to go around, plenty of ways that many Lefts can flourish. Some might call this pluralism. We would call it a rational response to pain and suffering. And working on different sites does not mean that things never add up. Whether they do or do not, is a matter of making the right connections, sharing structures of feeling, sustaining the gains made. This is why we have chosen to focus on the mastery of certain political arts in this book: it is through them that this accretion of concern can take place.

Much has been written recently about revitalizing the notion of "the common," and we must regard this as a vital task, too. The legacy of neoliberalism has been to produce a world in which the individual curriculum vitae has become a model of citizenship, and yet at the same time, a notion of the common has become even more important to capitalism as a means of sharing knowledge and intellect for gain. Rescuing the notion from this kind of advanced reductionism requires a recasting of how the common as a shared plenitude must itself be a cause of collective concern. If the common — whether in the form of public ownership and functioning services or a plural public sphere and shared public spaces or an acceptance that other actors must be included other than human beings—does not return as a wellspring of possibility for those without means, as well as a limit on greed and cant and over-accumulation, there can be no open and equal society and no push against the ungenerous, unforgiving tenor of our times.

With the help of this kind of repopulation of the environment by principle, the Left can begin to tackle the pressing developments of our time in a heterodox but still concerted way.

Left Materials

One major development of the past few decades has been the spread of the market economy, which has clearly had some positive effects in some locations. In India, Brazil, and China, for example, liberalization has sparked immense entrepreneurialism, new markets, and economic inventiveness and innovation, underpinned by family savings, thrift, hard work, new capital markets, personal sacrifice, science, technology, and education. The result is work, prosperity, opportunity, and advancement for many millions of people previously trapped by state, clientelist, familial, or rudimentary systems of provision and control. But liberalization can and often does remove market controls; push down wages and living standards; displace people from subsistence and subsistence economies; leave many subjects stranded in the indigent misery of the shadow, informal, or spent economy; and increase the gap between the haves and the have-nots.

Indeed, contra many a leftist argument stressing the homogeneity or wholly negative nature of the market economy, it would be possible to argue that what we face at the moment might be called "baroque capitalism"—that is, capitalism with so many different and variegated forms that it can no longer be approached as a collective. What, for example, does the kind of primitive accumulation to be found in Nigeria around oil have to do with the rise of family firms in India, of corporations in China and Russia run by armies or security services, or of firms that cleave to corporate social responsibility and may even, at the limit, question the profit motive itself? Market logic comes in many organizational guises that cannot be reduced to one another and, indeed, demand different political responses. In other words, an effective response to the ills of market society could not consist of any simple return to uniform forms of property rights and regulation. The answers will have to be as baroque as the problem.

This is not to diminish the scale of the problems posed. The intense corporate rivalry and adventurism promoted by poor market regulation have produced giant economic crashes with devastating effects. At the same time, economic imperialism clearly continues, but in many more forms than before. Whether we are talking about the rush of Chinese firms into Africa, the sharing of the spoils of war in the Middle East among U.S. corporations, or the degradation of rainforests as a result of corporations' investing in crops as various as soya or palm oil, it is surely difficult to say that the same problems do not continue but by different means.

A second development is the "financialization" of everything. As more and more assets have become tradable, either directly or indirectly through world financial markets that themselves have increased in scope and scale, market failure has become endemic. Only the most determined proponent of market efficiency can claim that all is for the best in the current international financial system. Lack of control has itself become a controlling feature, with all of the effects that we have seen recently: unbridled financial contagion; proliferation of financial instruments whose net effects are understood by few, if any, actors; and, most recently, financial meltdown. The financial system has dug deeper and deeper into the conduct of everyday life, producing a situation in which many citizens are given responsibility without control. This is more than a regulatory problem. It goes to the heart of what societies are thought to be about and the degree to which orderly conduct is defined as necessary.

Financialization has also made its way into the corporate sphere, producing a demand for permanent restructuring, which may be in the interests of increasing value for shareholders but does little for employees and other stakeholders. The economy of permanent restructuring is a key part of baroque capitalism, typified by armies of consultants, financial advisers and intermediaries, management gurus, and elaborate software packages whose main goal is to continually initiate change. The political challenge is to produce a more orderly financial system that has the welfare of citizens at its heart, not simply opportunities for profit.

An associated development, our third, is rising global inequality. There is considerable evidence that the position of the billions of poor people in the world has worsened relatively and maybe absolutely. Their dire position interacts with a raft of other challenges to produce extreme insecurity and marginality, to the point at which very small changes in climate or market position can have catastrophic consequences. The rawest manifestations of marginality are in the ever expanding slums of the world, along with new forms of abject poverty in a rural world deprived of its means of subsistence. The state of the bottom billions therefore has not only proved intractable but may sometimes have worsened. At the same time, those living in the strata above the absolutely marginalized can still very rapidly find themselves in a difficult situation. Their position is by no means secure, either.

The global capitalist economy as currently constituted provides no cure—indeed, it sails close to exacerbating the problem—and international efforts to alleviate poverty and stimulate growth remain patchy and thin as local energy is sapped by corporatist or corrupt interests. The efforts of millions of households seeking to improve their lot through thrift, hard work, education, and entrepreneurship are daily undermined by a bewildering nexus of forces: an aggressive neoliberalism that makes no room for anything other than market force, local regimes that thrive on want and scarcity, an international elite bent on defining the terms of "development" in the narrowest and most self-interested ways, the cruelties of environmental degradation and climate change, infrastructural collapse and state neglect, warfare and other forms of conflict, and economic insecurity and instability.

A fourth, and perhaps the most threatening, development is global climate change. While the exact contours of the problem may remain obscure, global warming is undoubtedly occurring, and its progress provides a salutary lesson in cosmopolitics in that various collectives of human and nonhuman actors have been triggered whose existence had not been understood and whose characteristics often remain unclear. The work of political recognition, in other words, remains incomplete, but the effects are clear: water shortages, desertification, crop failure, rising sea levels and flooding, species extinction, increases in extreme climatic events, and other cataclysmic developments that threaten the future of human being. There is no shortage of prognostications on climate change. Equally, a raft of policy initiatives have appeared, some market-driven, others technological, and yet others attempting to induce lifestyle change.

But no distinctive politics of climate change has emerged that acknowledges all actors and their power. This is different from the more common observation that this absence is due to disagreements over the appropriate interventions and about who should take responsibility. Acknowledging all actors and their powers means seeing a world in which they can be represented as more than just inconveniences or ciphers, a world in which the world itself can speak back. In this form of environmental politics, the actors in nature — from trees to rivers — may even be able to exercise some rights, including voice (through the placement of sensors of one sort or another that speak when crossed and that address particular assemblies of concern and act as focuses for new collectives). This is a politics — in an "Anthropocene" shaped by humans as the prime geological agent — that must go to the heart of making mankind act as a species dependent on other species and environments for its very survival (Chakrabarty 2009).

A fifth development must also be mentioned: the technological reconfiguration of human life. The nature of being human is being brought into question, and the answer is necessarily political. Thus, human beings may well find their memory expanded, their ability to feel changed, their genetic makeup altered, their environment becoming ever more active, and their bodies worked on according to norms that are simultaneously moral and biological, with tools migrating into the body and the body being distributed through various locative technologies across space and time. Each and every one of these changes requires debate and decision about what it is to be human and how human beings relate to one another and to the world. We can put these changes in a different way: the atmospheres within which human life exists will become more crowded, more variegated, and more ambiguous. A whole politics of what Peter Sloterdijk (2009) calls the human zoo becomes increasingly clearly demarcated day after day.

The standard philosophical question "How do we live?" becomes written into the environment we inhabit and open to explicit decision. However, this will be no promised land. It is already clear that an active political economy of human life is coming into existence, with all of the resonances this term has. There will be unequal access to particular powers and worlds. There will be new forms of exploitation, such as the trade in body parts from South to North. There will be new ways to ignore suffering as all manner of devices become available to keep inconvenient truths at bay. There will be a new regime of justification based on artificially created biological and technological worth that, in turn, will assign different degrees of human worthiness to different populations. What it means to be human is a changing and disputed question with a long history. However, what does seem distinctive about the present is the degree to which human manipulation now holds the potential for replication in ways that hand biological advantage to privileged populations.

Leftist Grounding

No doubt, there are other developments we have omitted — for example, the rise of the surveillance state and the increasing individualization of social life. We have focused on a limited selection of deeply rooted contemporary changes to make a general point: that newness, heterogeneity, and ambiguity necessitate a good measure of experimentation in advance of any programmatic manifesto. The developments are themselves a forcing of the political into new territory, substantive and tactical, demanding new means of survey and assay, new means of making journeys, new means of drawing up boundaries, new ways of capturing political agency and subjectivity. Leftist worlding in these circumstances has to begin with an audit of possible interventions, including marginal ones from which more can be acquired.

If the conservative response to these developments has been to work their energy to the benefit of the rich and the powerful, without much regard for the humans and nonhumans sacrificed or compromised along the way, the counter response has been to rein in these developments' excesses and harms, work them to the benefit of the many, and alter their composition so that a slower, fairer, and more responsible futurity can arise. The kinds of grounded response to the five developments we have outlined are summarized in table 1. They are so diverse, and in many cases so extraordinary, that we often wonder whether the Left underestimates its own power to produce change.

But to reorder the granularity of human being in specific sites is not enough. It remains the case that the corrosive machinations behind these developments persist. The progressive experiments remain fragmented and dispersed, frequently at the margin of organized harm. So the task of bringing them into the center ground of world politics and human am-

TABLE 1. Contemporary Global Developments and Left Experiments

DEVELOPMENTS	EXPERIMENTS
Market capitalism	Fiscal parity, basic wage, employee ownership, cooperatives, social enterprises, not-for-profit foundations, fair/ethical trade, anti-corporatist regulation, ethical consumption, profit sharing, non-monetary exchange, corporate social responsibility, microfinance, low-cost housing, socially useful commodities, workplace democracy, gifting, land borrowing
Financialization	Socially enabling credit and money, ethical pension funds and ethical investment, Islamic finance, non-intermediated payment, social accounting, circuit breakers to slow down transactions, public ownership, risk sharing, financial transparency, limits to pay differentials and dividends, shareholder activism, tax profiling, anti-monopoly
Global inequality	Tobin tax, women's empowerment, alternative trading blocs, open-access patent banks, paid schooling for underage workers, affordable basic provisions, consumer boycotts, antislavery/people-smuggling campaigns, expanded rights agendas, human security measures, rights of displaced peoples, indigenous peoples movements, antiviolence legislation
Climate change	Carbon trading, new forms of ecological identity, reproducible farming, environmental justice for the poor, low-energy technological acceleration, sustainable lifestyles, deliberative environmentalism, planetary responsibility, sustainable cities, environmental audits, alternative energy, protecting the commons (e.g., forests), slow food
Technological reconfiguration of human life	Genetic distributive justice, anti-profiling in insurance and health care, access to new technology for the poor, equal access to human augmentation, intelligent environments available to all, democratic forms of human mapping, treatment against unequal bodily life chances, animal rights and trans-human initiatives, new forms of empathy enabled by technology (e.g., bringing distant humans and nature up close), immersive environments

bition remains. But what does this mean? We do not think it can mean gathering the particularities into a fixed world emancipatory program. There is too much heterogeneity, difference, change, autonomy, variety of interest, and compulsion in the world to permit this, as should have become amply clear from the stance taken in this book.

Art of Resonance

We believe that if the varied examples of democratic practice around the world that we point to in table 1 are to animate and compel, the Left clearly needs to focus on the arts needed to give traction to the impetus behind these initiatives. "Traction" is the right word, so that the gains add up, count, become contagious. For too long, the Left has thought that its main task is to weave all of its resistances into one coherent program or movement. Or it has thought that insurgency alone will suffice, only to be disappointed when activism yields few reforms and gains for those who most need them in their daily lives (as we are learning from the blockades of the "occupy" movements). We think, instead, that the imperative is to find traction, even around the Left's smallest experiments.

Table 2 summarizes how the Left can begin to do this by working through matters of concern (we stick to the examples cited) as material for distinctive arts of world making. Following the selections made in this book, this means taking the politics of invention (disclosure *and* innovation), affect (including contagion), and organization as not just incidental but formative. The illustrations of traction in table 2 offer no comprehensive itinerary, only one that starts to put flesh on the bones of our argument. Our chief concern is that the Left learn to see the problem of resonance and radiation as the challenge of crafting traction and in ways that allow the problems tackled to be reframed, clothed in a language of difference and new hope that the Left can claim as its own.

Take the examples of market capitalism and financialization. If there is one thing that the current financial crash has illustrated, it is that affect is a key moment in how markets function. Even economists are warming to this notion (Akerlof and Shiller 2010). Knowing this makes it possible to open up a new political terrain in which markets are redefined as emotional entities, working not just to rules of exchange but to moments of contagion built around very specific emotions such as anxiety or desire.

TABLE 2. Contemporary Global Developments and Examples of Left Political Arts

DEVELOPMENTS	POLITICAL ARTS	
	Disclosure	Affect
Market capitalism	Markets as not invisible Markets that are regulated and do actually work as social markets	Positive uses of anxiety New forms of justification and worth
Financialization	New legal structures Multiple networks of finance Salaries and bonuses	New means of tracking market sentiments Dissipating greed and instant gratification
Global inequality	Quasi-experience of the harms of inequality	Fairness, building on behavioral dispositions Meeting needs and sharing
Climate change	Experience global warming closely New notions of hazard and risk End-of-world scenarios	Care of place/Earth futurity Mobilizing trauma of ecological meltdown
Technological reconfiguration of human life	Revealing the material composition of the body in new ways (e.g., imaging) Environments where humans and nature coexist	Making the monstrous normal Affinity

Contagion	Organization	Innovation
Build on success of ethical consumerism "Viral" campaigns	Politics of design (active construction of ecologies of worth)	Redefining exchange (e.g., barter, auctions) Social economy/plural economy Social tag to market relations (e.g., showing origins of products)
Filters (e.g., trading moratoriums) Press regulation to stop panics and booms	Global regulatory structures More surveillance of settlement Tracking trading models and practices	New forms of currency New market and regulatory structures
Action against child labor Minimum wage Action against sexual slavery Action against trade in body parts	State welfare Global taxation Human capabilities and empowerment	Social economy New deal Tobin tax Living wage Social services and public goods
Capacity for metamorphosis and mutability New kinds of ecological habitat and ecological living	Public controversies and unfamiliar shapes of organization Making new ecologies fixed and demanding	Individual and subcontracted responsibility (e.g., eco-homes) Local energy companies and distributed energy Making carbon markets work Reworking notions of closeness
Replicating new technology that expands communication, community, and human wellbeing	New forms of sorting/software Techno-welfare extended and protected	Bio-art Prosthetics and technologies for life New forms of parliament

These are emotions that a leftist politics of hope not only deplores but also works with in a positive way to generate new feelings of worth and expectation from markets. We might then begin to see previously unconsidered policy alternatives not just hove into view but also felt by publics as sensible and as important for their lives. The alterity of experiments that today seem marginal will begin to find grip and resonance as a new repertoire of market practices finds its way into the center of calculation and expectation: from very simple measures such as expanding the register of market sentiments to include affects such as ethical conduct or employee satisfaction, to new rules for global competition that legislate against harm in emerging or vulnerable markets. This is how the Left can take credit for altering the terms on which exchange, value, and worth are calculated not only by institutions, but also by citizens and consumers.

Take, next, the issue of global inequality. No one can genuinely defend the differences in life chances that currently exist in the world, but building an affective push in which the populations of rich countries become willing to make sacrifices to mend a broken system is clearly problematic. Interestingly, though, research on the affective foundations of inequality is beginning to show that people can be persuaded to such a cause if the issues are put in the right way. This means disrupting mechanisms of social comparison by inserting new measures of human being and deservingness into the affective calculus (e.g., the right to means of life and the means of association, boundaries of tolerable absolute and relative disparities in wealth). As momentum builds, it might become possible to enshrine some of these desires in actual bureaucracies (e.g., that girls in all parts of the world have access to education, that the drift toward charging the poor for clean water and sanitation is stopped, that labor is fairly rewarded), so that practices of inequality are progressively cut back through a machinery of subject formation in which a high degree of inequality is regarded simply as a moral slur. The Left has to work on the things that produce such a strong affective push that collective conduct will include an instinctive inclination that no bureaucracy needs to police or, equally, can fail to ignore.

We could go on, but we hope that our point has been made. It is possible to start systematically deriving forms of politics and political organization that have often been seen as consequences rather than as causes or have simply been neglected, and it is possible to do this in a way that conforms to leftist tenets. We will conclude with the challenge of reworking human being. What we know is that human beings are malleable and can be culturally and biologically produced. Let us say straight off that we are not heading toward a politics of bio-cultural engineering. But it cannot be denied that all human institutions form human conduct; therefore, there seems to be no reason not to intervene to cultivate different dispositions and personas. After all, education does this all the time. We could see a form of politics arising in which the disclosure of the multiple ways of human being is made more explicit and therefore open to self-fashioning in ways that are often denied currently. This would involve a combination of different arts and sciences that could refashion both body and environment to make ethical living and regard for others on the planet a strongly felt motivation.

One might think of revealing the material composition of the body in new ways, producing environments in which the connection between people, nature, and technology is made much more explicit, devising new technologies that simulate conscience (e.g., "ethical pop-ups" on the Internet warning against egregious statements), and imagining new forms of sorting that produce unexpected confluences, closeness, and coalitions. In this way, we might find a steady drift taking place toward a more accommodating human being who builds houses that include, not exclude. After all, as Jane Bennett (2009, 4) notes, "There can be no greening of the economy, no redistribution of wealth, no enforcement or extension of rights, unless there are present human disposition, moods, and cultural ensembles hospitable to these effects."

It is time to conclude. The Left needs to reclaim its place as the vanguard of democratic change, the force that wants a freedom that all people can enjoy—as a right to autonomy, self-fulfillment, meaningful and rewarding employment, and the space and time to enjoy the flourishing of others both near and far. In the process, new structures of feeling—solidarity; empathy; mutuality; care for the world; desire to leave the earth untrammeled; visceral revulsion at division, discord, and harm—will have begun to force the compulsions and cruelties we too often observe on the sidelines. In the process, the claims of gender, racial, class, and territorial equality will become normalized. In the process, the city on the hill that the Left has always craved will come into view again, carried forward by the momentum of desire and by imaginative anticipation and by gradually instituting gain. This is the program that the Left needs to recover, not as what Karl Marx (1990, 99) called "recipes for the cook-shops of the future," not as a manifesto that can be ticked off point by point or as a battle with the Right on its terms and its territory. Is this not what pragmatist idealists such as Friedrich Engels, Karl Kautsky, Emmeline Pankhurst, and Ernst Wigforss wanted?

We hope, then, that we have made one point consistently throughout this book, a point that will stay with readers. We believe that there is a politics of the imagination, understood as new ways of yearning for and disclosing the world that can be systematically worked on to bring into being worlds in which some of the standard tenets of the Left can be brought to life. We can hold our hands out to the messy, perplexing future, and we can do it confidently. But we are also sure that a politics of imagination, by definition, has to be left open. We cannot, and we should not, prescribe every answer, legislate every action, lock down every idea. Orientations toward what the Left desires — practical, affective, imaginative, organizational, rhetorical — can only be just that: orientations, improvised and set to work in the mangle of practices of politics that have opened up to unthought-of possibilities that now demand to be thought. False confidence? No. Confidence that human beings can invent formations in which dreams of new worlds can come into existence and thrive? Yes, absolutely.

notes

Prologue

1. Modes of argumentation need to change, too. The Left has a long history of turning to modes of argument whose importance is asserted through the classic idealist ruse of explaining away anything that might complicate its judgments—that is, "The fountainhead will produce whatever we may need" (Stengers 2011b, 379).

CHAPTER ONE
The Grounds of Politics

1. In the past, the Left has too often taken emancipation to mean a world free of constraints. In fact, emancipation has nearly always produced new constraints, which are a part of the political equation.

2. The so-called aestheticization of the political is often taken to be the most problematic and contentious contribution of continental philosophy. What does it mean? How exactly does it operate? And how might it become the basis of a practical politics? Too often it is seen as a defeatist strategy. We aim to show that it is not. Most particularly, the general political stance that arises from the aestheticization of the political is an attack on passivity and the political agenda that arises from that agenda, including how ignoble feelings such as envy and paranoia damp down political engagement, how non-cathartic feelings can be just as important as the cathartic releases that so often seem to have been valued in the Western demos, and how resigned or pessimistic understandings act as their own results, as well as the general construction of a poetics of sympathy that is not the usual sentimental genre.

3. We are not, in other words, advocating active passivity or passive activity, as seems to have become popular among some intellectuals, such as Žižek.

4. So, for example, in a mediatized age like ours, the Left has to intervene imaginatively in the politics of public culture. This means not only recognizing

the power of the many sites in which public culture and opinion is formed—blogs, Twitter, etc.—but also being in tune with the ideas and expectations that circulate in these sites of public formation. This is no simple matter of imagining counter-publics to those publics deemed exclusionary or undemocratic; it is, rather, a complex matter of tuning into the concerns of people as they rise and fall to produce a world in which a leftist alternative is permanently available. This means, for example, responding sensitively and creatively to pro-life concerns, animal testing, the clamor for clampdowns on immigration, and even the perpetual construction of notoriety. It is the occupancy of the space that is important, as is direct engagement with the concerns that circulate within that space. The challenge now is to integrate all these spatial politics into something that is more than the sum of the parts. We do not think that a single entity—an umbrella politics—is either desirable or necessary. However, if there is one thing the Left needs to do, it is to build momentum, and this requires more than just variegated action. Such momentum must come from openness to the possibility of cross-ventilation between the various spaces of the political with a degree of careful engineering so that the conversations and alliances can be sustained. That task requires organization—perhaps bureaucracy, perhaps common standards, perhaps media that traverse a different domain. In other words, an active politics of joining-up is required. Another way forward is to find common cause among the concerns and interests circulating in different political arenas and spaces. In this book, it is not universalist utopias that we have in mind but, rather, a commons born out of shared feelings about and toward the world. In other words, principles must be laced with affect, and mutable concerns must be bound into a common ethical framework that consists of value orientations such as fairness, care for the world, and the value of pluralism itself.

CHAPTER TWO
Leftist Beginnings

1. The great ideological disputes of the SPD during this period are well known within leftist historiography. This includes Eduard Bernstein's rebuttal of scientific Marxism on the grounds that capitalism was unlikely to collapse under its own weight, having developed a structure capable of self-regulation, a supportive civic infrastructure, and rising prosperity for the masses. Bernstein's proposal for a gradualist and reformist approach was thrown out by the leadership, which was celebrated internationally for its doctrinaire attachment to a socialism born out of the ashes of capitalist contradiction and collapse. It is also well known, however, that in practice the SPD was never that far from Bernstein's vision, not only because leaders such as Kaustky believed that reformist victories and compromises would neither delay nor damage the social revolution

(Przeworski 1980), but also because the party knew that its success depended on combining doctrinaire commitment with tangible pragmatic reforms. Indeed, it was precisely this combination that drew Rosa Luxemburg's fierce attack in 1910 in the name of a revolutionary socialism freed from reformist compromise.

2. Although there were more than one hundred unions in Sweden in 1885, the majority of them covered the traditional crafts. Only about a dozen represented different categories of skilled workers. Craft loyalty and organization remained supreme, with factory workers and general laborers largely peripheral to the labor movement.

3. The woodworkers' and metalworkers' unions were two pioneering examples of the SDAP's encouragement of "open" organizations in which active local committees attempted to represent both skilled and unskilled workers across linked sectors.

4. The SDAP pursued a moderate agenda to maintain an alliance with nonsocialist trade unions and with liberals in Parliament and to secure a footing across and beyond its fragmented working-class base. It had little choice but to develop a politics of diplomacy at odds with Marxist doctrine. For example, the party's first congress in 1891 voted to support the liberals in the campaign for universal suffrage; its program in 1887 justified social reforms such as the eight-hour workday and the abolition of child labor as steps "by degree" toward socialism; and in 1904, Swedish representatives at the International Socialist Congress in Amsterdam abstained from Kautsky's victorious proposal opposing collaboration with bourgeois parties in government (Tomasson 1969).

5. It was felt that such checks and balances would suffice to eliminate capitalist wastefulness, exploitation, and inequality without necessitating the abolition of private ownership and wage labor.

6. For an account of how cars, steamships, and banners helped to redefine the woman as modern, mobile, and resourceful, see, e.g., Cresswell 2006.

7. According to Julie Greene (1998, 37), between the spring of 1893 and the end of the year alone, some 15,000 businesses and 400 banks had declared bankruptcy.

8. They include the revolutionary Socialist Labor Party, the Industrial Workers of the World union, and the pro-election Socialist Party. While these movements can claim some success, for example, in representing the weakest sections of American society or workers in certain industries (Dubofsky 1969; Weinstein 1975), they failed to generate mass interest in a socialist America. Mark Kann (1982) explains this as the inability of the radicals to grasp the tacit pact of co-dependence between the masses and the elites in American constitutionalism, while Aileen Kraditor (1981) argues that the embedded strength of family, neighborhood, and club ties in American civic culture prevented workers from becoming interested in the radical persuasion. Werner Sombart's

view in 1906 was that American workers were more prosperous and lived better than their European counterparts, had a stronger sense of belonging to a more egalitarian society protected by the American constitution, and could dream of escape into the vast rural hinterland, cajoled by the lure of various homestead settlement schemes (see Sombart 1976). His account was rebutted by later socialists who argued that the material conditions of workers and the poor were far worse than he had portrayed them; that leftist politics in the hands of the unions and major political parties worked for a labor aristocracy at the expense of women, blacks, minorities, and rural populations; and that the ideology of the American dream obscured the true long-term interests of the working class (Laslett and Lipset 1974). In turn, the non-socialist left—progressives, liberals, and democrats of different hues—argues that it was the refusal of American socialists to relinquish sectarian purity in face of an American public motivated by very different collective ideals that prevented socialism from gaining mass appeal in America (Kraditor 1981; Rorty 1998; Rossiter 1960).

9. Croly (1963 [1909], 14, 22) argued that "American confidence in individual freedom has resulted in a morally and socially undesirable distribution of wealth," tied to "an economic system which starves and mutilates the great majority of the population, and under such conditions, its religion becomes a spiritual drug, administered for the purpose of subduing the popular discontent and relieving the popular misery."

10. However, the movement never fully pursued the cause of black emancipation and racial equality.

CHAPTER THREE
Reinventing the Political

1. Not least because of the contemporary "decentering of the human by its imbrication in technical, medical, informatic and economic networks" (Wolfe 2009, xv).

2. Some care needs to be taken with this statement. For example, William James has often been criticized for lacking a political theory, but it is more accurate to say that he lacked a normative political theory, a stance that was at odds with the dominant liberalism of his day and that many commentators on the left still find difficult to comprehend (Ferguson 2007).

3. But this does not imply relativism. Rather, it is a condition that requires concerted acts of diplomacy.

4. We will concentrate on Whitehead, but it is important to understand his links to this philosophical bloodline—most notably, to naturalism, typified by Spinoza's outline of a world in which all kinds of forces could be understood

as natural vectors susceptible to a geometrical analysis, and to empiricism—as well as the disagreements they held. In particular, Whitehead rejected Spinoza's monism and notion of the *conatus* in favour of William James's pluralism and sense of continual process (or what James calls creativity).

5. Whitehead is intent on producing a metaphysics that is non-anthropomorphic and non-anthropocentric, in which entities on different scales and different levels of reflexivity are all treated in the same manner. As Steven Shaviro (2009, 23) puts it, for Whitehead a "flat" ontological principle holds—namely, that "actual entities are the only reasons" (Whitehead 1978, 24). "The search for a reason is always the search for an actual fact which is the vehicle for that reason" (Whitehead 1978, 40), for "there is nothing which floats into the world from nowhere. Everything in the actual world is referable to some actual entity" (Whitehead 1978, 244).

6. Thus, Whitehead gives consciousness no special privileges. This is not to say that sentience is an illusion. Rather, it is a matter of degree (Shaviro 2009).

7. Not coincidentally, about one-third of the text of these wall newspapers seems to have been involved with anti-Jewish statements.

8. We should add that although this account strikes us as right in its essentials, it has some problems. In trying to describe a plane, Lazzarato, like others, tends to gloss over the way in which capitalism is coming to understand this plane by making it visible and thereby making it the subject of spatial and temporal variation. Again—too dramatically, perhaps—Lazzarato, like Virno and Antonio Negri, insists that the plane of machinic enslavement is immeasurable. But this is not the case. It might be more accurate to say that it has been immeasurable but that it is becoming more measurable over time. With the advent of a world encased in numbers—in which everything counts and is counted, in which quantification has become qualculation (Thrift 2007), in which many insights are numerical, even by proxy—it is no surprise that the plane of the pre-personal is increasingly metered. No doubt, many of the measurements are dubious, but their very existence points to a project that is ongoing and that will allow affect and other such qualities to be technologized.

9. But note here that in talking of large and small, we are not making an easy correlation between size and geographical extent. A "large" entity might be relatively nebulous. Think of many international political organizations that can function only because of multiple alliances. Equally an entity can be "small" and have remarkable effects: think of the contraceptive pill or the credit card. Both of these objects have been extruded from enormous and seemingly shadowy infrastructures; their "footprint" is correspondingly enormous.

10. This distinction can be traced back to Aristotle.

11. This may be why so many authors have turned to forms of materialism that

add in such qualities. For example, the Lucretian idea of the clinamen or swerve has become popular (see Bennett and Entman 2001).

12. In using the term "concerted agency," we are making it clear that there is no class of agents that functions as an island. All gain their force from alliances with others. At the same time, rather like Harman (2009), we are also trying to make it clear that we are wary of Latour's apparent insistence that different objects cannot therefore have different capacities. They surely can.

13. As Jacques Derrida (2008) pointed out, the category is self-evidently absurd, putting all manner of diverse species into a univocal class.

14. Thereby also indirectly pointing out how important insects have been in human history (Parikka 2010; Raffles 2010).

15. There are many other examples—for example, tobacco, a substance with which all manner of politics is associated.

16. Sloterdijk models his view of spatiality on the maternal relation borrowed from Julia Kristeva, which is both an analytic moment and a stance to the world, although many other symbiotic models are no doubt equally possible.

17. This is, of course, a key area of current debate about human history. When and how did the oral arrive, and was it as significant as has so often been assumed (see Smail 2008)?

18. Nigel Thrift's (2011) work on the current psychophysical regime of capitalism argues something similar.

CHAPTER FOUR
Contemporary Leftist Thought

1. The challenges have put many old certitudes to the test, including ideas of universal community, solidarity, and well-being; notions of progress and liberation linked to grand narratives and schemes; certainty about capitalist collapse and socialist transition; faith in the purity and public resonance of the politics of the oppressed; and clarity about the subjects and objects of political cause.

2. The coverage of the Left is not intended to be comprehensive or multifaceted. More reviews of this kind are beginning to appear (for an insightful critical account, see, e.g., Therborn 2007). In turn, our interest in focusing on clearly discernible leftist positions inevitably runs the risk of over-categorizing or mis-categorizing diversity of opinion held by individual thinkers or movements.

CHAPTER FIVE
Organizing Politics

1. Vocation as the gradual accumulation of knowledge and skills and the ever-stronger conviction that this path was the right one to take in one's life.

2. The popularity of these kinds of accounts by French authors may, of course, be specific to the French case, where *l'état* occupies a singular position.

3. Some have argued that a disconnection has occurred within radical feminism that has prevented it from passing its traditions along, the result of the growth of discourses of empowerment that have been offered as substitutes (McRobbie 2009).

4. At this time, a number of European states brought in legislation restricting acceptable names.

5. All that said, there have been societies in which identification has become close to a mania. Think of state socialist countries such as the former Soviet Union. There, documents took on a life of their own. The "documented self" came to acquire immense meaning. In particular, the proliferation of identification documents meant that it was difficult to take on full personhood without papers. It is possible to go further. Documents affected and even constituted the geographical movement of people across the vast post-Soviet terrain. Documents left a vast legacy of territorial residence that is still being worked out to this day.

6. Subsequent laws introduced in 1794 and 1803 ruled that it was prohibited to assume any name other than one's own — that is, any name other than the one recorded at birth.

7. Some commentators have argued that Gustave Le Bon's "era of crowds" is coming to an end, but given the events of the Arab Spring and many similar effusions, which suggest that the defining collectivities of the new millennium often appear to be online masses, this may well prove to be a premature judgment (Schnapp and Tiews 2006).

CHAPTER SIX
Eurocracy and Its Publics

1. Our aim is not to idealize the EU or its bureaucratic and political machinery. In many of the EU's dealings and entities, the problems of opacity, remoteness, unaccountability, elitism, and unfairness or inequality remain. The EU is not even remotely the perfect political formation. Instead, our aim is to draw on particular examples of progressive policy negotiation and outcome that illustrate our arguments about the powers of organization.

2. Jeremy Rifkin (2004, 368, 385) sees Europe as a "city upon the hill," the "beacon of light in a troubled world" rapidly "going dark" under the shadow of a U.S.-led "ethics of cold evil" under George Bush, marked by kneejerk condemnation of distant wrongs and contempt for the connections that bind. Rifkin's invocation forgets Europe's unreconciled diversities; its troubled history of war, violence, and empire; and its tarnished reputation among peoples of the

postcolonial world (Amin 2004, 2012; Gilbert 2004). Europe is not immune to the wind of self-interest and advancement, cultural and ethnic intolerance, and disengagement from a troubled globe. It is no new city on the hill, perched there because of its superior cultural traditions.

3. This section is based largely on the detailed account of the negotiations involved in passing the WFD in Kaika and Page 2003a, 2003b.

4. For a similar reading of the politics and counterpolitics of major scientific controversies in France, see Callon et al. 2009.

5. For a similar treatment of phenomenological motifs, see Hansen and Kozel 2007.

CHAPTER SEVEN
Affective Politics

1. Including, first, a lack of the resources to be able to see beyond bias and censorship; second, a lack of contact and opportunity; third, a shortage of time and attention; and fourth, a simple inability to understand the issues.

2. "Daisy" aired only once, to much criticism, but was still decisive.

3. Indeed, there are now even statistical panics, brought about by the teeming information that we have to negotiate as part of everyday life (Igo 2007).

4. The connection between cartography and the exercise of political power dates from the fifteenth century and sixteenth century in Europe (Buisseret 1992), when ruling elites first turned with some regularity to mapping as a means of managing state affairs (Akerman 2009). In particular, maps became a means of asserting control over far-flung lands. For example, bureaucratically organized topographic mapping played an important practical and symbolic part in the extension of European power over newly established colonies and dependencies. The imperial impulse also clearly hastened the adoption of mapping as a bureaucratic tool in the homelands. Then, more generally, maps sank into the popular imagination, as literary and journalistic mapping contributed to the formation of an imaginative impulse at home, as a means of framing far-flung lands and their legitimation as a part of the imperial domain, and to how the colonized thought about themselves. Later, colonized peoples developed their own cartographic traditions that drew on a response to imperialism and indigenous means of representing space (Ramaswamy 2004). Finally, maps stabilized states. By providing solid images of what had once been volatile spaces with indistinct geographic and cultural frontiers, maps produced well-defined spaces in which bureaucracies could more easily hold sway.

Epilogue

1. Traditional and unambiguous modes such as slavery, forced and bonded labor, child labor, and hyper-exploitation of labor jostle with new modes such as the organ trade, data invasion and surveillance, and widespread limits to movement. Many other modes can be mentioned, including state-sponsored violence, patriarchal and racial violence, wanton acts of terror, workplace depradations, and the many ways in which so much of the world's population continues to go without. The violence toward nature also continues unabated, up to and including the extermination of whole ecosystems. And the exact meaning of all manner of sites is contested — for example, genetic modification of humans and nature, the nature of work in the knowledge economy, and the pleasures and pains of modern consumption.

references

Agamben, Giorgio. 2005. *State of Exception*. Chicago: University of Chicago Press.

Agrawal, Arun. 2005. *Environmentality: Technologies of Government and the Making of Subjects*. Durham: Duke University Press.

Ahmed, Sara. 2010. *The Promise of Happiness*. Durham: Duke University Press.

Akerlof, George A., and Robert J. Shiller. 2010. *Animal Spirits: How Human Psychology Drives the Economy, and Why It Matters for Global Capitalism*. Princeton: Princeton University Press.

Akerman, James R. 2007. "Finding Our Way." *Maps: Finding Our Place in the World*, ed. James R. Akerman and Robert W. Karrow Jr., 19–64. Chicago: University of Chicago Press.

———, ed. 2009. *The Imperial Map: Cartography and the Mastery of Empire*. Chicago: University of Chicago Press.

Alliez, Éric, and Andrew Goffey, eds. 2011. *The Guattari Effect*. London: Continuum.

Althusser, Louis. 2006. *Philosophy of the Encounter: Later Writings, 1978–87*. London: Verso.

Amin, Ash. 2002. "Spatialities of Globalisation." *Environment and Planning A* 34, no. 3, 385–99.

———. 2004. "Multi-Ethnicity and the Idea of Europe." *Theory, Culture, and Society* 21, no. 2, 1–24.

———. 2012. *Land of Strangers*. Cambridge: Polity.

Anderson, Perry. 2009. *The New Old World*. London: Verso.

Archer, Margaret. 2007. *Making Our Way Through the World*. Cambridge: Cambridge University Press.

Arrighi, Giovanni. 2003. "The Social and Political Economy of Global Turbulence." *New Left Review* 20, 5–71.

Azmanova, Albena. 2011. "After the Left–Right (Dis)continuum: Globalization and the Remaking of Europe's Ideological Geography." *International Political Sociology* 5, 384–407.

Bachman, David M. 1991. *Bureaucracy, Economy, and Leadership in China: The Institutional Origins of the Great Leap Forward*. Cambridge: Cambridge University Press.

Badiou, Alain. 2001. *Ethics: An Essay on the Understanding of Evil*. New York: Verso.

———. 2005. *Metapolitics*. New York: Verso.

———. 2009. *Logics of Worlds: Being and Event*. London: Continuum.

Barrows, Susanne. 1981. *Distorting Mirrors: Visions of the Crowd in late Nineteenth-Century France*. New Haven: Yale University Press.

Barry, Andrew. 2001. *Political Machines: Governing a Technological Society*. London: Continuum.

Barry, Andrew, and Nigel Thrift, eds. 2007. *Gabriel Tarde: Special Issue of Economy and Society*. London: Routledge.

Barry, Brian. 2001. *Culture and Equality: An Egalitarian Critique of Multiculturalism*. Cambridge: Polity.

Bartolini, Stefano. 2000. *The Political Mobilization of the European Left, 1860–1980: The Class Cleavage*. Cambridge: Cambridge University Press.

Bauman, Zygmunt. 2003. "Utopia with No Topos." *History of the Human Sciences* 16, no. 1, 11–25.

Beck, Ulrich. 2005. *Power in the Global Age*. Cambridge: Polity.

Beirne, Piers. 1987. "Between Classicism and Positivism: Crime and Penality in the Writings of Gabriel Tarde." *Criminology* 25(4), 785–820.

Benhabib, Seyla. 2004. *The Rights of Others: Aliens, Residents, and Citizens*. Cambridge: Cambridge University Press.

Bennett, Jane. 2009. *Vibrant Matter: A Political Ecology of Things*. Durham: Duke University Press.

Bennett, W. Lance, and Robert M. Entman. 2001. *Mediated Politics: Communication in the Future of Democracy*. Cambridge: Cambridge University Press.

Berger, Stefan. 1995. "Germany." *The Force of Labour: The Western European Labour Movement and the Working Class in the Twentieth Century*, ed. Stefan Berger and David Broughton, 71–106. Oxford: Berg.

Berlant, Lauren G. 2008. *The Female Complaint: The Unfinished Business of Sentimentality in American Culture*. Durham: Duke University Press.

———. 2011. *Cruel Optimism*. Durham: Duke University Press.

Berlin, Isaiah. 1979. *Selected Writings: Against the Current*. London: Hogarth Press.

Bérubé, Michael. 2009. *The Left at War*. New York: New York University Press.

Bieling, Hans-Jürgen. 2006. "EMU, Financial Integration, and Global Economic Governance." *Review of International Political Economy* 13, no. 3, 420–48.

Boltanski, Luc. 2002. "The Left after May 1968 and the Longing for Total Revolution." *Thesis Eleven* 69, no. 1, 1–20.

Brader, Ted. 2006. *Campaigning for Hearts and Minds: How Emotional Appeals in Political Ads Work*. Chicago: University of Chicago Press.

Braidotti, Rosi. 2006. *Transpositions: On Nomadic Ethics*. Cambridge: Polity.

Brown, Wendy. 2006. *Regulating Aversion: Tolerance in the Age of Identity and Empire*. Princeton: Princeton University Press.

Bryant, Levi, Nick Srnicelk, and Graham Harman, eds. 2011. *The Speculative Turn: Continental Materialism and Realism*. Melbourne: Re.Press.

Buisseret, David. 1992. *Monarchs, Ministers, and Maps: The Emergence of Cartography as a Tool of Government in Early Modern Europe*. Chicago: University of Chicago Press.

Bull, Malcolm. 2006. "States of Failure." *New Left Review* 40, 5–25.

Butler, Judith. 2005. *Giving an Account of Oneself*. New York: Fordham University Press.

Caine, Barbara. 1997. *English Feminism, 1780–1980*. Oxford: Oxford University Press.

Callon, Michael. 2004. "Europe Wrestling with Technology." *Economy and Society* 33, 121–34.

Callon, Michael, Pierre Lascoumes, and Yannick Barthe. 2009. *Acting in an Uncertain World: An Essay on Technical Democracy*. Cambridge: MIT Press.

Campbell, David, and Michael J. Shapiro. 1999. *Moral Spaces: Rethinking Ethics and World Politics*. Minneapolis: University of Minnesota Press.

Carruthers, Mary. 1998. *The Craft of Thought: Meditation, Rhetoric, and the Making of Images, 400–1200*. Cambridge: Cambridge University Press.

Castells, Manuel. 2009. *Communication Power*. Oxford: Oxford University Press.

Castro, José E., and Léo Heller. 2009. *Water and Sanitation Services: Public Policy and Management*. London: Earthscan.

Castronova, Edward. 2007. *Synthetic Worlds: The Business and Culture of Online Games*. Chicago: University of Chicago Press.

Caute, David. 1966. *The Left in Europe since 1789*. London: World University Library.

Chakrabarty, Dipesh. 2002. *Habitations of Modernity: Essays in the Wake of Subaltern Studies*. Chicago: University of Chicago Press.

———. 2009. "The Climate of History: Four Theses." *Critical Inquiry* 35, 197–222.

Chalcraft, John T. 2005. "Pluralizing Capital, Challenging Eurocentrism: Toward Post-Marxist Historiography." *Radical History Review*, no. 91, 13–39.

Chandler, Alfred D. 1977. *The Visible Hand: The Managerial Revolution in American Business*. Cambridge: Harvard University Press.

Chatterjee, Partha. 2004. *The Politics of the Governed: Reflections on Popular Politics in Most of the World*. New York: Columbia University Press.

Clunas, Craig. 2007. *Empire of Great Brightness: Visual and Material Cultures of Ming China, 1368–1644*. London: Reaktion.

Connolly, William E. 2005. *Pluralism*. Durham: Duke University Press.

———. 2008. *Capitalism and Christianity, American Style*. Durham: Duke University Press.

Cresswell, Tim. 2006. *On the Move: Mobility in the Modern Western World*. London: Routledge.

Croly, Herbert D. 1963 (1909). *The Promise of American Life*. New Haven: Archon.

Crouch, Colin. 2004. *Post-Democracy*. Cambridge: Polity.

———. 2011. *The Strange Non-Death of Neo-liberalism*. Cambridge: Polity.

Dahl, Robert A. 2006. *On Political Equality*. New Haven: Yale University Press.

Daston, Lorraine J., and Peter Galison. 2007. *Objectivity*. Cambridge: Zone.

Dawley, Alan. 2003. *Changing the World: American Progressives in War and Revolution*. Princeton: Princeton University Press.

Deardorff, Alan V., and Robert M. Stern. 2002. "What You Should Know about Globalization and the World Trade Organization." *Review of International Economics* 10, no. 3, 404–23.

DeLanda, Manuel. 2006. *A New Philosophy of Society: Assemblage Theory and Social Complexity*. London: Continuum.

Delanty, Gerard, and Chris Rumford. 2005. *Rethinking Europe: Social Theory and the Implications of Europeanization*. London: Routledge.

Deleuze, Gilles, and Félix Guattari. 1994. *What Is Philosophy?* London: Verso.

Delli Carpini, Michael X., Leonie Huddy, and Robert Y. Shapiro. 2002. *Political Decision-Making, Deliberation and Participation*. Greenwich, Conn.: JAI.

Derrida, Jacques. 2000. *Of Hospitality*. Stanford: Stanford University Press.

———. 2008. *The Animal That Therefore I Am*. New York: Fordham University Press.

Dewey, John. 1954. *The Public and Its Problems*. Athens, Ohio: Swallow.

Diken, Bülent, and Carsten B. Laustsen. 2005. *The Culture of Exception: Sociology Facing the Camp*. London: Routledge.

Disch, Lisa. 2008. "Representation as 'Spokespersonship': Bruno Latour's Political Theory." *Parallax* 14, no. 3, 88–100.

Dubofsky, Melvyn. 1969. *We Shall Be All: A History of the Industrial Workers of the World*. Chicago: Quadrangle.

Du Gay, Paul. ed. 2005. *The Values of Bureaucracy*. Oxford: Oxford University Press.

———. 2008. "Max Weber and the Moral Economy of Office." *Journal of Cultural Economy* 1, no. 2, 129–44.

Dunning, John H. 2007. "Worlds of Capitalism: Institutions, Governance, and Economic Change in the Era of Globalization." *Economica* 74, no. 294, 374–75.

Eliasoph, Nina. 1998. *Avoiding Politics: How Americans Produce Apathy in Everyday Life*. Cambridge: Cambridge University Press.

Esposito, Roberto. 2008. *Bíos: Biopolitics and Philosophy*. Minneapolis: University of Minnesota Press.

Farmer, Kenneth C. 1992. *The Soviet Administrative Elite*. Westport, Conn.: Praeger.

Ferguson, Kennan. 2007. *William James: Politics in the Pluriverse*. Lanham, Md.: Rowman and Littlefield.

Foucault, Michel. 2007. *Security, Territory, Population. Lectures at the College de France, 1977–1978*. Basingstoke: Palgrave Macmillan.

———. 2008. *The Birth of Biopolitics: Lectures at the Collège de France, 1978–1979*. Basingstoke: Palgrave Macmillan.

Fraser, Nancy, and Axel Honneth. 2003. *Redistribution or Recognition?: A Political-Philosophical Exchange*. London: Verso.

Fulcher, James. 1991. *Labour Movements, Employers, and the State: Conflict and Co-operation in Britain and Sweden*. Oxford: Oxford University Press.

Fuller, Matthew, ed. 2008. *Software Studies: A Lexicon*. Cambridge: MIT Press.

Gallop, Jane. 2006. "Introduction: Envy." *Women's Studies Quarterly* 34, nos. 3–4, 12–21.

George, Susan. 2004. *Another World Is Possible if—*. London: Verso.

Geuss, Raymond. 2008. *Philosophy and Real Politics*. Princeton: Princeton University Press.

Gibson-Graham, J. K. 2006. *A Postcapitalist Politics*. Minneapolis: University of Minnesota Press.

Gilbert, Mark. 2004. "Europe: Paradise Found?" *World Policy Journal* 21, no. 4, 8–12.

Gillingham, John. 2006. *Design for a New Europe*. Cambridge: Cambridge University Press.

Gilly, Adolfo. 2010. "Interview: What Exists Cannot Be True." *New Left Review* 64, 29–45.

Gilmore, James H., and B. Joseph Pine. 2007. *Authenticity: What Consumers Really Want*. Cambridge: Harvard University Press.

Gilroy, Paul. 2004. *After Empire: Melancholia or Convivial Culture?* London: Routledge.

Glyn, Andrew. 2005. "Imbalances of the Global Economy." *New Left Review* 34, 5–37.

Goffey, Andrew. 2011. "Introduction: In the Witch's Broomstick." *Capitalist*

Sorcery: Breaking the Spell, ed. Pierre Pignarre and Isabelle Stengers, i–xxlv. Basingstoke: Macmillan.

Goldfarb, Jeffrey C. 2006. *The Politics of Small Things: The Power of the Powerless in Dark Times*. Chicago: University of Chicago Press.

Gordon, Scott P. 2002. *The Power of the Passive Self in English Literature, 1640–1770*. Cambridge: Cambridge University Press.

Gratton, Lynda. 2011. *The Shift: The Future of Work Is Already Here*. London: HarperCollins.

Green, Sarah, Penny Harvey, and Hannah Knox. 2005. "Scales of Place and Networks: An Ethnography of the Imperative to Connect through Information and Communications Technologies." *Current Anthropology* 46, no. 5, 805–26.

Greene, Julie. 1998. *Pure and Simple Politics: The American Federation of Labor and Political Activism, 1881–1917*. Cambridge: Cambridge University Press.

Groebner, Valentin. 2007. *Who Are You? Identification, Deception, and Surveillance in Early Modern Europe*. New York: Zone.

Gross, Daniel M. 2006. *The Secret History of Emotion: From Aristotle's Rhetoric to Modern Brain Science*. Chicago: University of Chicago Press.

Grossberg, Lawrence. 2009. "The Conversation of Cultural Studies." *Cultural Studies* 23, 177–82.

Guerrina, Roberta. 2002. *Europe: History, Ideas and Ideologies*. Oxford: Oxford University Press.

Hansen, Lone K., and Susan Kozel. 2007. "Embodied Imagination: A Hybrid Method of Designing for Intimacy." *Digital Creativity* 18, no. 4, 207–20.

Haraway, Donna Jeanne. 2008. *When Species Meet*. Minneapolis: University of Minnesota Press.

Harding, James. 2008. *Alpha Dogs: The Americans Who Turned Political Spin into a Global Business*. New York: Farrar, Straus, and Giroux.

Hardt, Michael, and Antonio Negri. 2001. *Empire*. Cambridge: Harvard University Press.

———. 2005. *Multitude: War and Democracy in the Age of Empire*. London: Penguin.

Harman, Graham. 2005. *Guerrilla Metaphysics: Phenomenology and the Carpentry of Things*. Chicago: Open Court.

———. 2009. *Prince of Networks: Bruno Latour and Metaphysics*. Melbourne: Re.press.

Harvey, David. 2003. *The New Imperialism*. New York: Oxford University Press.

———. 2005. *A Brief History of Neoliberalism*. New York: Oxford University Press.

Hauser, Marc D. 2006. *Moral Minds: How Nature Designed Our Universal Sense of Right and Wrong*. New York: Ecco Press.

Heise, Ursula K. 2008. *Sense of Place and Sense of Planet: The Environmental Imagination of the Global*. Oxford: Oxford University Press.

Held, David. 1999. *Global Transformations: Politics, Economics and Culture*. Stanford: Stanford University Press.

Herf, Jeffrey. 2006. *The Jewish Enemy: Nazi Propaganda during World War II and the Holocaust*. Cambridge: Harvard University Press.

Herzfeld, Michael. 2005. *Cultural Intimacy: Social Poetics in the Nation-State*, 2d ed. New York: Routledge.

Hird, Myra J. 2009. *The Origins of Sociable Life: Evolution after Science Studies*. London: Palgrave Macmillan.

Hirst, Paul Q., and Grahame Thompson. 2002. "The Future of Globalization." *Cooperation and Conflict* 37, no. 3, 247–65.

Hofstadter, Richard. 2008. *The Paranoid Style in American Politics*. New York: Vintage.

Hrdy, Sarah Blaffer. 2009. *Mothers and Others: The Evolutionary Origins of Mutual Understanding*. Cambridge: Harvard University Press.

Humphrey, Caroline. 2008. "The 'Creative Bureaucrat': Conflicts in the Production of Soviet Communist Party Discourse." *Inner Asia* 10, no. 1, 5–35.

Hurd, Madeleine. 1996. "Education, Morality, and the Politics of Class in Hamburg and Stockholm, 1870–1914. *Journal of Contemporary History* 31, no. 4, 619–50.

Hutton, Will. 2003. *The World We're In*. Preston: Abacus.

Igo, Sarah E. 2007. *The Averaged American: Surveys, Citizens, and the Making of a Mass Public*. Cambridge: Harvard University Press.

Ihde, Don. 2008. "Introduction: Postphenomenological Research." *Human Studies* 31, no. 1, 1–9.

International Labour Organisation (ILO). 2009. *The Financial and Economic Crisis: A Decent Work Response*. Geneva: International Labour Organization.

Irigaray, Luce. 2000. *Democracy Begins between Two*. London: Athlone.

Jacoby, Russell. 2005. *Picture Imperfect: Utopian Thought for an Anti-Utopian Age*. New York: Columbia University Press.

Jaggar, Alison M., 1983. *Feminist Politics and Human Nature*. London: Routledge.

James, William. 1995. *Pragmatism*. Mineola, N.Y.: Dover.

———. 2003. *Essays in Radical Empiricism*, Mineola, N.Y.: Dover.

Jameson, Frederic. 2007. "Lenin and Revisionism." *Lenin Reloaded: Toward a Politics of Truth*, ed. Sebastian Budgen, Stathis Kouvelakis, and Slavoj Žižek, 59–73 Durham: Duke University Press.

Jay, Martin. 2010. *The Virtues of Mendacity: On Lying in Politics*. Charlottesville: University of Virginia Press.

Jessop, Bob. 2004. "The European Union and Recent Transformations in Statehood." In Sonja Puntscher Riekmann, Monika Mokre, and Michael

Latzer, eds. *The State of Europe: Transformations of Statehood from a European Perspective*. Frankfurt am Main: Campus Verlag, 75–94.

Jonsson, Stefan. 2008. *A Brief History of the Masses: Three Revolutions*. New York: Columbia University Press.

Joselit, David. 2007. *Feedback: Television against Democracy*. Cambridge: MIT Press.

Judt, Tony. 2007. *Postwar: A History of Europe since 1945*. London: Pimlico.

Kaika, Maria, and Ben Page. 2003a. "The EU Water Framework Directive, Part 1: European Policy-Making and the Changing Topography of Lobbying." *European Environment* 13, no. 6, 314–27.

———. 2003b. "The EU Water Framework Directive, Part 2: Policy Innovation and the Shifting Choreography of Governance." *European Environment* 13, no. 6, 328–43.

Kaldor, Mary. 2007. *New and Old Wars*. Stanford: Stanford University Press.

Kann, Mark E. 1982. *The American Left: Failures and Fortunes*. New York: Praeger.

Keane, John. 2009. *The Life and Death of Democracy*. London: Simon and Schuster.

Keith, Michael. 2005. *After the Cosmopolitan?: Multicultural Cities and the Future of Racism*. London: Routledge.

Kelty, Christopher. 2005. "Geeks, Social Imaginaries, and Recursive Publics." *Cultural Anthropology* 20, no. 2, 185–214.

Kraditor, Aileen S. 1981. *The Radical Persuasion, 1890–1917: Aspects of the Intellectual History and the Historiography of Three American Radical Organizations*. Baton Rouge: Louisiana State University Press.

Krasner, David, ed. 2000. *Method Acting Reconsidered: Theory, Practice, Future*. New York: St. Martin's Press.

Kristeva, Julia. 1991. *Strangers to Ourselves*. Hemel Hempstead: Harvester Wheatsheaf.

Kymlicka, Will. 1995. *Multicultural Citizenship: A Liberal Theory of Minority Rights*. Oxford: Oxford University Press.

Lakoff, George. 2008. *The Political Mind: Why You Can't Understand 21st-Century Politics with an 18th-Century Brain*. New York: Viking.

Lamoreaux, Naomi R. 1985. *The Great Merger Movement in American Business, 1895–1904*. Cambridge: Cambridge University Press.

Landauer, Carl A. 1959. *European Socialism: A History of Ideas and Movements from the Industrial Revolution to Hitler's Seizure of Power*. Berkeley: University of California Press.

Landry, Donna. 2009. *Noble Brutes: How Eastern Horses Transformed English Culture*. Baltimore: Johns Hopkins University Press.

Laslett, John H. M., and Seymour M. Lipset, eds. 1974. *Failure of a Dream?: Essays in the History of American Socialism*. Garden City, N.Y.: Anchor.

Latour, Bruno. 1993. *The Pasteurization of France.* Cambridge: Harvard University Press.

———. 1999. *Pandora's Hope: Essays on the Reality of Science Studies.* Cambridge: Harvard University Press.

———. 2004. *Politics of Nature: How to Bring the Sciences into Democracy.* Cambridge: Harvard University Press.

———. 2005. "From Realpolitik to Dingpolitik, or How to Make Things Public." *Making Things Public: Atmospheres of Democracy,* ed. Bruno Latour and Peter Weibel. Cambridge: MIT Press, 14–41.

———. 2007a. "A Plea for Earthly Sciences." Keynote lecture delivered at the annual meeting of the British Sociological Association, East London, April 2007.

———. 2007b. "Can We Get Our Materialism Back, Please?" *Isis* 98, no. 1, 138–42.

———. 2012. *Enquête sur les Modes d'Existence: Une Anthropologie des Modernes.* Paris: La dé couverte.

Latour, Bruno, and Peter Weibel, eds., 2005. *Making Things Public: Atmospheres of Democracy.* Cambridge: MIT Press.

Lazarfield, Paul, Berelson, Bernard, and Hazel Gaudet. 1944. *The People's Choice: How the Voter Makes up his Mind in a Presidential Campaign.* New York: Columbia University Press.

Lazzarato, Maurizio. 2004. "From Capital-Labour to Capital-Life. *Ephemera* 4, 187–208.

———. 2006. "The Machine." *Transversal* 10, available online at http://eipcp .net/transversal/1106/lazzarato/en.

Leadbeater, Charles. 2000. *Living on Thin Air: The New Economy.* London: Penguin.

Lefebvre, Henri. 2009. *State, Space, World: Selected Essays,* ed. Neil Brenner and Stuart Elden. Minneapolis: University of Minnesota Press.

Leys, Ruth. 1993. "Mead's Voices: Imitation as Foundation, or the Struggle against Mimesis." *Critical Inquiry* 19, no. 2, 277–307.

———. 2000. *Trauma: A Genealogy.* Chicago: University of Chicago Press.

Li, Tania Murray. 2007. *The Will to Improve: Governmentality, Development, and the Practice of Politics.* Durham: Duke University Press.

Lippmann, Walter. 1921. *Public Opinion.* London: Allen and Unwin.

———. 1961 (1914). *A Preface to Politics,* repr. ed. New York: Prometheus.

Lloyd, Geoffrey E. R. 2007. *Cognitive Variations: Reflections on the Unity and Diversity of the Human Mind.* Oxford: Oxford University Press.

Loury, Glenn C., Tariq Modood, and Steven M. Teles, eds. 2005. *Ethnicity, Social Mobility, and Public Policy: Comparing the US and UK.* Cambridge: Cambridge University Press.

Mackenzie, Adrian. 2002. *Transductions: Bodies and Machines at Speed*. London: Continuum International.

MacKenzie, Donald. 2010. "Constructing Carbon Markets: Learning from Experiments in the Technopolitics of Emissions Trading Schemes." *Disaster and the Politics of Intervention*, ed. Andrew Lakoff, 130–48. New York: Columbia University Press.

Mair, Peter. 2006. "Ruling the Void: The Hollowing of Western Democracy." *New Left Review* 42, 25–51.

Majone, Giandomenico. 1996. *Regulating Europe*. New York: Routledge.

———. 2005. *Dilemmas of European Integration: The Ambiguities and Pitfalls of Integration by Stealth*. Oxford: Oxford University Press.

Marcus, George, Newman, W. Russell, and Michael MacKuen. 2000. *Affective Intelligence and Political Judgement*. Chicago: University of Chicago Press.

Margulis, Lynne. 1998. *Symbiotic Planet: A New Look at Evolution*. Amherst, Mass.: Perseus Books.

Marres, Noortje. 2005. "No Issue, No Public: Democratic Deficits after the Displacement of Politics." Ph.D. diss., University of Amsterdam.

Marx, Karl. 1990. *Capital, Volume 1*. Harmondsworth: Penguin.

Massumi, Brian. 2009. "National Enterprise Emergency: Steps toward an Ecology of Powers." *Theory, Culture, and Society* 26, 153–85.

Mayhall, Laura E. N. 2000. "Defining Militancy: Radical Protest, the Constitutional Idiom, and Women's Suffrage in Britain, 1908–1909." *Journal of British Studies* 39, no. 3, 340–71.

McGregor, Richard. 2010. *The Party: The Secret World of China's Communist Rulers*. London: Allen Lane.

McLuhan, Marshall. 1964. *Understanding Man: The Extensions of the Media*. New York: Signet.

McRobbie, Angela. 2009. *The Aftermath of Feminism: Gender, Culture, and Social Change*. London: Sage.

Melitopoulos, Angela, and Maurizio Lazzarato. 2011. "Machinic Animism." Available online at http://www.europhilosophie.eu/recherche/IMG/pdf/Melitopoulos_-_Lazzarato._Machinic_Animism.pdf (accessed July 23, 2012).

Merrifield, Andy. 2011. *Magical Marxism: Subversive Politics and the Imagination*. London: Pluto.

Michie, Jonathan, and John G. Smith, eds. 1995. *Managing the Global Economy*. Oxford: Oxford University Press.

Milward, Alan S. 2005. *Politics and Economics in the History of the European Union*. London: Verso.

Modood, Tariq. 2007. *Multiculturalism: A Civic Idea*. Cambridge: Polity.

Mol, Annemarie, Ingunn Moser, and Jeanette Pols, eds., 2010. *Care in Practice: On Tinkering in Clinics, Homes, and Farms*. Bielefeld: Transcript Verlag.

Monbiot, George. 2007. "Environmental Feedback: A Reply to Clive Hamilton." *New Left Review* 45, 105–13.

Moravcsik, Andrew. 2002. "In Defence of the 'Democratic Deficit': Reassessing Legitimacy in the European Union." *Journal of Common Market Studies* 40, no. 4, 603–24.

Morton, Timothy. 2010. *The Ecological Thought*. Cambridge: Harvard University Press.

Moscovici, Serge. 1985. *The Age of the Crowd: A Historical Treatise on Mass Psychology*. Cambridge: Cambridge University Press.

Mühlmann, Heiner. 1996. *The Nature of Cultures: A Blueprint for a Theory of Culture Genetics*, Vienna: Springer.

———. 2005. *MSC Maximal Stress Cooperation: The Driving Force of Cultures*. Vienna: Springer.

Netz, Reviel. 2009. *Barbed Wire: An Ecology of Modernity*. Middletown, Conn.: Wesleyan University Press.

Ngai, Sianne. 2005. *Ugly Feelings*. Cambridge: Harvard University Press.

Nussbaum, Martha C. 2007. *The Clash Within: Democracy, Religious Violence, and India's Future*. Cambridge: Harvard University Press.

Oakeshott, Michael. 1991. *On Human Conduct*. Oxford: Oxford University Press.

Parekh, Bhikhu C. 2005. *Rethinking Multiculturalism: Cultural Diversity and Political Theory*. Basingstoke: Palgrave Macmillan.

———. 2008. *A New Politics of Identity: Political Principles for an Interdependent World*. Basingstoke: Palgrave Macmillan.

Parikka, Jussi. 2010. *Insect Media: An Archaeology of Animals and Technology*. Minneapolis: University of Minnesota Press.

Peck, Jamie, and Nik Theodore. 2010a. "Mobilizing Policy: Models, Methods, and Mutations." *Geoforum* 41, no. 2, 169–74.

———. 2010b. "Recombinant Workfare, across the Americas: Transnationalizing 'Fast' Social Policy." *Geoforum* 41, no. 2, 195–208.

Pignarre, Philippe, and Isabelle Stengers. 2011. *Capitalist Sorcery: Breaking the Spell*. Basingstoke: Palgrave Macmillan.

Popkin, Samuel, L. 1991. *The Reasoning Voter: Communication and Persuasion in Political Campaigns*. Chicago: University of Chicago Press.

Power, Michael. 1997. *The Audit Society: Rituals of Verification*. Oxford: Oxford University Press.

———. 2007. *Organized Uncertainty: Designing a World of Risk Management*. Oxford: Oxford University Press.

Prigogine, Ilya. 1997. *The End of Certainty: Time, Chaos, and the New Laws of Nature*. New York: Free Press.

Protevi, John. 2009. *Political Affect: Connecting the Social and the Somatic*. Minneapolis: University of Minnesota Press.

Przeworski, Adam. 1980. "Social Democracy as a Historical Phenomenon." *New Left Review* 122, 27–58.

Rabinbach, Anson. 1985. *The Austrian Socialist Experiment: Social Democracy and Austromarxism, 1918–1934*. Boulder: Westview.

Raffles, Hugh. 2010. *Insectopedia*. New York: Vintage.

Ramaswamy, Sumathi. 2004. *The Lost Land of Lemuria: Fabulous Geographies, Catastrophic Histories*. Berkeley: University of California Press.

Rancière, Jacques. 1999. *Dis-agreement: Politics and Philosophy*. Minneapolis: University of Minnesota Press.

———. 2006. *The Politics of Aesthetics*. London: Continuum International.

Rancière, Jacques, Davide Panagia, and Rachel Bowlby. 2001. "Ten Theses on Politics." *Theory and Event* 5, no. 3. Available online at http://muse.jhu.edu/journals/theory_and_event/v005/5.3ranciere.html (accessed September 8, 2011).

Raunig, Gerald. 2010. *A Thousand Machines: A Concise Philosophy of the Machine as Social Movement*. Los Angeles: Semiotext(e).

Read, Alan. 2008. *Theatre, Intimacy, and Engagement: The Last Human Venue*. London: Palgrave Macmillan.

Rhodes, R. A. W., Sarah A. Binder, and Bert A. Rockman, eds. 2008. *The Oxford Handbook of Political Institutions*. Oxford: Oxford University Press.

Richardson, Robert, ed. 2010. *The Heart of William James*. Cambridge: Harvard University Press.

Rifkin, Jeremy. 2004. *The European Dream: How Europe's Vision of the Future Is Quietly Eclipsing the American Dream*. Cambridge: Polity.

Robbins, Paul. 2007. *Lawn People: How Grasses, Weeds, and Chemicals Make Us Who We Are*. Philadelphia: Temple University Press.

Rodowick, David N. 2007. *The Virtual Life of Film*. Cambridge: Harvard University Press.

Roessler, Johannes, and Naomi Eilan, eds., 2003. *Agency and Self-Awareness: Issues in Philosophy and Psychology*. Oxford: Oxford University Press.

Rogers, Everett M. 2003. *Diffusion of Innovations*. New York: Free Press.

Rorty, Richard. 1998. *Achieving Our Country: Leftist Thought in Twentieth-Century America*. Cambridge: Harvard University Press.

Rosamond, Ben. 2000. *Theories of European Integration*. Basingstoke: St. Martin's Press.

Rosanvallon, Pierre. 2006. *Democracy Past and Future*, ed. Samuel Moyn. New York: Columbia University Press.

Rossiter, Clinton. 1960. *The American Presidency: The Powers and Practices, the Personalities and Problems of the Most Important Office on Earth*. New York: Harcourt, Brace, and World.

Saldanha, Arun. 2010. "Politics and Difference." *Taking-Place: Non-representational Theories and Geography*, ed. Ben Anderson and Paul Harrison, 283–302. Farnham, Surrey: Ashgate.

Sassoon, Donald. 1996. *One Hundred Years of Socialism: The West European Left in the Twentieth Century*. London: I. B. Tauris.

Savoie, Donald J. 2010. *Power: Where Is It?* Montreal: McGill-Queen's University Press.

Schnapp, Jeffrey T., and Matthew Tiews, eds., 2006. *Crowds*. Stanford: Stanford University Press.

Sennett, Richard. 2008. *The Craftsman*. New Haven: Yale University Press.

———. 2012. *Together: The Rituals, Pleasures, and Politics of Cooperation*. London: Allen Lane.

Shaviro, Steven. 2009. *Without Criteria: Kant, Whitehead, Deleuze, and Aesthetics*. Cambridge: MIT Press.

Shaw, Tamsin. 2007. *Nietzsche's Political Skepticism*. Princeton: Princeton University Press.

Shipman, Pat. 2011. *The Animal Connection: A New Perspective on What Makes Us Human*. New York: W. W. Norton.

Simondon, Gilbert. 1992. "The Genesis of the Individual." *Incorporations*, ed. Jonathan Crary and Sanford Kwinter, 297–319. Cambridge: Zone.

Singer, Peter W. 2008. *Corporate Warriors: The Rise of the Privatized Military Industry*. Ithaca: Cornell University Press.

Slaughter, Anne-Marie. 2004. *A New World Order*. Princeton: Princeton University Press.

Sloterdijk, Peter. 2005. "Foreword to the Theory of Spheres." *Cosmograms*, ed. Melik Ohanian and Jean-Christophe Royox, 223–40. Berlin: Lukas and Sternberg.

———. 2007. "What Happened in the Twentieth Century?: En Route to a Critique of Extremist Reason." *Cultural Politics* 3, no. 3, 327–55.

———. 2009. "Rules for the Human Zoo: A Response to the Letter on Humanism." *Environment and Planning D: Society and Space* 27, no. 1, 12–28.

———. 2011. *Neither Sun nor Death*. New York: Semiotext(e).

Smail, Daniel L. 2008. *On Deep History and the Brain*. Berkeley: University of California Press.

Solnit, Rebecca. 2005. *Hope in the Dark: The Untold History of People Power*. Edinburgh: Canongate.

Sombart, Werner. 1976. *Why Is There No Socialism in the United States?* Armonk, N.Y.: M. E. Sharpe.

Stengers, Isabelle. 2010a. *Cosmopolitics I*. Minneapolis: University of Minnesota Press.

―――. 2010b. "Including Nonhumans in Political Theory: Opening Pandora's Box?" *Political Matter. Technoscience, Democracy, and Public Life*, ed, Bruce Braun and Sarah J. Whatmore, 3–34. Minneapolis: University of Minnesota Press.

―――. 2011a. "Relaying a War Machine?" *The Guattari Effect*, ed. Éric Alliez and Andrew Goffey, 134–55. London: Continuum.

―――. 2011b. "Wondering about Materialism." *The Speculative Turn: Continental Materialism and Realism*, ed. Levi Bryant, Nick Srnicek, and Graham Harman, 368–80. Melbourne: Re.press.

Stengers, Isabelle and Andrew Goffey. 2009. "William James: An Ethics of Thought?" *Radical Philosophy* 157, 9–19.

Sterelny, Kim. 2003. *Thought in a Hostile World: The Evolution of Human Cognition*. Oxford: Wiley-Blackwell.

Stewart, Kathleen. 2007. *Ordinary Affects*. Durham: Duke University Press.

Stiegler, Bernard. 2010. *For a New Critique of Political Economy*, trans. Daniel Ross. Cambridge: Polity Press.

Stiglitz, Joseph E. 2003. *Globalization and Its Discontents*. London: W. W. Norton.

Strang, Veronica. 2004. *The Meaning of Water*. Oxford: Berg.

Szerszynski, Bronislaw. 2005. *Nature, Technology, and the Sacred*. Oxford: Wiley-Blackwell.

Tarde, Gabriel. 2012. *Monadology and Sociology*, trans. Theo Lorenc. Melbourne: Re.press.

Therborn, Göran, ed. 2006. *Inequalities of the World: New Theoretical Frameworks, Multiple Empirical Approaches*. London: Verso.

―――. 2007. "After Dialectics." *New Left Review* 43, 63–114.

Thomas, Keith. 1983. *Man and the Natural World: Changing Attitudes in England, 1500–1800*. London: Allen Lane.

Thrift, Nigel J. 2007 *Non-Representational Theory: Space, Politics, Affect*. London: Routledge.

―――. 2010. "Halos: Finding Space in the World for New Political Forms." *Political Matter: Technoscience, Democracy, and Public Life*, ed. Bruce Braun and Sarah J. Whatmore, 139–74. Minneapolis: University of Minnesota Press.

―――. 2011. "Lifeworld, Inc.—And What to Do about It." *Environment and Planning D: Society and Space* 29, no. 1, 5–26.

Tilley, Christopher. 2008. "From the English Cottage Garden to the Swedish Allotment: Banal Nationalism and the Concept of the Garden." *Home Cultures* 5, no. 2, 219–49.

Tilton, Timothy A. 1974. "The Social Origins of Liberal Democracy: The Swedish Case." *American Political Science Review* 68, no, 2, 561–71.

———. 1979. "A Swedish Road to Socialism: Ernst Wigforss and the Ideological Foundations of Swedish Social Democracy." *American Political Science Review* 73, no. 2, 505–20.

Tomasello, Michael. 2008. *Origins of Human Communication*. Cambridge: MIT Press.

———. 2009. *Why We Cooperate*. Cambridge: MIT Press.

Tomasson, Richard F. 1969. "The Extraordinary Success of the Swedish Social Democrats." *Journal of Politics* 31, no. 3, 772–98.

Trüby, Stephan. 2008. *Exit-Architecture: Design between War and Peace*. Vienna: Springer.

Tsing, Anna Lowenhaupt. 2004. *Friction: An Ethnography of Global Connection*. Princeton: Princeton University Press.

Turkle, Sherry, ed. 2009. *Simulation and Its Discontents*. Cambridge: MIT Press.

Turner, Stephen P., ed. 2000. *The Cambridge Companion to Weber*. Cambridge: Cambridge University Press.

Urbinati, Nadia. 2006. *Representative Democracy: Principles and Genealogy*. Chicago: University of Chicago Press.

Van Tuinen, Sjoerd. 2007. "Critique beyond Resentment: An Introduction to Peter Sloterdijk's Jovial Modernity." *Cultural Politics* 3, no. 3, 275–306.

Venn, Couze. 2006. *The Postcolonial Challenge: Towards Alternative Worlds*. London: Sage.

Veyne, Paul. 2010. *Foucault: His Thought, His Character*. Cambridge: Polity Press.

Vibert, Frank. 2001. *Europe Simple, Europe Strong: The Future of European Governance*. Oxford: Wiley-Blackwell.

Virno, Paolo. 1996. "The Ambivalence of Disenchantment." *Radical Thought in Italy: A Potential Politics*, ed. Paolo Virno and Michael Hardt, 189–209. Minneapolis: University of Minnesota Press.

———. 2004. *A Grammar of the Multitude*. Cambridge: MIT Press.

———. 2009. "Facing a New 17th Century." Available online at http://www.generation-online.org/p/fpvirno4.htm (accessed July 23, 2012).

Viveiros de Castro, Eduardo. 1998. "Cosmological Deixis and Amerindian Perspectivism." *Journal of the Royal Anthropological Institute* 4, no. 3, 469–488.

Wacquant, Loïc. 1996. "Foreword." In Pierre Bourdieu, *The State Nobility: Elite Schools in the Field of Power*, ix–xxii. Stanford: Stanford University Press.

Wallerstein, Immanuel. 2006. "The Curve of American Power." *New Left Review* 40, 77–94.

Walzer, Michael. 1998. *Spheres of Justice*. Oxford: Blackwell.

Wasik, Bill. 2009. *And Then There's This: How Stories Live and Die in Viral Culture*. New York: Viking.

Waterton, Claire. 2002. "From Field to Fantasy: Classifying Nature, Constructing Europe." *Social Studies of Science* 32, no. 2, 177–204.

Weber, Max. 1978. *Economy and Society: An Outline of Interpretive Sociology*. Berkeley: University of California Press.

———. 1994. *Weber: Political Writings*, ed. Peter Lassman and Ronald Speirs. Cambridge: Cambridge University Press.

Wedel, Janine R. 2009. *Shadow Elite: How the World's New Power Brokers Undermine Democracy, Government, and the Free Market*. New York: Basic.

Wegner, Daniel M. 2002. *The Illusion of Conscious Will*. Cambridge: MIT Press.

Weinstein, James. 1975. *Ambiguous Legacy: The Left in American Politics*. New York: New Viewpoints.

Wershler-Henry, Darren S. 2005. *The Iron Whim: A Fragmented History of Typewriting*. Ithaca: Cornell University Press.

Westen, Drew. 2008. *The Political Brain: The Role of Emotion in Deciding the Fate of the Nation*. Cambridge: Public Affairs.

Wheeler, Wendy. 2006. *The Whole Creature: Complexity, Biosemiotics, and the Evolution of Culture*. London: Lawrence and Wishart.

Whitehead, Alfred North. 1933. *Adventures of Ideas*. New York: Free Press.

———. 1978. *Process and Reality: An Essay in Cosmology*, ed. David Ray Griffin and Donald W. Sherburne. New York: Free Press.

Wiebe, Robert H. 1967. *The Search for Order, 1877–1920*. New York: Hill and Wang.

Wilkinson, Iain. 2005. *Suffering: A Sociological Introduction*. Cambridge: Polity Press.

Will, Pierre-Étienne. 1990. *Bureaucracy and Famine in Eighteenth-Century China*. Stanford: Stanford University Press.

Williams, Raymond (1977) *Marxism and Literature*, Oxford: Oxford University Press.

Winter, Nicholas J. G. 2005. "Framing Gender: Political Rhetoric, Gender Schemas, and Public Opinion on U.S. Health Care Reform." *Politics and Gender* 1, no. 3, 453–80.

Wolfe, Cary. 2009. *What Is Posthumanism?* Minneapolis: University of Minnesota Press.

Wolfram, Stephen. 2002. *A New Kind of Science*. Champaign, Ill.: Wolfram Media.

Wolin, Sheldon S. 2008. *Democracy Incorporated: Managed Democracy and the Specter of Inverted Totalitarianism*. Princeton: Princeton University Press.

Woodward, Kathleen M. 2009. *Statistical Panic: Cultural Politics and Poetics of the Emotions*. Durham: Duke University Press.

Zakaria, Fareed. 1997. "The Rise of Illiberal Democracy." *Foreign Affairs* 76, no. 6, 22–43.

Žižek, Slavoj. 2000. *The Fragile Absolute: Or, Why Is the Christian Legacy Worth Fighting For?* London: Verso.

———. 2008. *In Defense of Lost Causes.* London: Verso.

———. 2009. "Berlusconi in Teheran." *London Review of Books* 31, no. 14, 3–7.

index

accomplishment, as structure of feeling, 181–84
actors. *See* political actors
Addams, Jane, 32, 34
advertising, political, 159, 167. *See also* media
aesthetics, 14, 51, 201n2
affect: artificial, 59; definitions of, 46, 47; differentiating from emotion, 46–47; envy and competition, 52–53, 67, 68; and imitation, 160–61; as political art, xiii, 14–15; role in financial markets, 195; as semi-conscious process, 161. *See also* affective politics; emotions; mood
affective politics: construction of commonplaces in, 159–65; influence of, 14–15, 52–54, 157; need for Left to reclaim, 14–15, 68, 158, 174–86; and Obama campaign, 186; and technological change, 168–74; technologies of mood, 166–68. *See also* affect
Africa, 189, 190
Agamben, Giorgio, 49
alcohol, 59–60, 69
Althusser, Louis, 7, 116
American Federation of Labor, 32
Amsterdam Treaty, 142
Anderson, Perry, 149–50
anger, 54, 68, 95, 172. *See also* affect
animals: agency of, 57–58; and cognition, 182; Derrida on, 206n13; horses, 58; and human responsibility, 182; as

political entities, 40–41, 44, 58–59, 60. *See also* insects
anti-capitalism, 79–83
anti-globalization movement, 82–83
Aquinas, Saint Thomas, 124
Arab Spring, 111, 207n7
Archer, Margaret, 51
Arendt, Hannah, 53, 98, 128
Aristotle, 54, 163, 205n10
Art of Rhetoric, The (Wilson), 165
Atwater, Lee, 169
Austen, Jane, 58
automatisms, 64, 161, 166. *See also* publics
Azmanova, Albena, 2, 3

Bachelard, Gaston, 99
Bachman, David, 121–22
Badiou, Alain, 82, 94, 100–101
Balkans, 99
barbed wire, 52, 61–62, 64
Barry, Andrew, 149
Bebel, August, 19, 20, 23, 24
Beck, Ulrich, 88, 90–91
Benhabib, Seyla, 100
Bennett, Jane, 52, 199
Bentham, Jeremy, 126–27
Berger, Stefan, 24
Bergson, Henri, 40
Berlant, Lauren, 1, 40, 43, 52, 164
Berlin, Isaiah, 42, 109
Berlusconi, Silvio, 163, 171
Bernstein, Eduard, 202n1

Bérubé, Michael, 2
biopolitical realm, 159
Bismarck, Otto Fürst von, 20
blame, modern culture of, 183–84
Bloch, Ernest, 109
blogs, 71, 107, 159, 171. *See also* Internet
Boer War, 62
Boltanski, Luc, 80–81
Bosnia, 101
Bourdieu, Pierre, 113, 123–24, 125
Brader, Ted, 168
Braunthal, Julius, 23
Brazil, 189
Britain: political communications, 169–
    70; and political fairness, 177; political
    history of animals, 58; political history
    of plants, 59–60; on social empower-
    ment, 3. *See also* British feminism;
    European Union; United Kingdom
British feminism: inventiveness of, 9,
    28–32, 35–37; New Woman campaign,
    28–29; political alliances in, 28, 29–30,
    31–32, 36; and women's suffrage, 28,
    29–31
Brown, Gordon, 168
Brown, Wendy, 100
Buber, Martin, 99, 109
bureaucracies: Bourdieu on, 113, 123–24,
    125; in China, 121–22, 124; ethics of,
    128–29, 155–56; habitus of, 113, 123–25;
    identity control efforts, 125–27; im-
    pact on democracy, 152–53; impact on
    political sphere, 113, 120–21, 127–28, 151,
    152–53; in India, 128; organizational
    changes in, 129–30; in Soviet Union,
    122–23, 124; Weber on, 128–29, 155
Butler, Judith, 96, 99–100, 102

Caddell, Pat, 171
caffeine, 59–60, 69
Callaghan, James, 168
Callon, Michael, 149
Cameron, David, 172
campaigns. *See* political campaigns

capitalism: "baroque," 189–90; and Ger-
    man socialism, 20–21, 22–23; and
    global economy, 191; and modern
    labor, 175–76; and pre-personal realm,
    49; resilience of, 81–82; and Swedish
    social democracy, 26–27; world-
    making capacity, 186. *See also* anti-
    capitalism; capitalism reform; corpo-
    rate interests; post-capitalism
capitalism reform, 83–91
carbon trading, 84
Carruthers, Mary, 50
Castro, Eduardo Viveiros de. *See* Viveiros
    de Castro, Eduardo
Caute, David, 20
China: bureaucracies of, 118, 121–22, 124;
    economy, 86, 189, 190; statecraft, 117,
    118
Chomsky, Noam, 50, 162
Christian Right, 104–5. *See also* Right
Cicero, 164
Civilization and Its Discontents (Freud), 51
Clayton Act, 34
climate change: as global threat, 81, 191–
    92; Left's engagement with, 192, 194,
    196–97; and markets, 81, 84
Clinton, Bill, 170
coffee, 59, 60
commonplaces, 151, 158, 165
the "commons": definition, 131; as force
    for democratic change, 131; revitaliza-
    tion of, 144, 188–89
communication. *See* political communi-
    cation
communism, 17, 18, 45, 74
competition, 52–53, 68
Connolly, William, 102, 104, 108
consensus, 132. *See also* manufacturing
    consent
conservatives. *See* Right
contagion. *See* psycho-social contagion
Coordination des Intermittents et Pré-
    caires, 133
CORINE Biotopes initiative, 144–46, 148

corporate interests: and economic imperialism, 190; and financialization,
190; impact on leftist renewal, 35–36;
impact on political sphere, 117, 151; and
Progressive Movement, 32, 34
cosmopolitanism, 90–91, 99. *See also* eco-
cosmopolitanism
Cotton, John, 55
Council of Environment Ministers, 141
Council of Ministers, 135, 138, 139, 140,
141–42, 144
counter-organization, 130–34
Croly, Herbert, 33, 204n9

Dahl, Robert, 177
"Daisy" ad, 167, 208n2
Daston, Lorraine, 43
databases: and mapping, 172–74,
208nn3–4; tracking of emotional landscapes, 172. *See also* polls; technologies
Davies, Margaret Llewellyn, 30
Dawley, Alan, 33
Dean, Howard, 169
Deleuze, Gilles, 46, 47, 48, 49, 67, 130, 133
democracy: and the "commons," 131;
Dewey on, 33, 102, 104; Latour on,
102, 104–7, 109; and pluralism, 102–5;
and Progressive Movement, 33, 34–35;
promise of, 152–53; role of political
activism in, 154–55; role of representation in, 56–57, 153–54; totalitarian, 117,
151, 162–63
Derrida, Jacques, 96, 98, 101, 206n13
Descartes, René, 58
Descola, Philippe, 43
designed environments, 72–73
Dewey, John, 32, 33, 102, 104
Dichter, Ernest, 169
Dingpolitik, 104, 106–7
diplomacy: role in European Union,
13–14, 87–88, 135, 136–37, 139, 140, 143,
144; role in politics, 12, 13–14
DNA profiling, 125, 127. *See also* identity
labeling

Du Gay, Paul, 129, 155
Durkheim, Émile, 52

eco-cosmopolitanism, 74
ecology of practices, 72–73, 131–34
economic crisis. *See* financial crisis
Économie psychologique (Tarde), 71
elections: and German socialism, 20–21;
leftist critique, 152. *See also* political
campaigns
Eliasoph, Nina, 166, 171
Ellison, Ralph, 43
emotions: distinguishing from affect,
46–47; mapping of public, 173–74; and
political decision-making, 157–58, 172;
and rhetoric, 164–65; role in thinking,
160; and statecraft, 163–64, 172. *See also*
affective politics; mood; structures of
feeling
Engels, Friedrich, 20, 200
environmentalism: and gardening, 60;
and globalization, 2; and interconnection, 74–75; role of Left in, 3, 85, 86,
187. *See also* climate change
environments, designed, 72–73
envy, 52–53, 67, 68
ethics: of bureaucracies, 128–29, 155–56;
of European Union, 139–40; of human
conduct, 97–99; of personal conduct,
99–100; of political organization, 129;
politics based on, 100–102
ethnicity: and politics of difference, 97;
and Progressive Movement, 33, 34
Europe: and historical mapping, 208n4;
identity labeling, 126–27; and identity
politics, 3; and language of belonging,
99; leftist movements, 9–10. *See also*
British feminism; European Union;
German socialism; Swedish social
democracy
European Commission, 138, 139, 141,
145–46, 148
European Parliament, 138, 139, 140, 141,
142, 144

European Union: concept of commons in, 144–48; critiques of, 136, 149–50, 207nn1–2; and ecology of practices, 134; ethics of care, 139–40; European Water Framework Directive, 140–44; as example for Left, 149–51; governing bodies of, 135; Infocities (information society program), 147–48; invention and innovation, 113, 134, 135–48, 149; and organization, 13–14, 137–40; re-mapping of Europe, 146–48; role of diplomacy in, 13–14, 87–88, 135, 136–37, 139, 140, 143, 144; unity in diversity, 139, 140; vegetation classification (CORINE Biotypes), 144–46, 148

European Water Framework Directive (WFD), 140–44

Fabian Women's Group, 29, 30
fairness, as structure of feeling, 177–79
Farmer, Kenneth, 122
fascism, 45
Fawcett, Millicent, 31
fear, 46, 68
Federal Reserve System, 34
Federal Trade Commission, 34
feeling. See structures of feeling
feminism: coining of "feminist," 28; and Progressive Movement, 33; transmission of traditions, 207n3. See also British feminism; feminist political theory
feminist political theory: on envy and competition, 52–53; on rationality, 41–42
Ferenczi, Sándor, 71
Fichte, Johann Gottlieb, 126
financial crisis, 3, 178–79, 190, 195
financialization, 16, 190, 194, 195–98
Foucault, Michel, 115–16, 119–20, 144
Fourier, Charles, 109
France, 84, 127, 207n6
Freewoman (magazine), 28
French Legislative Assembly of 1791, 2
Freud, Sigmund, 51, 52, 71

Galison, Peter, 43
Gallop, Jane, 52
German Marxism, 9
German socialism: emergence of, 19, 20–21; "free" unions, 21, 22–23, 24; political arts of, 21–24; success of, 21–22; and utopianism, 19, 23; world-making by, 35–36
German Socialist Party (SPD): doctrine of scientific socialism, 21; emergence of, 20; ideological disputes, 23, 202n1; inventions by, 22–24, 35; moral commitment, 36; torchbearers for, 22. See also German socialism
German Workers' Association, 20
Germany: Anti-Socialist period, 20; "Christian" unions, 21; fragmentation in late nineteenth century, 25; industrialization in, 21, 22, 25; Third Way thinking in, 84. See also German socialism; Nazi Germany
Geuss, Raymond, 116
Gibson-Graham, J. K., 92–93, 95
Gilly, Adolfo, 5
Gilroy, Paul, 96
Gingrich, Newt, 171
Giving an Account of Oneself (Butler), 99–100
global developments/challenges: anti-globalization movement, 82–83; financialization, 16, 190, 194, 195–98; global inequality, 190–91, 194, 196–97, 198; globalization, 2–3, 84, 91; leftist experiments/engagement with, 78, 193–95, 206nn1–2; market capitalism, 189–90, 194, 195–98; technological reconfiguration of human life, 192–93, 194, 196–97. See also climate change
Gompers, Samuel, 32
Gratton, Lynda, 130
Great Leap Forward, 121–22
Greece, ancient, 45, 159, 164, 165
Green, Sarah, 147
Greene, Julie, 203n7

Groebner, Valentin, 43, 125–27

Grossberg, Lawrence, 46–47

Grunwald, Mandy, 169

Guattari, Félix, 49, 130, 133

habitus, of bureaucracies, 113, 123–25

Haraway, Donna, 132

Harding, James, 171

Hardt, Michael, 82, 130–31

Harman, Graham, 7, 60–61, 62, 206n12

Harvey, Penny, 147

Hauser, Marc, 50

Heidegger, Martin, 40, 65

Held, David, 88

Herf, Jeffrey, 48

Herzfeld, Michael, 116

heterogeneity: engagement by Left, 179–81, 188; as structure of feeling, 179–81

Hinduism, 59, 101

Hobbes, Thomas, 46, 54

Hofstadter, Richard, 164

Hooker, Thomas, 55

Hrdy, Sarah Blaffer, 43

human beings: and cognition, 50–51; ethic of recognition, 96–102; and free will, 49–50; and intelligence, 43; models of personhood, 43–44; models of political behavior, 41–47; and morality, 50; political definition of, 39–41, 204n1; practice orientation, 51; pre-personal realm, 41, 47–55; and rationality, 41–44; and subconscious, 51–52; and technological reconfiguration of life, 192

Humphrey, Caroline, 122–23

Hurd, Madeleine, 27

Husserl, Edmund, 40

"hylomorphism," 62–63

identity labeling, 125–27, 207nn5–6

identity politics. See politics of difference

imagination: needed by Left, 16, 78, 200, 201n4; as political art, x

imitation: and human behavior, 70, 160–61; role in politics, 70–71, 160–61, 167

income inequality. See inequality

Independent Labour Party, 30

India: bureaucracies of, 128; and capitalism, 86; Hindu violence toward Muslims, 101; market economy, 189; shadow states of, 118–19; treatment of animals, 58–59

Indonesia, 116

inequality: global, 2, 190–91; income, 3, 178, 204n9; and Swedish social democracy, 26; worker, 2

Infocities (information society program), 147–48

information technology, 64, 72, 133, 173–74. See also Internet

insects, 58, 206n14

institutions, as political actors, 111–12. See also bureaucracies; organization; the state

interconnection, 74–75

International Labour Organisation, 86

International Monetary Fund, 87

Internet: blogs, 71, 107, 174; political uses of, 64, 120, 169, 171, 174, 201n4; and pre-personal realm, 52; use by Left, 174, 201n4; as viral space, 71

invention/inventiveness: in British feminism, 9, 28–32, 35–37; of early American Left, 9, 17–20, 35–37, 77; in European Union, 113, 134, 135–48, 149; in German socialism, 21–24, 35; and Obama campaign, 186; as political art, xii-xiii, 10–11, 36–37; in Progressive Movement, 9, 33–35; in Swedish social democracy, 9, 25–26, 36, 203n4. See also leftist renewal; political reinvention

Iraq War, 152

Irigaray, Luce, 96, 101

Islam, 59

Italy: and Berlusconi, 163, 171; craft districts, 85

Jacobs, Jane, 67

Jains, 58

James, William: on imitation, 70; influence of psychology on, 51; on perfection, xii; on pluralism, xiii, 40, 44, 102–4, 204n2, 204n4
Jameson, Fredric, 116
Jessop, Bob, 139
Johnson, Lyndon, 167
Jonsson, Stefan, 131
juxtapolitical domain, 1, 40, 59

Kafka, Franz, 113
Kaika, Maria, 141, 143
Kann, Mark, 203n8
Kant, Immanuel, 46
Kautsky, Karl, 19, 20, 24, 200, 202n1, 203n4
Keane, John, 152
Kennan, Ned, 169
Kenney, Annie, 31
Knox, Hannah, 147
Kosovo, 101
Kraditor, Aileen, 203n8
Kristeva, Julia, 96, 101, 206n16
Kung Fu Panda (cartoon), 163

labor: changing face of, 176; Left's engagement with, 175–77; as structure of feeling, 175–77. See also labor unions/ organizations
labor unions/organizations: and British feminism, 29, 30; changing face of, 176; "free" unions, 21, 22–23, 24; and German socialism, 20, 21, 24; and Progressive Movement, 32. See also labor
Labour Party (Britain), 30
La Follette, Robert, 34
Landauer, Carl, 23–24, 39
Lassalle, Ferdinand, 20
Latour, Bruno: as actant, 56; on democracy, 102, 104–7, 109; on political actors/relationships, 41, 57, 61, 73–74, 105, 106–7, 206n12; on political representation, 56–57, 153
Lazarsfeld, Paul, 164
Lazzarato, Maurizio, 48–49, 67, 205n8

Le Bon, Gustave, 207n7
Lefebvre, Henri, 124
Left: and interconnection, 74–75; loss of momentum, 1–3, 19, 108–9; modes of argument, xiv, 201n1; opposition to oppression, 5, 108, 187–88; origin of term, 2; political experimentation by, 193–95, 201ch.1n1; vs. progressive politics, 1; world-making capacity, xii–xiii, 4–5, 8–9, 19, 77, 78–79, 185–86. See also global developments/challenges; leftist history; leftist renewal; leftist thought; political arts
leftist history: inventiveness in, 9, 17–20, 35–37, 77; organizational strengths, 36, 37. See also British feminism; German socialism; Progressive Movement; Swedish social democracy
leftist renewal: expansion into new sites, 109, 188, 201n4, 209n1; four processes important for, 169–71; global challenges faced by, 16, 189–200; inventiveness needed in, 5–6, 9–10, 11, 19, 35, 37, 40–41, 109; mobilization of publics, 3–5, 109; and political theory, 8–10; reclaiming of structures of feeling, 15, 158, 174–86, 199; revitalization of the "commons," 144, 188–89; world-making ability, 5–6, 9–10, 11, 78–79, 199–200. See also political arts; political reinvention
leftist thought: anti-capitalism, 79–83; capitalism reform, 83–91; human recognition, 95–102; on new publics, 11, 103–8; post-capitalism, 92–95; redistributive justice, 85–86
Leibniz, Gottfried Wilhelm, 46, 66
Lenin, Vladimir, 7, 116–17
Levinas, Emmanuel, 99, 101
Libet, Benjamin, 49–50
Lilydale, xii
Lippmann, Walter, 15, 104, 162–63
Li, Tania Murray, 116
Lloyd, Geoffrey, 45

Luntz, Frank, 171
Luxemburg, Rosa, 203n1

Machiavelli, Niccolò, 46
Majone, Gianfranco, 138–39
Making Things Public (Latour and
    Weibel), 102, 104
manufacturing consent, 15, 162
Mao, Zedong, 121–22
mapping, 172–74, 208nn3–4
Marcus, George, 164
Margulis, Lynn, 63–64
markets: and capitalism, 189–90, 194, 195–
    98; and climate change, 81, 84; as emo-
    tional entities, 195; regulation of, 3, 189
Marsden, Dora, 28
Marx, Karl, 20, 200
Marx Brothers, 163
Marxism: on capitalism, 81; and German
    socialism, 20; on labor, 59, 175, 177; on
    nature, 64; scientific, 202n1; structural
    approach to politics, 46; on utopia, 181.
    See also German socialism
Massumi, Brian, 46, 115
materialism, 56–57, 205n11
McCann, H. E., 165
McKinnon, Mark, 169
McLuhan, Marshall, 69
media: affective power of, 166–68; de-
    cline of traditional, 71; and German
    socialism, 23; and manufacturing con-
    sent, 162; in Nazi Germany, 48; and
    paranoia, 151; and reception speed,
    166; role in politics, 151, 159, 162, 169–
    70, 201n4. *See also* Internet; political
    communication
Merleau-Ponty, Maurice, 72
Middle Ages, 50, 164
Middle East, 99, 190
Miller, Scott, 169
mobilization: and globalization, 2–3; of
    publics, 3–5, 109
mood: influence on politics, 159, 161–62,
    163–64, 165, 167; technologies of, 165,

166–68; Weber on, 159, 161–62. *See also*
    emotions
Morris, Dick, 169
Morris, William, 177
Morton, Timothy, 57–58
Moscovici, Serge, 167
Moses, Robert, 67
Mühlmann, Heiner, 71
multiculturalism, 97, 98

names. *See* identity labeling
National Union of Women's Suffrage
    Societies (NUWSS), 30, 31
Nazi Germany, 48, 62, 99, 128, 205n7
Negri, Antonio, 82, 130–31, 205n8
neoliberalism, 83, 86, 90, 95, 188, 191
Netz, Reviel, 61, 62
New Woman campaign, 28–29, 33
Ngai, Sianne, 14, 52–53, 68
Nietzsche, Friedrich, 42
Nigeria, 189
nongovernmental organizations (NGOs),
    88, 139, 178
non-human actors, 55–64. *See also* ani-
    mals; objects; plants
North Africa, 150
Nussbaum, Martha, 101

Oakeshott, Michael, 42
Obama, Barack, 3, 117, 186
objects: barbed wire, 52, 61–62, 64; and
    concerted agency, 57, 206n12; Latour
    on, 57, 105, 106–7, 206n12; as political
    entities, 52, 60–64, 205n9
"occupy" movements, 195
organization: and counter-organization,
    130–34; as ecology of practices, 131–34;
    and German socialism, 22–24, 36; and
    Obama campaign, 186; as political art,
    xiii, 11–14; role in statecraft, 116–17;
    and Swedish social democracy, 25–26,
    36. *See also* bureaucracies; institutions;
    the state
organizations (institutions). *See* institu-
    tions

Page, Ben, 141, 143
Pankhurst, Christabel, 31
Pankhurst, Emmeline, 200
Pankhurst family, 30–31, 200
paranoia, 151
Parekh, Bhikhu, 96
passports, 125, 126, 127. *See also* identity labeling
People's Liberation Army, 118
People's Stage, 24
plants, as political entities, 40, 41, 59–60, 206n15
pluralism: and democracy, 102–5; James on, xiii, 40, 44, 103–4, 204n2, 204n4
Pluralism (Connolly), 102, 104
the political: as an art form, x–xi; definitions, x, 39–41. *See also* political arts; political reinvention
political activism, 154–55
political actors: crowds as, 130, 207n7; equal consideration of all, 6, 40–41; institutions as, 111–12; Latour on, 41, 57, 61, 73–74, 105, 106–7, 206n12; non-human, 55–64; terrain as, 65, 72–73. *See also* animals; human beings; objects; plants; space; the state
political agency, 53–55
political arts: aesthetics as, 51; Left's need for mastery of, x–xiv, 10–16, 158, 188, 196–97; and Obama campaign, 186. *See also* affect; invention/inventiveness; organization
political campaigns: appeal to emotions in, 165, 172; data collection in, 171–72; Internet techniques, 169, 171; low-information signaling, 168, 170; "permanent," 171–72; polling techniques, 168, 169, 170
political communication, 64, 71. *See also* Internet; media
political contract theory, 41, 46
political reinvention: of the "commons," 144, 188–89; five main directions for, 67–75; and human beings, 41–47; and

non-human actants, 55–64; ongoing process of, 6; and pre-personal field, 47–55; of space, 64–67, 72, 74–75. *See also* human beings; leftist renewal
political skepticism, 42
politicians: compromises of, 56–57; interactions with public, 159, 168, 170; and political representation, 56–57, 153–54
politics: and evolution, 43; as mimetic canvas, 70–71; original meaning of, 58. *See also* the political
politics of difference (identity politics), 2, 3, 96–97
polls, 168, 169
Popkin, Samuel, 167–68
post-capitalism, 91–95
Postcapitalist Politics, A (Gibson-Graham), 92
poststructuralism, 91
poverty: global, 190–91. *See also* inequality
practices, ecology of, 72–73, 131–34
pragmatic utopianism, 18–19
pre-personal field, 41, 47–55. *See also* human beings
Prince, Morton, 71
Progressive Movement: anti-corporatist reforms, 32, 34; emergence of, 32–33; inventiveness of, 9, 33–35; and organization, 36; political arts of, 9, 33–35, 36; socialist impulses preceding, 32, 203n8; world-making by, 35–36
Proletarian Freethinker's League, 24
Promise of American Life, The (Dewey), 33
Protevi, John, 68
Prozac, 69
psycho-social contagion, 70, 81, 159, 160, 167–68, 195, 198
psychotopical dynamics, 41, 67, 71–72, 166
psychotropics, 59, 68–70
publics: and automatisms, 64, 161, 166; and construction of commonplaces, 151, 158, 159–65; and imitation, 160–61;

influences on thinking, 160–61; politician interactions with, 159, 168; and rhetoric, 164–65. *See also* emotions; mood; societies

Qing dynasty, 121
Quakers, 154

race: and politics of difference, 97; and Progressive Movement, 204n10
Rancière, Jacques, 82
rationality, 41–44
Reagan, Ronald, 167, 170
Reasoning Voter, The (Popkin), 167–68
Republican Party, 3, 167. *See also* Right rhetoric, 164–65
Rhetoric (Aristotle), 163
Rifkin, Jeremy, 139–40, 207n1
Right: and affective politics, 158; Christian Right, 104–5; mastery of political arts, xiii, 10; origin of term, 2; and politics of conviction, 184; response to global challenges, 193; role in contemporary politics, 108, 109. *See also* Republican Party
Ritalin, 69
Roman Empire, 164
Roosevelt, Theodore, 32
Rorty, Richard, 33
Rove, Karl, 169
Ruskin, John, 177
Russia, 171, 189
Russo-Japanese War, 62
Rwanda, 99, 101

Sassoon, Donald, 21–22
Sawyer, David, 169
Scandinavia, 84, 159
Second International, 20, 24
Sennett, Richard, 114
Shafts (magazine), 28, 29
Shaviro, Steven, 205n5
Shaw, Tamsin, 42
Shipman, Pat, 58
Silicon Valley, 85

Simondon, Gilbert, 62–63, 64
Sloterdijk, Peter: on politics of human zoo, 192; on psychotopical dynamics, 67, 73, 74, 166; theory of spheres, 5, 65–67, 165, 173, 206n16
Smail, Daniel, 59, 68–69
social democracy, 3, 17, 26–27. *See also* Swedish social democracy
Social Democratic Federation, 30
Social Democratic Workers Party (SDAP), 25–26, 203nn3–4. *See also* Swedish social democracy
socialism, 3, 18, 26, 30, 80. *See also* German socialism; Swedish social democracy
Socialist International, 24
societies: as semi-conscious, 161; Tarde on, 70–71, 160, 161. *See also* publics
Solnit, Rebecca, 95
Somalia, 99
Sombart, Werner, 203n8
Sophists, 164
sovereignty: and political theater, 72; theories of, 46. *See also* statecraft
Soviet Union: bureaucracies of, 122–23, 124; identity documents, 207n5
space: and the political, 41, 64–67, 72, 74–75; state, 65; viral, 71
Sphären (Sloterdijk), 65–67
spheres, theory of. *See* Sloterdijk, Peter
Spinoza, Benedictus de, 46, 53, 204n4
Stalinism, 99
the state: as political actor, 112–13, 114. *See also* bureaucracies; statecraft
statecraft: attention to public emotions, 163–64, 172; and democratic audit, 119–20; and organization, 116–17; outsourcing of government functions, 112, 117–18; role in political process, 112–13, 114–16, 123, 151; shadow states, 118–19
steadfastness, as structure of feeling, 184–85
Stengers, Isabelle, 7, 57, 95, 131–33
Sterelny, Kim, 43

Stewart, Kathy, 52

Stiglitz, Joseph, 86–87

structures of feeling: accomplishment as, 181–84; creation of new, 199; definition of, 174; fairness as, 177–79; heterogeneity as, 179–81; labor as, 175–77; reclaiming by Left, 15, 158, 174–86, 199; steadfastness as, 184–85

"stuplimity," 14, 68

subjectivity: inventions by historical Left, 21–22, 35; planes of, 48–49, 205n8

suffrage: and British women's movement, 28, 29–31; and German socialism, 20–21; in late nineteenth-century Sweden, 25; and Progressive Movement, 34; and Swedish social democracy, 27

Sullivan, Andrew, 71

Sweden, 25, 26, 203n2. See also Swedish social democracy

Swedish national union organization (LO), 25, 26

Swedish social democracy: emergence of, 19–20, 24–26; and good society, 24–25; inventiveness and organization, 9, 25–26, 36, 203n4; political arts of, 25–28; six tenets of, 26–27; and unions, 25–26, 203n2–4; and utopianism, 26, 28; world-making by, 35–36. See also Social Democratic Workers Party (SDAP)

symbiogenesis, 64

Talking Points Memo (blog), 71

Tarde, Gabriel, 48, 52; on imitation, 66, 70–71, 153, 160, 167; on psycho-social contagion, 160; on societies, 70–71, 160, 161; on subjectivity, 48

Taussig, Michael, 116

tea, 60

technologies: advances in political sphere, 168–74; and changing face of labor, 176; of identity control, 125–27; of mood, 165, 166–68. See also information technology

temperance movements, 27, 34

terrain, as political actor, 65, 72–73. See also space

Thomas, Keith, 58

Thrailkill, Jane, 52

Thrift, Nigel, 49, 206n18

Tomasello, Michael, 43

totalitarian democracy, 117, 151, 162–63

Trade Union Congress, 30

transduction, 63

Uexkull, Jakob von, 73

unions. See labor unions/organizations

United Kingdom: permanent campaigns, 171–72; Third Way thinking, 84. See also Britain; European Union

United Nations, 88, 89

United States: great depression of 1893–97, 32, 203n7; income inequality, 204n9; inverted totalitarianism, 117; Left vs. Right agenda in, 3, 159; outsourcing of government functions, 112, 117–18; permanent campaign, 171–72; polling techniques, 168, 169, 170; turn-of-century labor unions, 32; World War I, 62. See also Progressive Movement

Utopia, xii

utopianism: and anti-capitalism, 80; envisioned by Left, 108; pragmatic, 18–19

vegetarianism, 58, 60

Virno, Paolo, 53–54, 130–31, 186, 205n8

Viveiros de Castro, Eduardo, 43, 44–45

volksbühne (People's Stage), 24

Wacquant, Loïc, 124

Walzer, Michael, 154

War on Terror, 98

Waterton, Claire, 145

Webb, Beatrice, 30

Weber, Max: on bureaucracies, 123–24, 128–29, 155; on statecraft, 116, 121, 122, 123–24; on states of mood, 159, 161–62; on vocation, 114, 206n1

Wegner, Daniel, 161

Weibel, Peter, 102, 107

welfare: and German socialism, 20, 21, 22; and reformist Left, 85; and Swedish social democracy, 26, 27

Whitehead, Alfred North, 40, 46, 61, 204nn4–6

Wigforss, Ernst, 26, 200

Williams, Raymond, 15, 174

Wilson, Thomas, 165

Wilson, Woodrow, 34

Wolin, Sheldon, 162

Woman and Socialism (Bebel), 23

Women's Co-operative Guild, 29, 30

Women's Industrial Council, 29, 30

Women's Labour League, 29

women's movement, 9, 17, 18, 23, 34, 96. *See also* British feminism; suffrage

Women's Social and Political Union (wspu), 28, 30–31

Women's Trade Union Association, 29

Women's Trade Union League, 29

workers' recreational movements, 23–24

working class: and British women's movement, 28, 30; and German socialism, 21, 22; "invention" of, 22; and Swedish social democracy, 25; and workers' rights, 9, 26

World Bank, 86

world-making capacity: definition of, 5, 9; as key to progressive success, 9–10; political arts of, xii–xiii. *See also* Left; leftist renewal; political arts

World Social Forum, 93

World Trade Organization, 86–87

World War I, 62

Yates, Francis, 50

Yeltsin, Boris, 171

Yemen, 59

Young, Iris Marion, 96

Yugoslavia, 150

Žižek, Slavoj, 7, 162, 163, 201n3